Visual Programming
with HP VEE

Hewlett-Packard Professional Books

Blinn	Portable Shell Programming: An Extensive Collection of Bourne Shell Examples
Blommers	Practical Planning for Network Growth
Costa	Planning and Designing High Speed Networks Using 100VG-AnyLAN, Second Edition
Crane	A Simplified Approach to Image Processing: Classical and Modern Techniques in C
Fernandez	Configuring CDE—The Desktop Environment
Fristrup	The Essential Web Surfer Survival Guide
Fristrup	USENET: Netnews for Everyone
Grady	Practical Software Metrics for Project Management and Process Improvement
Grosvenor, Ichiro, O'Brien	Mainframe Downsizing to Upsize Your Business: IT-Preneuring
Gunn	A Guide to NetWare₍ for UNIX®
Helsel	Graphical Programming: A Tutorial for HP VEE
Helsel	Visual Programming with HP VEE
Kane	PA-RISC 2.0 Architecture
Knouse	Practical DCE Programming
Lewis	The Art & Science of Smalltalk
Lund	Integrating UNIX® and PC Network Operating Systems
Madell, Parsons, Abegg	Developing and Localizing International Software
Malan, Letsinger, Coleman	Object-Oriented Development at Work: Fusion in the Real World
McFarland	X Windows on the World: Developing Internationalized Software with X, Motif®, and CDE
McMinds/Whitty	Writing Your Own OSF/Motif Widgets
Phaal	LAN Traffic Management
Poniatowski	The HP-UX System Administrator's "How To" Book
Poniatowski	HP-UX 10.x System Administration "How To" Book
Thomas	Cable Television Proof-of-Performance: A Practical Guide to Cable TV Compliance Measurements Using a Spectrum Analyzer
Witte	Electronic Test Instruments

Visual Programming
with HP VEE

Robert Helsel

Hewlett-Packard Company

For book and bookstore information

http://www.prenhall.com

Prentice Hall PTR
Upper Saddle River, New Jersey 07458

Editorial/production supervision: *Craig Little*
Manufacturing manager: *Alexis R. Heydt*
Acquisitions editor: *Karen Gettman*
Editorial assistant: *Barbara Alfieri*
Cover design: *Design Source*
Cover design director: *Jerry Votta*
Patricia Pekary, Manager Hewlett-Packard Press

Published by Prentice Hall PTR
Prentice-Hall, Inc.
A Simon & Schuster Company
Upper Saddle River, New Jersey 07458

The publisher offers discounts on this book when ordered in bulk quantities.
For more information, contact:

Corporate Sales Department
Prentice Hall PTR
1 Lake Street
Upper Saddle River, NJ 07458

Phone: 800-382-3419, Fax: 201-236-7141
E-mail: corpsales@prenhall.com

Printed in the United States of America
10 9 8 7 6 5 4 3 2 1

ISBN 0-13-533548-5

Prentice-Hall International (UK) Limited, *London*
Prentice-Hall of Australia Pty. Limited, *Sydney*
Prentice-Hall Canada Inc., *Toronto*
Prentice-Hall Hispanoamericana, S.A., *Mexico*
Prentice-Hall of India Private Limited, *New Delhi*
Prentice-Hall of Japan, Inc., *Tokyo*
Simon & Schuster Asia Pte. Ltd., *Singapore*
Editora Prentice-Hall do Brasil, Ltda., *Rio de Janeiro*

Contents

Part II: Common Tasks Using HP VEE

Appendices and Index

Index

PREFACE

What is HP VEE?

Hewlett-Packard Visual Engineering Environment (HP VEE) is a visual programming language optimized for instrument control applications. (See next page for more detail.)

Why Learn HP VEE?

- Increase productivity dramatically. Customers report reducing their program development time up to 80%.

- Leverage your investment in textual languages. HP VEE integrates with textual languages including C, C++, Visual Basic, Pascal, Fortran, HP BASIC.

- Use HP VEE on a variety of platforms such as PCs running MS Windows, Windows 95, Windows NT, HP-UX workstations, and Solaris workstations.

- Use HP VEE in a wide range of applications such as test and measurement, data acquisition, monitoring and control, science and education. HP VEE controls GPIB, VXI, Serial, GPIO, PC Plug-in, and LAN instruments over the interfaces directly or using instrument drivers.

Why Use This Book To Learn HP VEE?

This book is the fastest and easiest way to learn HP VEE.

Grasp the fundamentals in a single day. Complete the entire book in a week. Your key benefit in doing so would be to double your productivity. You can even use the free evaluation software included in the back cover of this book to learn HP VEE before purchase.

Visual vs. Textual Programming Languages

With HP VEE you create programs by connecting icons together using the mouse; with a textual language you use keywords following rules of syntax. The result in HP VEE resembles a data-flow diagram, which is easier to use and understand than traditional lines of code. There is no laborious edit-compile-link-execute cycle using HP VEE.

The following two figures compare a simple function programmed first in a textual language (ANSI C) and then in HP VEE. The function creates an array of 10 random numbers, finds the maximum value, and displays the array and maximum value.

```
/* Program to find maximum element in array */

#include <math.h>
main( )
{
 double num[10], max;
 int i;

  for (i=0; i<10; i++){
   num[i]=(double) rand( )/pow(2.0,15.0);
   printf("%f\n",num[i]);
  }
  max=num[0];
  for (i=1; i<10; i++){
   if (num[i] > max) max=num[i];
  }
  printf("\nmax: %f\n",max);
}
```

Figure P-1. An ANSI C Program

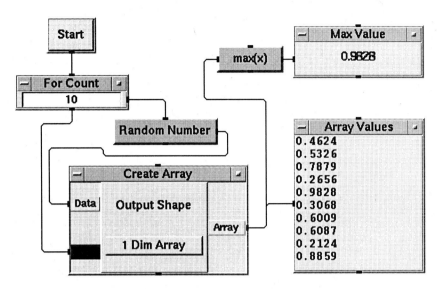

Fig. P-2. An HP VEE Program

You can see that each icon performs a specific function. For example, there are icons to create arrays or to obtain the maximum value from an array. Time-consuming tasks such as controlling instruments, creating customized data displays, or developing operator interfaces become very easy using HP VEE. This method of test development leads to productivity gains up to five times greater than conventional techniques.

Create Operator Interfaces in Minutes

With HP VEE it's easy to perform certain tasks in minutes that might take days in a textual language.

- Create colorful, intuitive front-ends to your programs.

- Exercise complete keyboard control — in addition to mouse control — for manufacturing functional test.

- Choose from a complete assortment of user input and data display features.

- Use pop-up panels to create focus and conserve screen space.

- Secure your programs from unwanted tampering.

- Use labels with color and font selection, beepers, notepads, buttons, switches in a variety of formats, to name a few in HP VEE's arsenal of interface features.

Leverage Your Existing Test and Measurement Software

HP VEE runs on PCs running MS Windows, Windows 95, Windows NT, HP-UX workstations, or Solaris workstations. (See Appendix A for ordering information.) On each of these platforms HP VEE provides mechanisms for linking conventional test programs as well as commercial applications. For example, you could use HP VEE to sequence existing tests in HP BASIC, C, C++, Visual Basic, Fortran, or Pascal (or any compiled or interpreted language on your operating system). HP VEE also provides a number of interprocess communication features to share data with commercial applications such as databases or spreadsheets.

HP VEE supports standard ties to standard languages: Dynamic Data Exchange and Dynamic Link Libraries on PCs; Named Pipes and Shared Libraries on HP or Sun platforms. HP VEE also supports TCP/IP for sharing data in mixed environments - moving HP VEE data into a large database, for example.

Maintain a Flexible I/O Strategy Based on Standards

- Use instrument drivers for over 450 instruments from different vendors plus all drivers available that are VXI*plug&play* compatible in the WIN, WIN95, or WIN-NT frameworks.

- Use HP VEE's Direct I/O icon to send instrument command strings over standard interfaces such as HP-IB (IEEE488), GPIO, RS 232, VXI, LAN-based instruments for remote testing.

- Control PC plug-in boards from any manufacturer that supplies a Dynamic Link Library with the board. Data Translation also sells a

Visual Programming Interface for their boards to make programming plug-ins easier in HP VEE. (See Appendix A.)

- Use the instrument driver monitor for current monitoring of a number of instruments at once with state store or recall capability.

- Enjoy direct VXI backplane control using embedded PCs or workstations.

Exploit HP VEE Manufacturing Test Capabilities

- Reduced development and maintenance time with visual programming.

- Test executive tools included with the product.

- Integration with conventional languages like C, C++, Visual Basic, Pascal, Fortran, and HP BASIC.

- Convenient and flexible operator interface capabilities.

- Platform support for HP and SUN workstations as well as PCs.

- Remote test capabilities.

- Interprocess communication tools to link with other applications such as relational databases or statistical analysis packages.

- HP's excellent array of support options.

- Unlimited run-time option.

- Low cost site licenses.

- Instrument driver monitor.

- Easy documentation tools.

- Easy to port test data to standard spreadsheets and word processors for reports.

The Best Way to Use This Book

> *Note:* *Use the free HP VEE evaluation software in the back cover of this book, or for more information on buying the complete HP VEE, see Appendix A.*

This book provides a tutorial in two parts. Part I teaches the fundamentals of HP VEE in a single day. Each chapter will take approximately two hours or less to complete. Part II is task-oriented, so you can go directly to the chapters that suit your application. If you work through the entire book, it will take you about a week to complete. To teach you HP VEE as quickly as possible, we have used guided examples for the most part. If you can spare the time, you should also work through the examples in Appendix B, which challenge you to solve problems on your own. Solutions are provided with explanations.

You can use the HP VEE software on any of the supported platforms for the purposes of this tutorial. Although you don't need HP VEE documentation for this course, we encourage you to consult it for more information on any given topic. The goal of this tutorial is to enable you to program your applications with HP VEE as soon as possible. It covers most of the same material as the HP VEE customer class, but in a self-paced format. If you want to achieve expert capability, you may want to continue your study with the product documentation after this book.

Let's get started.

Robert Helsel

Measurement Systems Engineer

Hewlett-Packard Company

Acknowledgments

I would like to thank all the people within HP who offered suggestions on this book — especially the HP VEE team, T&M customers, and the Field.

Special thanks go to Susan Wolber in the lab for her thorough review, to Bruce Hebert for materials on DDE and DLLs, and John Dumais in the lab for the information on compiled functions, and to Jim Armentrout and Van Walther for examples and material from the HP VEE class.

Special thanks go to the sponsor and champion for this book: Bill Heinzman, the R&D HP VEE Project Mgr., and Donna Trinko Majcen, Automotive Marketing Manager.

Finally, I'd like to thank Karen Gettman, Senior Editor from Prentice Hall, Pat Pekary, HP Press Editor, and Sophie Papanikolaou, PH Production Manager for making the process of publishing smooth and enjoyable.

Part I: HP VEE Fundamentals

Using the HP VEE Development Environment

1

Average time to complete: 1.5 hrs.

Overview

HP VEE (Hewlett-Packard Visual Engineering Environment) is a visual programming language that produces dramatic reductions in test development time. Programs are constructed by connecting icons together on the screen. The resulting HP VEE program - which resembles a block diagram -may be run like a program in a textual language such as C or HP BASIC. The exercises in this chapter will introduce you to a style of program development that is not only efficient but intuitive and fun as well.

Please refer to the Preface for a more detailed discussion of HP VEE features and benefits.

*Note: You can use **free evaluation software** in the back cover of this book to learn HP VEE. For details on how to purchase HP VEE, see Appendix A.*

In this chapter you'll learn about:

- Environment components

- Selecting menu items

- Saving programs, exiting and starting HP VEE

- Getting help

- Using HP VEE objects

- Input and output pins

- Connecting objects to make programs

- Creating HP VEE UserObjects

An HP VEE Program

You can see an example of an HP VEE program in the figure below.

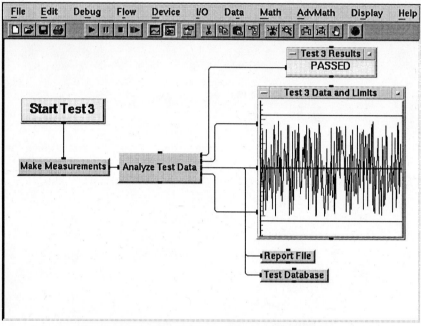

Fig. 1-1. An HP VEE Program (Detail View)

This is the "Detail" view of the program, which shows all the connections between icons ("objects") and is analogous to source code in a textual language. The objects perform various functions such as I/O operations, analysis, and display. All objects use their input and output pins in a consistent way: data input pins on the left, data output pins on the right, operational sequence pins on the top and bottom. Each object may be displayed as an icon or in its "open view". For example, in Fig. 1-1 the object labeled Analyze Test Data is shown as an icon; the object labeled Test 3 Data and Limits is shown using an open view. The open view is larger and more detailed. An object might also contain a subprogram, which can be viewed and changed. You start this program by clicking Start Test 3. This object triggers the Make Measurements object, which gathers test data and passes it to the next object for analysis. Analyze Test Data not only analyzes the test data, but also puts out a pass/fail message, sends the data and test limits to a display, and copies a record of the test data to a report file and a database. You can see how easy it is to follow the flow of the program. Make Measurements and Analyze Test Data are objects you can create and label yourself. HP VEE programs are modular and practically document themselves. You save the program to a file, which you can open, change, and run in HP VEE.

An additional benefit of programming in HP VEE is that it only takes a few minutes to create an operator interface (the one below took about 30 seconds to create). The figure below shows the "Panel" view of the program in Fig. 1-1. Only the Start object and displays are presented to the operator making the test extremely easy to use (as well as a subset of the menu and tool bar icons.) You can also secure the panel view from unwanted alterations.

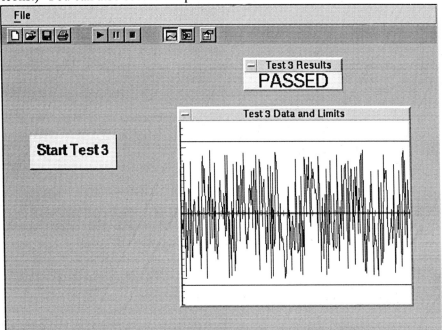

Fig. 1-2. An HP VEE Program (Panel View)

This chapter will teach you how to start and stop HP VEE, how to help yourself while you're learning, and the basic mechanics of getting objects from the menus and connecting them together to create programs. First, let's look at the basic components of the HP VEE development environment.

The Development Environment Components

After you've installed and started HP VEE, you will see the HP VEE development environment. See Figure 1-3. HP VEE is synchronized on all platforms, so that you can easily port programs from one environment to another. (Ordering information is located in Appendix A.)

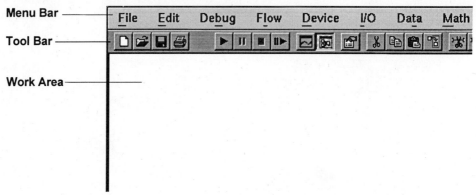

Fig. 1-3. The HP VEE Development Environment

- The *Menu Bar* provides menus holding the commands and icons used to build your programs.

- The *Tool Bar* displays buttons as shortcuts to the most common tasks in HP VEE. (Just place the mouse pointer over a button and HP VEE displays the button's function.)

- The *Work Area* is where you construct your program with icons.

    Note: This book focuses on the HP VEE 3.2. If you have an earlier version (click Help => About VEE... to find out), inexpensive upgrades are available. If you have a support contract for software updates, you will receive the new version automatically. Also, consult Help on enhancements after revision 3.2.

Using Menus

Let's use a specific example to explain how menus work. The process will be the same for all menus. First, you'll open the Device menu, select an object from the Virtual Source submenu, and place it in the work area. Next, you'll open the "object menu" and select Help to find out how the object operates. *(HP VEE objects will be highlighted in bold typeface, if you are supposed to practice doing something with them.)*

> **Note:** *"Click and hold" means that you should press the left mouse button, and hold it down, until you move the mouse pointer to a new location. "Click" means to quickly press and release the left mouse button. If you need to use the right mouse button, we will say so in the instructions. If you have a mouse with three buttons, you won't need the middle button using HP VEE.*

1. Click and hold **Device** to open the menu. A pull-down menu appears.

2. Move the mouse pointer down to the *Virtual Source* submenu, then right to **Function Generator,** and then release the mouse button.

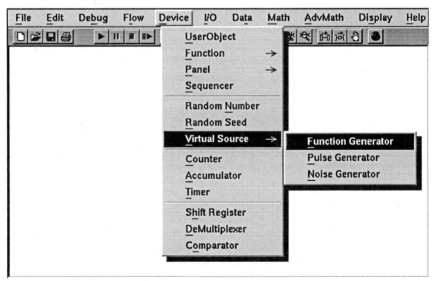

Fig. 1-4. The Device => Virtual Source Submenu

An outline of the Function Generator object appears.

3. Move the **Function Generator** to the center of the work area, and click to place the object.

The object appears where you placed it.

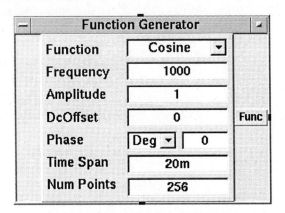

Figure 1-5. The Function Generator Object

Note: *In future exercises instructions similar to those above will be condensed into the following format: Select Device => Virtual Source => Function Generator, and place it in the center of the work area.*

The arrow to the right of Virtual Source indicates a submenu. Three dots after a menu item indicate that one or more dialog boxes will follow. For example, File => Save As ... operates this way.

4. Now open the **Function Generator** object menu by clicking the horizontal bar in the upper left-hand corner of the object.

You can see the object menu bar and the open menu in the following figure. Most object menus open the same way.

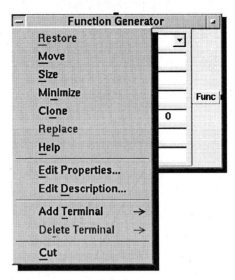

**Fig. 1-6. The Function Generator
Object Menu**

Tip: *Often a more convenient way to open an object menu is to simply place the mouse pointer over the object and click the right mouse button. Try this using the Flow => Start object. The menu will "pop up" at the location of the pointer.*

The Function Generator object is used to simulate test data. You can use it to generate waveforms such as sine, cosine, square, triangle, +ramp, -ramp, as well as DC only. If you want to know more about it, just open its object menu and click Help.

Saving Your Work, Exiting HP VEE, and Re-starting Your Program

To Save Your Work and Exit HP VEE

1. Select **File => Save As ...** and complete the dialog box.

   A dialog box entitled Save File appears. The following two figures show the PC and UNIX formats for this box.

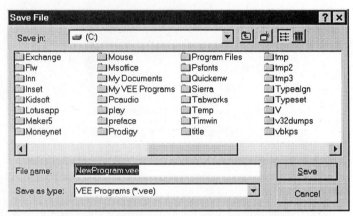

Fig. 1-7. The Save File Dialog Box (PC)

In the PC dialog box, if the default selections for a drive, folder, and file type are suitable, you can just type in a file name and click **OK**. Otherwise, double-click a folder to open it. Select a drive by opening the drop-down menu next to **Save in** and clicking on your choice. Open the menu labeled **Save as type**, and make a selection. (The default extension is **.VEE**.) Finally, double-click in the **File name** field, type in a file name, and click **Save**. HP VEE will automatically add the **.VEE** extension.

Note: *If you're using the evaluation kit software , HP VEE will only let you save your work to one file, EVAL.VEE, so just write over this file for the different programs in this book.*

For the UNIX version of the Save File dialog box, see the figure below.

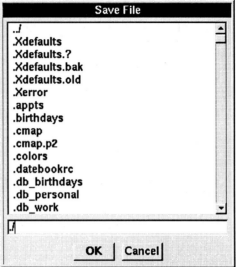

Fig. 1-8. The Save File Dialog Box (UNIX)

In the UNIX dialog box, just type the file name and click **OK**. Your home directory is the default. If you'd like to save the file in another directory, use the **Backspace** key to delete the characters ./, then type the file name with the complete path and click **OK**. In UNIX you need to add the **.vee** extension.

Tip: *A handy way to replace a typed entry in a dialog box is to click and drag the mouse pointer over the entry to highlight it. Or you can highlight the entry by double-clicking the input field. Then you can simply type your correction and click OK.*

2. Select **File => Exit** to close the HP VEE application window.

Shortcut: Press Ctrl-e to exit HP VEE.

To Re-start HP VEE and Run Your Program

1. **PC:** Double-click the **HP VEE for Windows** icon in MS Windows. In Win95, click **Start**, move to the **HP VEE** submenu, and select **HP VEE**.

   UNIX: From your home directory, enter **veetest**. (The executable is linked at install time to /usr/bin/veetest, which should be in your PATH. If it's not, you may have to change to that directory. If HP VEE has been installed in another directory, you may have to type the complete path.)

2. **Select File => Open** and complete the **Open File** dialog box.

   The PC and UNIX formats are the same as for the Save File dialog box. Note that in HP VEE for Windows, the default directory for user programs is the VEE_USER directory, unless you specified something else during installation.

   HP VEE will read your program into the work area.

3. Click the run button - which looks like a small arrowhead - on the tool bar (below the Debug menu).

Tip: *The command, veetest -r <filename>, will start HP VEE and automatically run the program specified by <filename>. (Again, if the HP VEE directory is not in your path, you need to enter the complete path, typically /usr/lib/veetest -r <filename>.) On MS Windows you can create your own icon to do this.*

Helping Yourself

- Click Help in an object menu to get specific information on that object.

- Click Help on the main menu bar to access the online help facility for HP VEE, which will give you information on features, instruments drivers, common tasks, short cuts, the version you're running, how to use the help facility, and release notes.

- Although you will not need to use HP VEE documentation to complete this self-paced training, consult the product documentation for more detailed information on any particular feature or concept.

- Use the Help system to search for HP VEE topics you need to locate. The Help system can also "jump" to related subjects.

- You could learn HP VEE entirely online through experimentation and consulting the Help system.

Using Objects

To Delete an Object from the Work Area

Let's use an example object. Get the **Function Generator** from the **Device** menu and put it in the work area.

1. Place the mouse cursor over the object and press **Ctrl-d**.

          - OR -

1. Open the object menu, and select **Cut**.

To Paste a Deleted Object
(To "Undo" a Cut)

1. After an object has been deleted, click **Edit => Paste**. An outline of the object appears. Place the object and click to release it.

   Note: *If the object has lines attached, these connections will be maintained. This action operates like an "undo" in other programs. It's not called "undo", because it doesn't apply to all HP VEE programming actions. (It also works on groups of objects that have been deleted.)*

To Duplicate an Object

The Clone operation duplicates an object exactly including any changes you've made such as sizing or renaming.

1. Open the object menu and select **Clone**.

   An outline of the duplicated object appears.

2. Move the outline to the desired location, and click to place the object.

To Move an Object

   Note: Select File => New to open a new file and clear your work area before starting a new exercise, if necessary. If an exercise builds on a former one that you need to retain, we'll say so.

Let's use one of the display objects for an example. Select Display => Waveform(Time) and place it on the right side of the work area.

1. Open the object menu and select **Move**.

   The mouse pointer becomes a small square with cross hairs.

2. Place the mouse pointer over the object, press and hold the left mouse button (called "dragging"), while you move the object to the desired location.

3. Release to place the object.

   Shortcut: You can also click and drag the object.

To Edit the Name of an Object

1. Open the object menu and select **Edit Properties...** .

   A Properties dialog box appears with the current title highlighted.

2. Type the new title and click **OK**.

To Switch an Object Between Iconic and Open Views

HP VEE displays objects either in an iconic or "open view," as shown in the figure below.

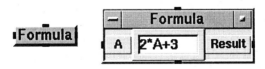

Fig. 1-9. Object in Iconic and Open Views

The iconic view conserves space in the work area and makes your programs more readable. The open view provides more detail and allows you to edit the internals of an object.

1. To switch from an open to iconic view, click the dot on the right end of the object's title bar. To return to an open view, double-click the icon.

   Note: *The object menu also has Minimize and Restore selections.*

To Size an Object

1. Place the mouse pointer over the lower right-hand corner of the object until you see a left angle, then click-and-drag to the desired position.

- OR -

   Open the object menu and click **Size**.

   You will see a small left angle on the cursor.

2. Move the left angle to desired position of the lower-right corner and click.

   Note: *You can also size an object when you first select it from a menu. After you've placed the object outline, just click and drag to indicate the desired position of the lower-right corner of the object.*

To Select or Deselect an Object

1. An object is selected when you click it; HP VEE puts a shadow behind it (see Fig. 1-11). To deselect it, just move the mouse pointer over the work area and click.

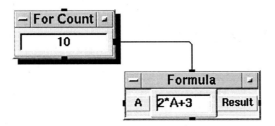

Fig. 1-10. Selected and Deselected Objects

> *Note:* *We will also use the word "select" to indicate choosing a menu item, but the context will make the meaning obvious.*

You select an object to let HP VEE know that you want to do something to that object in particular. For example, if you select an object, then click Edit => Cut, that object alone will be deleted.

To Select Several Objects

You'd want to do this when performing an operation on multiple objects such as *Edit => Cut* or *Edit => Move Objects*.

1. Press **Ctrl,** then click-and-drag a rectangle around the objects to be selected.

-OR-

Click **Edit => Select Objects**. The cursor becomes a right angle, then click-and-drag a rectangle around the objects to be selected.

> *Tip:* *If the objects cannot be grouped in a rectangle, you can select several objects by pressing Ctrl and clicking the desired objects. Notice this and other shortcuts are in the menus. "LB" stands for the left button of the mouse, Ctrl - LB is the shortcut for the Select Objects menu item.*

To Deselect All Objects

1. Click anywhere on the HP VEE work area.

To Edit Objects

1. Click **Edit** on the menu bar and select the operation you want.

   - OR -

   Place the mouse pointer anywhere on blank work area space and click the
   right mouse button.

   A pop-up Edit menu appears.

   *Note: Any menu items that are inactive appear in a different shade than
   active items. For instance, the Cut, Copy, and Clone operations
   in the Edit menu appear in a different shade from active menu
   items, until at least one object is highlighted in the work area.*

To Create Data Lines Between Objects

1. Click on the data output pin of one object, then click on the data input pin
   of another, as shown below. (A line appears behind the pointer as you
   move from one pin to the other.)

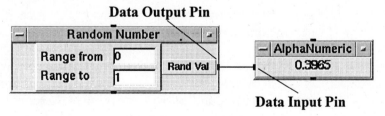

Note: *For more information on pins, see the next section.*

To Move the Work Area

1. (Make sure there is at least one icon in the work area.) Place the mouse pointer anywhere on the background of the work area, press and hold the left mouse button, and move the work area in any direction.

   Note: Scroll bars appear if your program is too big for the work area.

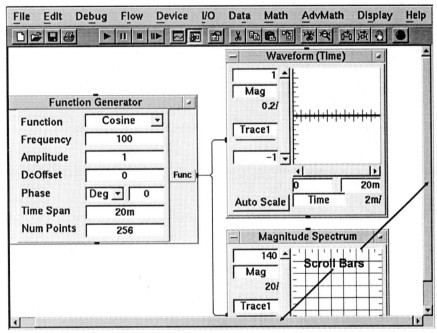

Fig. 1-11. Scroll Bars Appearing in Work Area

To Clear the Work Area

1. Select **File => New**.

To Delete Lines

1. Press **Shift-Ctrl** and click the line you want to delete. (Shift + Ctrl + LB, or select **Edit => Delete Line** and click the line you want to delete.

Object Pins and Terminals

You create an HP VEE program by connecting objects together with data lines. These lines are attached to "pins" on the objects.

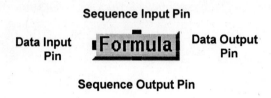

Fig. 1-12. Input and Output Pins

You connect the data input and output pins to carry data between objects. The sequence pin connections are optional. If connected, they will dictate an execution order flowing from the top of the work area to the bottom.

Terminals are simply the open view representation of the data pins. They carry detailed information such as the name of the terminal, the type and value of the data being transmitted. (To display this information, double-click the terminal.)

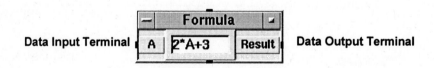

Fig. 1-13. Input and Output Terminals

To Add Data Input Terminals to an Object

1. Open the object menu and select **Add Terminal => Data Input**.

   If the data inputs are tied to particular functions - as with instrument drivers, for example - you will be given a menu of these functions; otherwise, the terminals will be named A, B, C, ...

   Shortcut: *Just place the mouse pointer over the terminal input area and press CTRL-a.*

To Delete Data Input or Output Terminals from an Object

1. Open the object menu and select **Delete Terminal => Input...**, choose the input to delete, and click **OK**.

   Shortcut: *Just place the mouse pointer over the terminal and press CTRL-d. Ctrl-d is context sensitive. Over a terminal area, it will delete a terminal; over an object, it will delete the object.*

To Examine or Alter Terminals

1. Double-click on the terminal. Change any of the fields, if appropriate, then click **OK**. You can also check the data type this way.

To Edit the Terminal Name

1. Double-click the terminal. The **Name** input field is highlighted.

2. Type the new name and click **OK**.

Connecting Objects to Make Programs

Let's work through a few simple examples. The principles will be the same for all programs. This program simply generates and displays a random number. It will give you practice in connecting objects and documentation.

Note: The exercises are designed to teach certain programming principles, and the programs themselves may serve no practical purpose.

Lab 1-1. First Program

1. Document your program:

   a. Select **Display => Note Pad** and place it at the top center of the work area. Click on the editing area to get a cursor, then enter:

   Display Random Number generates a real number between 0 and 1, then prints it to a display box.

2. Select **Device => Random Number** and place it on the left side of the work area.

3. Select **Display => AlphaNumeric** and place it to the right of the **Random Number** object.

4. Open the object menus and select **Help** to understand the objects better. Double-click on **Random Number** to get the open view.

5. Connect the objects by clicking the **Random Number** data output pin. Move the mouse pointer to the **Alphanumeric** data input pin and click.

You should get a data line connecting the two objects.

Note: *As you move the mouse pointer with the line attached near the target pin, a box highlights the pin. Then you click again to complete the connection.*

Note: *If for some reason you want to terminate the line connecting operation before you've completed the link, just double-click the mouse and the line will disappear.*

6. Click the **Run** button on the tool bar (below the Debug menu) and you will see a random number displayed, as shown below.

Select **File => Save As ...**, type **DISPRAND.VEE**, and click **OK**.   (Or save to EVAL.VEE, if you're using the evaluation kit software.) This name will appear next to HP VEE in the title bar when you open it in the future.

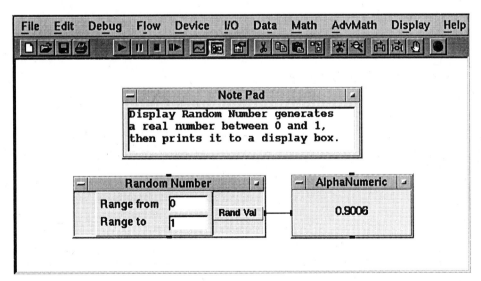

Figure 1-14. Display Random Number

Lab 1-2: Display Waveform

This program gives you additional practice in the basic mechanics of constructing an HP VEE program. You'll generate a cosine waveform and display it.

> *Note: We will assume that you select File => New to clear your work area before all lab exercises. If you need to revise a former program, we will say so.*

1. First, let's document the program. Select **Display => Note Pad** and place it at the top-center of the work area. Click on the editing area to get a cursor, then enter:

   Display Waveform generates a cosine waveform and sends it to a real time display.

   You may have to size the Note Pad depending on your screen. (Open the object menu, select **Size**, move the cursor - in the shape of a right angle - to the desired position of the lower-right corner of the object, then click.)

2. Select **Device => Virtual Source => Function Generator** and place it on the left side of the work area. Edit **Frequency** to **100**.

3. Select **Display => Waveform (Time)** and place it on the right side of the work area.

4. Click the **Function Generator** data output pin, move the mouse pointer to the data input pin of the **Waveform (Time)** object, and click again.

5. Click the **Run** button on the tool bar (below the Debug menu). Your program should look like the figure on the next page.

6. Select **File => Save As ...**, type in **DISPWAVE.VEE**, then click **OK**.

> *Note: If you're using the evaluation software, you can only save to one file, EVAL.VEE, so just overwrite what's there.*

Note: *To conserve space we will just print the program without the*
surrounding HP VEE environment.

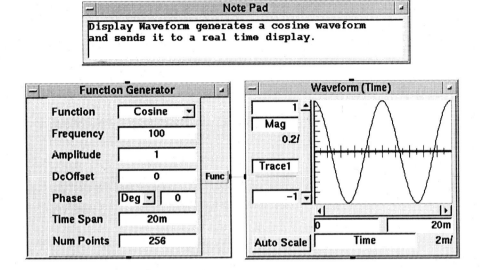

Fig. 1-15. The Display Wave Program

Lab 1-3: Set and Get a Global Variable

This program gives you more practice in the basic mechanics of building an
HP VEE program while introducing global variables. You can use the Set
Global object to create a variable that can be retrieved later in the program
using a Get Global object. You can use any HP VEE data type. This
example uses a number of type Real. Chapter 4 discusses all of the HP VEE
data types.

1. Select **Display => Note Pad** and place it at the top-center of the work
   area. Click on the upper left-hand corner of the editing area to get a
   cursor, then enter:

   **Set and Get a Global Variable prompts the user to enter a real
   number. The variable, num, is set to this real number. Then num is
   recalled and displayed.**

2. Select **Data => Constant => Real** and place it on the left side of the
   work area. Open the object menu and examine the **Help** entry.

3. Open the **Real** object menu and select **Edit Properties...** . Change the
   title to the prompt, **Enter a Real Number:**, then click **OK**.

   *Note: We're using one of the Constant objects for an input dialog box by
   simply changing its title to a prompt. This is a common technique
   for getting user input. You could use Data => Dialog Box =>
   Real Input. Also, you can double-click on the title bar to get the
   Edit Properties dialog box.*

4. Select **Data => Global => Set Global** and place it to the right of the **Real**
   object. Double-click **globalA** to highlight it, then enter **num**.

   This means that the user will enter a real number in the Real object.
   When they click the Run button (below the Debug menu), that number
   will be set to the global variable, num.

5. Connect the data output pin of the **Real** object to the data input pin of the
   Set Global object.

6. Select **Data => Global => Get Global** and place it below the **Set Global** object. Change the variable name to **num**.

7. Connect the **Set Global** sequence output pin to the **Get Global** sequence input pin.

   Note: A global variable has to be set, before you can use it; therefore, we need to use the sequence pins in this case to make sure that the variable num has been set, before you retrieve it with Get Global.

8. Select **Display => AlphaNumeric** and place it to the right of the **Get Global** object.

9. Connect the **Get Global** data output pin to the **AlphaNumeric** data input pin.

10. Enter a real number and click the run button on the tool bar.

11. Select **File => Save As ...** and name your program **global.vee**. (Or save to EVAL.VEE using the evaluation kit software.)

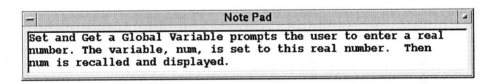

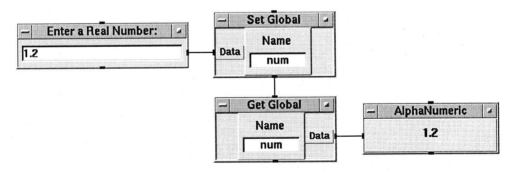

Figure 1-16. Set and Get a Global Variable

Conserving Screen Space

There is an object in the Device menu called a UserObject, which is essentially another HP VEE environment inside the main work area. Think of it as a subroutine or your own customized object that you use like any other object HP VEE provides. See the figure below.

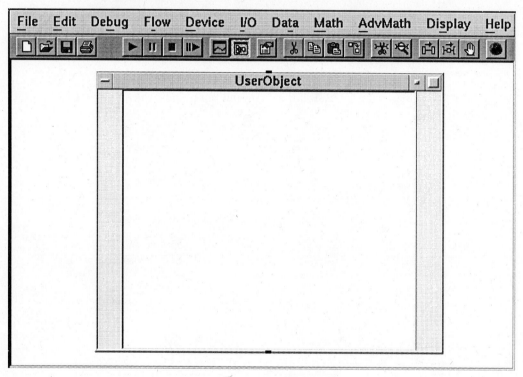

Figure 1-17. A UserObject

If you put parts of your program into UserObjects, they can be iconized to conserve screen space. You can also label that UserObject in a way that describes its functionality. Let's try a simple example.

Lab 1-4: Noisy Cosine Program

This lab shows how a UserObject can conserve screen space. You'll add a cosine waveform to a noisy waveform inside a UserObject named Noisy Cos. The resultant wave will then be displayed.

1. Select **Device => UserObject** and place it to the left side of the work area. To change the title, open the **UserObject** menu and click **Edit Properties...**. Type **Noisy Cos** and click **OK**. Open the object menu again and select **Add Terminal => Data Output**.

   The UserObject is now named Noisy Cos, and it has a data output pin with the default label X.

2. Select **Device => Virtual Source => Function Generator** and place it in **Noisy Cos**. Highlight the **1000** in the **Frequency** input field and type **100** instead. Iconize the **Function Generator** by clicking on the iconize button in the upper right corner of the object.

3. Select **Device => Virtual Source => Noise Generator** and place it below the **Function Generator** in the **UserObject**. Open its **Help** entry to find out what it does. Iconize the **Noise Generator**.

4. Select **Math => + - * / => a + b** and place it to the right of the generators in the **UserObject**. Consult the **Help** entry for +. Connect the data output pins of both generators to the two input pins on the + object.

   HP VEE will now add the two waveforms. You want to send this resultant wave to the UserObject data output pin.

5. Connect the data output pin of the **a + b** object to the **UserObject** data output **X**. Position the icons in the upper left of Noisy Cos.

6. Select **Display => Waveform (Time)** and place it to the right of the **Noisy Cos UserObject**. Connect the **Noisy Cos** data output to the **Waveform (Time)** data input. Open the **Waveform (Time)** object menu and select **Edit Properties...**. Under **Layout** select **Graph Only** and click **OK**.

7. Click the run button on the tool bar. Your program should look like Figure 1-18.

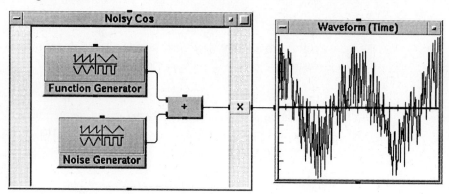

Fig. 1-18. The Noisy Cosine Program

8. Iconize **Noisy Cos** now. You have the same functionality, but you've conserved a lot of work space and simplified your program. See Figure 1-19.

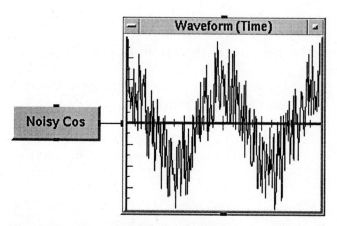

Fig. 1-19. The Noisy Cosine Program After Iconizing

To Stop HP VEE by Brute Force

Most of the time you can just select File => Exit to stop HP VEE. You probably will never need to use the following techniques, but occasionally you might do something very creative, and HP VEE stops responding to the mouse or keyboard.

In MS Windows or Win95:

1. Press **Ctrl-Alt-Delete** and a window pops up giving you various options. Just follow the instructions in the window for MS Windows, or click End Task in Win95.

In Windows NT, you might lock up an application, but you'll still have control of the mouse, so:

1. Double-click on the background and select **End Task** from the pop-up window.

In UNIX you need to "kill" the process (UNIX terminology is not very polite about these things):

1. Enter **ps -ef | grep vee** in HP-UX or Solaris (or **ps -aux|grep vee** in SunOS) at a prompt to identify the process identification number. You will see a line with **veetest** on the end. The number following your login is the process number you want. In my case it's **bobh <number> ... veetest**.

2. Enter **kill -9 <number>** to stop the HP VEE application. Then you can simply enter **veetest** to start over again.This completes Chapter 1, which gives you a basic understanding of the HP VEE development environment and how to use it. The next chapter will unify the methods you've learned by building a simple program. The last page of each chapter provides a checklist of tasks covered. Use it to give yourself a quick test.

Chapter 1 Checklist

You should now be able to do any of the following tasks. Review topics as needed, before going on to Chapter 2.

- Identify the main menu bar, program execution buttons, and work area.

- Select menu items from the main menu and object menus.

- Simulate waveform data.

- Look up on-line help documentation from the main menu bar and from the object menus.

- Open an object menu in two different ways.

- Save your work, exit HP VEE, and restart your program.

- Perform the following operations on an object: moving, renaming, iconizing, expanding, sizing, selecting, deselecting, deleting.

- Identify data and sequence pins on an object and explain their purpose.

- Examine terminals and change their names.

- Move the work area; clear the work area.

- Explain a UserObject and its purpose.

- Write a small program within a UserObject.

- Minimize and restore a UserObject.

- Run and save a program.

- Set a global variable and retrieve it.

Creating a Simple
Test Program

Average time to complete: *2 hrs.*

Overview

In this chapter you'll create an HP VEE program that generates a pulse waveform, adds noise to it, then stores and displays the results. The user will be able to select the frequency of the pulses and the amount of noise added from a simple operator interface. You'll encapsulate this simulated test within a UserObject, so that it can be iconized and easily exported to another program. This lab exercise will also incorporate HP VEE debugging and documentation tools.

How long would it take you to create this program in a textual language like C? It should take you about an hour in HP VEE - even the first time. After that, it would take approximately 10 minutes.

In this chapter you'll learn about:

- Creating modular tests

- Getting user inputs

- Simulating test data

- Storing and displaying results

- Documenting your program

- Creating an operator interface

- Using debugging tools

- Using HP VEE online help

Lab 2-1: The Pulse Program

We'll partition the instructions under task headings to make it easier to apply the procedures to other programs.

To Give Your Program a Title

1. Click **File => Edit Properties**, type **Pulse Program** in the **Title** field, then click **OK**. (This title will be used by HP VEE's documentation tool.)

To Make a Test Procedure Modular

By storing your test procedure inside a UserObject, you can iconize the entire test to conserve screen space. Also, you can merge this program with another more easily, because it is an easily identifiable module. Finally, the UserObject could easily be converted to a function, which you could then call from any number of points in your program.

1. Select **Device => UserObject** and place it in the middle of the work area.

2. Maximize the **UserObject** by clicking on the maximize button at the upper right-hand corner of the object. (If you click on the iconize button by mistake, just double-click the icon to enlarge it again.)

To Document Your Program

Using File => Save Documentation... HP VEE will store all object names, object settings, entries from the Display => Note Pad objects, entries from the Edit Description dialog boxes, and nesting of objects. All objects have an Edit Description item in their object menus, which provides a dialog box to accept documentation on that particular object. This file also provides a way to correlate the documentation with screen dumps. Now, you'll make entries in the Edit Description dialog box. Later in this chapter you'll use this documentation tool.

1. Change the **UserObject** title to **PulseNoise**.

   There should be no spaces or unusual characters in the name, since you might want to convert this UserObject to a function in the future.

2. Open the object menu and click **Edit Description**.

3. Type the following text in the dialog box:

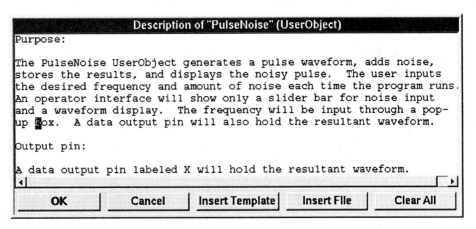

Fig. 2-1. The Edit Description Dialog Box

Click **OK**, when you're done.

Note: Your entries in the Edit Description dialog box will not be visible to a user unless they access them through the object menu for information; however, the documentation tool (File => Save Documentation...) will save them in your specified file Also, notice that you can insert a file or a template in this dialog box.

To Create a Dialog Box for User Input

In the Data => Dialog Box submenu are three choices for input (Text, Integer, and Real). In each case you'll get a dialog box to help you configure your prompt or label, default value, value constraints, and error message. Once you edit these choices, iconize the object. When you run your program a pop-up input box will appear, as you configured it.

1. Select **Data => Dialog Box => Integer Input** and place it in the upper-left work area of the **UserObject**.

2. Change the Prompt/Label field to **Enter Frequency:**. (Remember to click and drag over the field to highlight it first.) Change the Default Value, **5**, to **100**.

   Reminder: You can also double-click an input field to highlight an entry.

3. Change the Value Constraints to **1** on the low end to **193** on the high end. Also change the error message to reflect these new values. Iconize the Integer Input object.

To Set Up the Pulse Generator

We'll use a "virtual source" called a pulse generator to simulate data from an instrument. In chapter 3, we'll cover communication with real instruments. You'll need to add a data input pin to receive the frequency setting from the Integer object.

1. Select **Device => Virtual Source => Pulse Generator**, and place it to the right of the input box.

   You may need to use the Size command in the Pulse Generator object menu to conserve work area space.

2. Open the Pulse Generator object menu and click **Add Terminal => Data Input**.

A list box appears with the possible data input pins you may add to change the different functions on the **Pulse Generator. Frequency** is already highlighted, so just click **OK**. HP VEE adds the terminal.

> ***Shortcut:*** *You could also place the mouse pointer over the data input pin area and press Ctrl-a to get the list box.*

3. Connect the top data output pin of the **Integer Input** object to the **Pulse Generator** data input pin.

   Notice that Frequency can only be changed through the input pin now; you can no longer edit the Frequency input field.

4. Run this section of the program entering different values in the pop-up input box. See Figure 2-2 (shown at run-time with the pop-up input box.).

> ***Note:*** *You will get an error box, if you enter frequencies above 193 unless you reduce the Pulse Width. Notice that you get the exact error message that you configured. Simply click-and-drag on the pop-up box to control where it appears.*

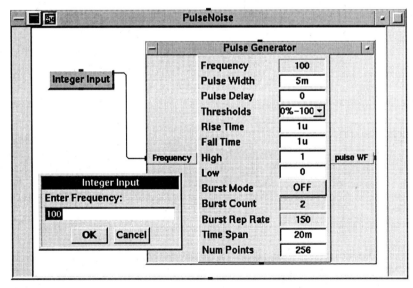

Fig. 2-2. The PulseNoise UserObject at an Early Stage

5. Iconize the **Pulse Generator** and move it closer to the input box to simplify the screen.

To Set Up the Noise Generator

HP VEE also includes a virtual instrument to generate a noise waveform, which you can add to other waves. The amount of noise is controlled by adjusting the amplitude.

1. Select **Device => Virtual Source => Noise Generator** and place it to the right of the noise input box.

2. Open the object menu and select **Add Terminal => Data Input**.

3. Select **Amplitude**.

Notice that the default values for Time Span and Num Points are the same for both of the generators.

To Create a Noise Input Box

Now that the Noise Generator has an amplitude input pin, you can input this data as a real number. HP VEE provides an object that makes this easy, a Real Slider, which is located in the Data menu. (You could also have used the Real Input object.)

1. Select **Data => Continuous => Real Slider** and place it to the left of the **Noise Generator**. (You could also use a Real Knob.)

   To select a value, just click and drag the slider bar up or down. The value chosen displays at the top. You can also change the range limits, if you want.

2. Edit the name, **Real Slider,** to be a user prompt: **Enter Noise:**.

(Use Edit Properties in the object menu.) Size the object to be smaller.

Shortcut: *Simply place the mouse pointer at the lower right corner of the object (until the pointer changes to a right angle) and click-and-drag to the desired size.*

3. **Access Help** in the object menu, if you have any questions about the object.

4. Connect the **Real Slider** data output pin to the **Noise Generator Amplitude** input pin.

5. Iconize the **Noise Generator** and move it closer to the input box.

   You can move an icon by simply clicking and dragging with the mouse.

To Add Two Waveforms

The addition object signified by the a + b symbol can be used to add waveforms as well as scalar numbers. If both inputs are arrays, the data must have the same size and shape. Size means the number of elements in an array. In this case, we know both waveforms have 256 points. Shape refers to the structure holding the data: a scalar, a one-dimensional array (ARRAY 1D), a two-dimensional array (ARRAY 2D), and so on. Waveforms from the generator objects are stored as one-dimensional arrays, which you can verify by opening the output terminal to examine the Shape field.

1. Select **Math => + - * / => a + b**, and place it to the lower-right of the **Pulse Generator**.

   Examine the **Help** entry for a + b in the object menu.

2. Connect the **Pulse Generator** data output pin to the upper-left data input pin of the **a + b** object.

3. Connect the data output pin from the **Noise Generator** to the lower data input pin of the + object.

So far your program should look like the one in Figure 2 - 3.

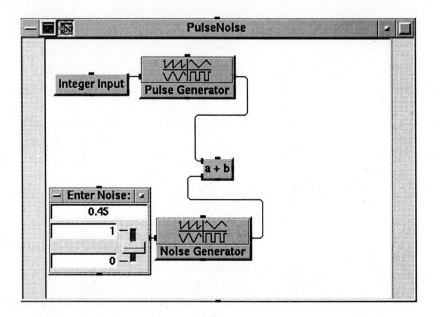

Fig. 2-3. Pulse Program After Adding Two Waveforms

Reminder: The Integer Input object will bring up a pop-up dialog box when your program runs.

To Display a Waveform in the Time Domain

1. Select **Display => Waveform (Time)**and place it to the right of the addition object. (You may need to use Size in the object menu.)

2. Connect the data output pin of the a + b object to the data input pin of the **Waveform (Time)** display.

   Check the connections by clicking the run button on the HP VEE tool bar. You should see a pulse displayed. Try entering different frequencies and moving the slider bar for the amount of noise you want before running the program again. Click **Auto Scale** on the **Waveform (Time)** object to scale the display quickly.

To Put the Program Results in a File

1. Select **I/O => To => File** and place it in the central work area.

   It doesn't matter if you overlap other objects, because you'll iconize the To File object in a moment.

2. Change the default filename, **myFile**, to **pulsnois.dat**.

3. If there is no check mark to the left of **Clear File At PreRun & Open**, then click on the small input box.

   To File defaults to appending data to the existing file. In this case, however, you want to clear the file each time you run the program.

4. Examine **Help** in the To File object menu. You can use the default settings, but double-click on **WRITE TEXT a EOL** anyway to examine the different choices you have. We'll go over this in detail in Chapter 5.

5. Iconize the **To File** object by clicking the iconize button at the upper right-hand corner of the object.

6. Connect the data output pin of the **a + b** object to the data input pin of **To File**.

   Note: You can connect one data output pin to several data input pins.

7. Click the run button on the tool bar again to test your program.

Double-click the **To File** object to get the open view, then double-click the input terminal **A** to examine its contents. You should see an array of 256 points.

To Add a Data Output Pin to the UserObject

You do this the same way you would for any HP VEE object.

1. Open the UserObject object menu by placing the mouse pointer on the title bar or input/output areas and clicking the right mouse button. Select **Add Terminal => Data Output**. HP VEE adds an output named **X**.

   Shortcut: You can add a data output pin by placing the mouse pointer on the output terminal area and pressing Ctrl-a.

2. Connect the data output pin of the **a + b** object to **X**.

3. Run your program, then double-click on **X** to examine the contents.

The **PulseNoise UserObject** should look like the figure below.

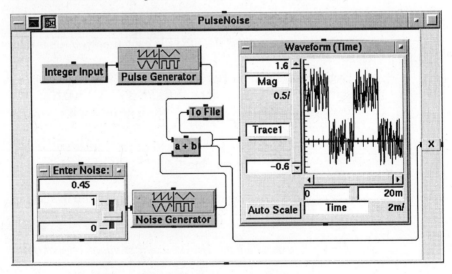

Fig. 2-4. The PulseNoise UserObject (Detail View)

To Create an Operator Interface

First, you're going to select the objects that you want to appear in the Panel view, which acts as your operator interface. Then simply selecting Edit => Add To Panel will create the panel.

1. Press and hold **Ctrl** while clicking on all of the objects you want to select. (Make sure no object is accidentally highlighted.) Click on the **Real Slider** and the **Waveform (Time)** object. Each will now have a shadow to indicate your selection. (The Integer Input object will pop up a dialog box in the Panel view when the program runs.)

   Note: You can also select Edit => Select Objects, click on the objects you want to select, then click on the background to stop.

2. Pop up the **PulseNoise Edit** menu by placing the mouse pointer over the **PulseNoise** background and clicking on the right mouse button. Click **Add to Panel**.

   Note: You can also open the UserObject Edit menu by selecting the object menu for PulseNoise and selecting Edit => Add to Panel.

   The selected objects will appear in the panel view, as shown in Figure 2-5 on the next page (program shown during execution with the pop-up dialog box).

   Your program is still intact. Just click detail view button on the left side of the PulseNoise title bar to return to the detail view. (And click the panel view button to go the other way, of course.)

   Shortcut: Press the "maximize" button (the large square button in the upper right-hand corner of the UserObject) from the detail view to go to full screen size.

3. Go to the panel view.

   You can move objects easily by dragging them to different locations. Experiment with different arrangements of objects.

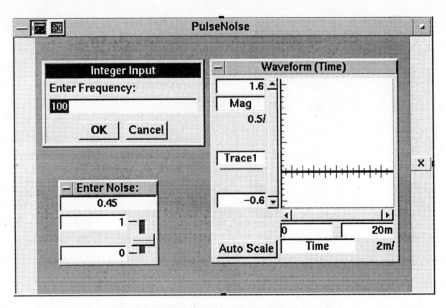

Fig. 2-5. The Panel View of PulseNoise

5. Enter various inputs for noise and run your program filling in the frequency as the program asks for it. Notice that your program operates the same way in the detail or panel view.

To Change Colors on the Panel

1. Select **Edit Properties** from the object menu (in panel view). Then choose **Colors**, click the **Panel View -Background:** button, and select the color you want.

To Save Your Program

1. Select **File => Save As...** and complete the dialog box, as you did in Chapter 1. Name the program **pulsnois.vee**.

To Print a Copy of Your Program

The following instructions presume that you configured a printer during installation. (File => Edit Default Preferences is used for setting default HP VEE preferences for all of your programs.)

1. Go to the detail view of the program.

2. Click the maximize button to expand the window.

3. Click **Edit => Clean Up Lines** in case the lines got messy in the development stage.

4. Select **File => Print Screen...** , edit the dialog box presented to suit your preferences, then click **OK**.

Easy Text Documentation of Your Program

By using the File => Save Documentation... command, you can specify a text file to hold your program documentation. HP VEE will list all objects, their key settings, their default and user names, their Edit Description entries, and their "nesting". For example, objects within a UserObject are nested one level from the main HP VEE environment, and these levels are indicated by numbers. The following exercises will clarify what we mean.

To Generate Documentation Automatically

1. Click **File => Save Documentation...**, name a file to hold the documentation using a **doc** suffix (pulsnois.doc, for example), then click **OK**.

2. Open the file in any text editor to view or print.

Using the Pulse Program yields the file shown in the following two figures.

```
Source file: "/users/bobh/ch2/pulsnois.vee"
File last revised: Fri Sep 29 07:21:38 1995
Date documented:  Mon Oct 30 09:28:59 1995
VEE revision: 3.2 (Beta - Fizzbin+)
SaveFormat: 2.0
Convert Infinity on Binary Read: no
Title: "pulsnois.vee"
Delete globals at PreRun: yes
Trig mode: Degrees

0: UserObject: "PulseNoise"
 Trig mode: Degrees
 Description:
  Purpose:

  The PulseNoise UserObject generates a pulse waveform, adds noise,
  stores the results, and displays the noisy pulse.  The user inputs the
  desired frequency and amount of noise each time the program runs.
  An operator interface will show only a slider bar for noise input and
  a waveform display.  The frequency will be input through a pop-up
  box.  A data output pin will also hold the resultant waveform.

  Output pin:

  A data output pin labeled X will hold the resultant waveform.

0.0:  Integer Input: "Integer Input"
 Prompt: "Enter Frequency:"
 Default Value: 100
 Value Constraint: 1<=value AND value<=193
 Error Message: "You must enter an integer between 1 and 193."
 Auto timeout: off
 Password Masking: off
```

Fig. 2-6. Documentation File for Pulsnois.vee

Notice the source file on top followed by the last revision date, the documentation date, and the HP VEE revision. Your program title appears here. The numbers before the decimal points indicate levels of nesting. Since there was only one level in this program, all numbers start with a **0**. The number after the decimal point indicates the order in which the objects were programmed. The title of the object follows the identification number plus a Edit Description entry, if there was one. The settings are documented.

```
0.1:  Pulse Generator: "Pulse Generator"
 Frequency: 100
 Pulse width: 0.005 sec
 Pulse delay: 0 sec
 Thresholds: 0%-100%
 Rise time: 1E-06 sec
 Fall time: 1E-06 sec
 High: 1
 Low:  0
 Burst mode: OFF
 Burst count: 2 pulses
 Burst repeat rate: 150
 Time span: 0.02 sec
 Num points: 256
 Error On Alias: yes

0.2:  Slider: "Enter Noise:"
 Constant Value: 0.341
 Lower Limit: 0
 Upper Limit: 1
 Detent Size: 0.001

0.3:  Noise Generator: "Noise Generator"
 Amplitide: 0.341
 Time span: 0.02 sec
 Num points: 256

0.4:  Formula: "a + b"
 Formula: A+B

0.5:  Y Plot: "Waveform (Time)"

0.6:  To File: "To File"
 Transactions:
```

Fig.2-7. The Remainder of the Documentation File

Note: *After running the Save Documentation command a File => Print All command will put the identification numbers on the objects, so you can match the text documentation to your printer output.*

Using Online Help and Debugging Tools

Now that you've created a simple program, we'd like to show you how to teach yourself HP VEE.

One of the best ways to learn about HP VEE is to examine the Help entries in the object menus, and then experiment with the objects until you understand how they work. These entries should be consulted first when something goes wrong.

If this doesn't solve the problem, and you would like to explore related topics, you should consult the Help facility on the main menu bar.

Using the Help Facility

Regardless of what operating system you're using, the help facility will provide information on the following topics:

- All menu items as well as shortcuts for most of them

- Instrument driver information

- Frequently performed tasks and many example programs

- Definition of HP VEE terms

- Using the help facility

- HP VEE version

You can browse, use the keyword index, use hyperlinks to related topics, or even do a search.

Exercises Using the Help Facility

- Find the help screen for the **For Count** object and read it.

- Do the same thing for the **Start** object.

- Look up the short-cut way to delete an object.

- Find detailed information on the HP 3325B Function Generator.

- Look up the word "terminal".

- Look up your HP VEE version number, and find out if there is any information specific to that version that's not covered in the manuals.

> *Note:* *HP VEE will give you two types of dialog boxes, when it doesn't understand what you're doing: a yellow-titled Caution box or a red-titled Error box. The error number given may be referenced in Error Codes in Contents under the main Help menu along with the message, cause, and recovery action.*

Debugging Programs in HP VEE

Let's use the Pulse Program to demonstrate debugging methods, so select **File => Open**, highlight **pulsnois.vee**, and click **OK**.

To Show Data Flow

1. Click the Show Data Flow button on the upper-right tool bar.

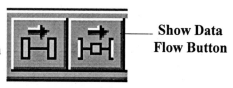

Show Data Flow Button

(To turn it off, click it again.) When you run your program you will see small squares moving along the data lines to indicate the flow of data in your programs.

Note: *You can create your programs in most cases by connecting data input/output pins alone without using any sequence pins. Notice that data moves from left to right in an HP VEE program, as shown below.*

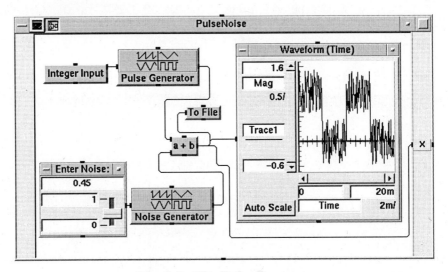

Fig. 2-8. The Pulse Program

Data moves from the input boxes to the Pulse and Noise Generators to the a + b object. Finally, it moves to the Waveform (Time) display, the output pin X, and the To File object.

To Show Execution Flow

1. Click the Show Execution Flow button on the tool bar.

Show Execution Flow Button

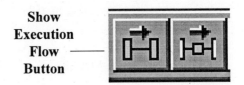

When you run the program, you will see a colored outline around the objects as they execute.

Use Data Flow and Execution Flow to understand how your program is operating, but turn them off to get higher performance. Combining these features with debugging tools such as breakpoints will help you understand how an HP VEE program works and where possible errors lie.

To Examine Data on a Line

Checking the data at different points in your program is a fast, useful way to debug your program. You already know how to double-click on terminals to examine the data. The Line Probe is a way to view the data on a given line.

1. Select the **Line Probe** button on the upper-right tool bar.

 **Line Probe Button**

The pointer becomes a small plus sign, which you place over a line and click to examine the data. A dialog box will present the data type and value(s). Click **OK** when you're done.

Shortcut: *Hold down Shift and click on the line to get the dialog box.*

Using the Alphanumeric Displays for Debugging

You can add the Alphanumeric or Logging Alphanumeric displays at certain points in your program to track the flow of data. When things are working correctly, just delete them. Remember that AlphaNumeric displays a single data container (a Scalar value, an Array 1D, or Array 2D); whereas, Logging AlphaNumeric (either a Scalar or Array 1D) displays consecutive input as a history of previous values. You can also use a Counter to see how many times an object ran.

To Set a Breakpoint on a Single Object

You set breakpoints in a program before a particular object operates to examine the data. A colored outline will highlight an object to indicate a breakpoint is set. When the program runs, it will pause before executing that object.

1. Double-click the title bar of an object to get the **Edit Properties** dialog box, then select **Breakpoint Enabled** under **Debug**.

To Set Breakpoints on Several Objects

1. Select the objects. (Press Ctrl and click on each object.)

Toggle
Breakpoint(s)
Button
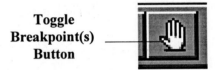

2. Click the **Toggle Breakpoint(s)** button on the upper-right tool bar. (Also in the Debug menu.)

To Resume a Program

1. Just click the **Resume** button on the tool bar. (Also in the Debug menu.)

Resume
Button
(same as Run
Button)

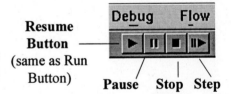

Pause   Stop   Step

To Clear Breakpoint(s)

Toggle
Breakpoint(s)
Button
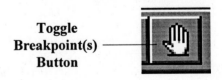

1. Select the objects with breakpoints.

2. Click the Toggle Breakpoint(s) button on the upper-right tool bar. (Also in the Debug menu.)

To Clear All Breakpoints

1. Click **Debug => Clear All Breakpoints**. (Or click the **Toggle Breakpoint(s)** button on the tool bar.)

To Pause, Stop, or Step Through a Program

1. Just click the **Pause**, **Stop**, or **Step** buttons on the upper-left tool bar. (Also in the Debug menu.)

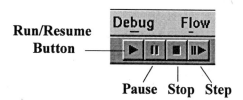

Run/Resume Button

Pause Stop Step

Note: *During an HP VEE program you might get an error message. HP VEE will automatically put an outline around the object where the error was found. You can either correct the error and the outline will disappear, or you can click the Stop button, which will remove the red outline, and then fix the error.*

The Order of Events Inside an Object

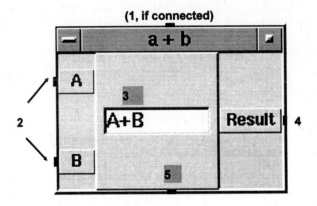

Fig. 2-9. The Order of Events in an Object

1. If the sequence input pin is connected, the object will not operate until it receives a message to execute (a "ping" in HP VEE terms). However, the sequence input pin does not have to be connected.

2. All data input pins must have data before the object operates. (Most objects may add data input/output pins to the object. Explore the Add/Delete Terminal menu in any object menu to find out what pins can be added.)

3. The object performs its task. In this case, **A** is added to **B**.

4. The data output pin fires. The object waits for a signal from the next object that the data is received, before its operation is completed.

   Therefore, a given object does not fire its sequence output pin until all objects connected to its data output pin have received data.

5. The sequence output pin fires.

There are two exceptions to this sequence of events:

First, control input pins may be added to some objects, which may cause an immediate execution of an object sub-function such as a Clear or Autoscale operation in the Waveform (Time) display. Control lines to an object are dashed lines. Note that the object is not required to have data on a control pin to execute. See the figure below. Notice that the display receives the waveform data and displays it, then the sequence output pin is fired, which in turn pings the Auto Scale control pin to adjust the Y axis scales.

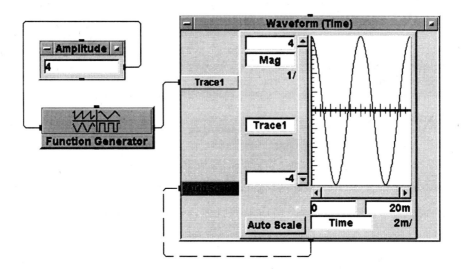

Fig. 2-10. Control Line Used to Execute Autoscale

Secondly, error output pins may be added to trap errors inside an object. They will override standard object behavior. If an error occurs during object execution, the error pin will send out a message, and the data output pins will not fire.

The Execution Order of Objects in a Program

1. **Start** objects operate first.

   Note: *Flow => Start is used to operate individual threads, as shown below. A thread is a set of objects connected by solid lines in an HP VEE program.*

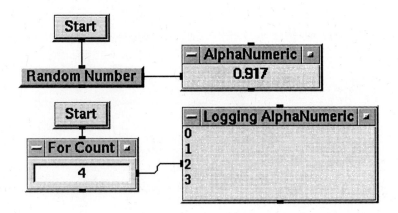

Fig. 2-11. Start Objects Executing Separate Threads

2. Objects with no data input pins operate next. **Data => Constant** objects are often in this category.

3. Objects with input pins operate when all connected inputs are satisfied. (Recall that connecting sequence inputs is optional.)

Stepping Through the Pulse Program

1. Get the **pulsenois.vee** program on your screen.

2. Click the **Step** button on the tool bar.

3. As you keep clicking **Step**, the colored outlines around the objects about to execute guide you through the program sequentially.

Since there is no Start object, the first object with no inputs connected is the UserObject, so it executes first. Within the PulseNoise UserObject the input boxes have no input pins connected, so they execute first in no defined order. If you wanted them to execute in a particular order, you could control this by connecting their sequence pins. Data flows left to right, so you will see the data generators executing next in no particular order. The addition (a + b) object cannot execute until both inputs are satisfied. Then the Waveform (Time) and To File objects execute in the order that they were added to the program. Again, you could mandate execution order anywhere in the program by using the sequence pins or the Flow => Do object. (To learn more about the Do object consult Help.)

On Your Own

Generate a sine wave. Add noise to it. The user should be able to control the amplitude of the wave as well as the amount of noise to add. Get the inputs using a Real Slider and a pop-up dialog box. Display the results graphically using a red trace. Add a control input pin to your display for AutoScale and connect it to the sequence output pin. (After the display has gathered the data, the sequence out pin fires, which triggers the AutoScale control pin.)

Store the results in a file called sinenois.dat. Put your test procedure in a module named SineNoise. Create a user interface that uses a pop-up box for amplitude input, uses a slider for the noise input, and shows a display of results. Give the operator precise instructions on how to proceed. Save your program as sinenois.vee. Print hardcopy of the detailed view of your program. Save textual documentation of your program in sinenois.dat and print a copy of this file.

EXTRA CREDIT!

Figure out how you would retrieve the program data from the sinenois.dat file and display it in a Alphanumeric display. You'll have to enlarge the display with Size in the object menu.

(HINT: You'll need to use sequence pins. When retrieving the data you'll be looking for an array, not a scalar.)

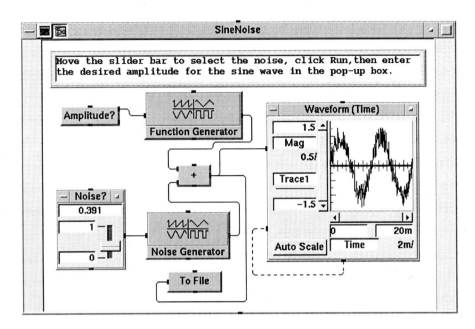

Fig. 2-12. The SineNoise UserObject (Detail View)

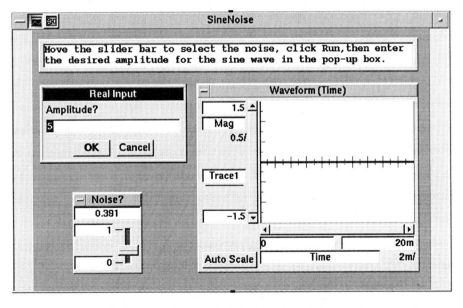

Fig. 2-13. The SineNoise UserObject (Panel View)

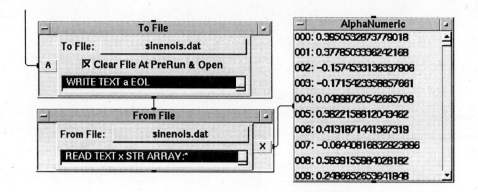

Fig. 2-14. Extra Credit Part of Sinenois Program

Notes on Different Versions of HP VEE

This book focuses on HP VEE 3.2. You could use this tutorial with future versions of HP VEE by consulting the entries in Help => Latest Information and the latest manuals to note any changes. HP VEE is synchronized on all platforms.

If you have an earlier version, upgrades are available at a very low cost. Contact your HP sales representative for details.

Chapter 2 Checklist

You should now be able to perform the following tasks. Review topics, if necessary, before proceeding to Chapter 3.

- Create a modular test program.

- Document your work.

- Generate a documentation file.

- Set up pop-up dialog boxes and sliders (or knobs) for user inputs.

- Simulate test data for prototyping.

- Add inputs to objects.

- Add inputs to control functions on the Pulse and Noise Generators.

- Use math operators.

- Store test results in a file.

- Create a UserObject that outputs a single result.

- Create an operator interface for a program.

- Save and print a program.

- Use online help.

- Show data and execution flow.

- Use the line probe to examine data.

- Use Alphanumeric displays for debugging.

- Use breakpoints.

- Step through a program.

- Explain the order of events inside an object.

- Explain the execution order of objects in a program.

Two Easy Ways
To Control Instruments

3

Overview

HP VEE provides two easy ways to control instruments: instrument drivers and the "Direct I/O" object. Instrument drivers give you a simple user interface to control an instrument from your computer screen. With a driver you don't need to know the unique software commands that control a particular instrument. Once you've set up the instrument using menu selections and dialog boxes, the driver will automatically send the right command strings over the bus.

With the Direct I/O object, on the other hand, you do have to know the instrument command strings. HP VEE provides you with a convenient method of transmitting commands and receiving data. Using Direct I/O you can communicate with any instrument that connects to one of the supported interfaces.

*In this chapter
you'll learn about:*

- Configuring an HP-IB instrument

- Using an instrument driver

- Using the Direct I/O object

- VXI*plug&play* drivers

- The Instrument Driver Monitor

- Other I/O Features

- Controlling PC plug-in boards

This chapter is designed to give you the fundamentals of controlling instruments to cover most situations using HP-IB, RS-232, or GPIO interfaces. For more information on communication with the VXI backplane, consult HP VEE documentation. VXI*plug&play* drivers are discussed later in this chapter. Data acquisition using PC plug-in boards is also discussed in a later section. Let's take a look at an instrument panel and a Direct I/O object.

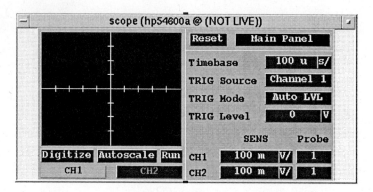

Fig. 3-1. The HP54600A Scope Instrument Panel

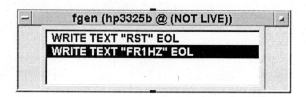

Fig. 3-2. A Function Generator Direct I/O Object

An instrument driver gives you maximum ease-of-use and saves the most development time. You get over 450 instrument drivers for different instrument vendors with HP VEE in addition to the numerous VXI*plug&play* drivers (WIN, WIN95, and WIN-NT frameworks) available from other VXI instrument companies.

If you want to control instruments from any vendor *without* drivers, you have a number of options:

- Use the Direct I/O object instead of an instrument driver.

- Use the Instrument Driver Language to write your own driver.

- Ask HP to add the driver to the queue of drivers under development.

- Ask HP to recommend contractors that could write the driver.

With Direct I/O you can communicate with any instrument from any vendor over standard interfaces. Although it requires slightly more effort than an instrument driver, it's still very easy to use. Also, Direct I/O yields faster execution speeds. Choosing the best method of instrument control will depend on driver availability, the need for fast test development, and your performance requirements.

Whether you use drivers or Direct I/O, you need to configure your instrument before you can talk to it from a program, so the first lab exercise covers configuration.

Lab 3 - 1: Configuring an HP-IB Instrument

With HP VEE you can develop your programs *without* the instruments present. For the purposes of this exercise, let's configure a multimeter (HP 3478A) for use with an instrument panel. Then we'll show you how easy it would be to add the physical instrument to the configuration.

To Configure a Multimeter Without the Instrument Present

1. Select **I/O => Other Instruments...** (instruments not VXI*plug&play* compatible). *Move the dialog box to the upper-left work area (click and drag its title bar). See the figure below.*

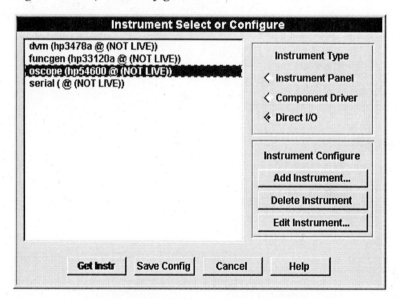

Fig. 3-3. The Instrument Select or Configure Box

The instruments on the left have already been configured on this system. To configure an instrument, you first choose the Instrument Type in the upper-right area of the box.

We've already described the differences between an Instrument Driver and a Direct I/O object. A Component Driver simply uses a subset of the functions provided by an instrument panel. (Consult HP VEE documentation for more information on Component Drivers.) After you've chosen an instrument type, you click Add Instrument... under Instrument Configure in the lower-right area of the box to get a Device Configuration dialog box.

2. Click **Add Instrument...**.

   The entries in the **Device Configuration** dialog box mean:

   Name: Any name you'd like to call the instrument in your program.

   Interface: Choose one from HP-IB, Serial, VXI. (GPIO available on the HP 9000, Series 300 and 700 workstations).

   Address: The select code of the interface (HP-IB is usually 7) plus the local bus address of the instrument (the default on the multimeter is 23). If you leave the address at 0, it means that you're developing without an instrument present.

   Gateway: Use **This Host** to control instruments locally, or enter a **Gateway** for remote control. (See HP VEE documentation for more information.)

   Device Type: This will be the name of the driver file for the instrument. HP VEE will enter this for you, as you will see in a moment.

   Timeout: The maximum number of seconds allowed without an instrument response, before you get an error message.

   Byte Ordering: Specifies the order the device uses for reading and writing binary data. You can toggle between Most Significant Byte first or Least Significant Byte first. All IEEE488.2-compliant devices must default to MSB order.

Live Mode: This will be set to the **OFF** position, unless you have an instrument present. If you've specified an address, HP VEE defaults to the **ON** setting, which signifies live communication with the instrument.

Direct I/O Config ... and Instrument Driver Config ... will present additional dialog boxes.

3. Edit **newDevice** to **Multimeter** making sure to use the **Tab** key instead of the **Enter** key. (If you hit the **Enter** key by mistake, just click **Edit Instrument...** and continue.)

Tip: *Pressing the Tab key after typing in a field will move you to the next field; Shift-Tab moves you to the previous field. Pressing Enter is equivalent to clicking OK, and HP VEE will close your dialog box.*

4. Leave all the other defaults as they are, and click **Instrument Driver Config ....** Your screen should look similar to Figure 3-4, except we've already selected an **ID Filename**.

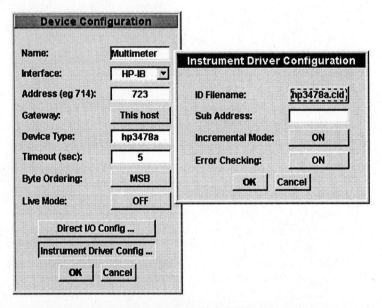

Fig. 3-4. The Instrument Driver Configuration Box

5. Click the field to the right of **ID Filename** to obtain a list box entitled **Read from what Instrument Driver?**. This list includes all of the instrument driver files loaded with your revision of HP VEE in the directory specified. Scroll down the list to highlight **hp3478a.cid**, then click **OK**.

   Tip: *You can also double-click on a highlighted file to select it.*

   The *.cid files signify the compiled instrument driver files. Notice that the ID Filename field in the Instrument Driver Configuration box has been filled in for you. Explanations of the other entries follow:

   Sub Address: This field is generally not used, so you can omit it. Sub addresses are used by non-VXI cardcage instruments for identifying plug-in modules.

   Incremental Mode: Leave the default, unless you'd like to send the entire instrument command string for your instrument state each time you change a setting.

   Error Checking: Leave the default, unless you need extra throughput or you're not worried about checking for I/O errors.

6. Click **OK** in both the **Instrument Driver Configuration** and **Device Configuration** boxes.

   Note: *An instrument object named Multimeter using the driver file hp3478a.cid is now in your list of available instruments. It does not have a bus address specified, because it is NOT LIVE at present. You can develop your program in this mode, and add an address later, when you're ready to connect the instrument to your computer.*

7. Click **Save Config** to close the **Instrument Select or Configure** box.

You have now added the HP 3478A Multimeter to your device list. You could use this driver while programming, even though the actual instrument was not present. The next exercise will show you how easy it is to add the instrument later.

To Add the Physical Instrument to your Configuration

1. Select I/O => Other Instruments..., and click **Edit Instrument...** with the Multimeter highlighted.

2. Double-click the **Address** field to highlight the current entry, type **723**, then click **OK**.

   (If the HP-IB select code is not 7, replace 7 with that number.)

3. Click **Save Config** to save your changes.

To Select an Instrument to Use in your Program

1. Select **I/O => Other Instruments....**

2. Highlight your selection, in this case the **Multimeter (hp3478a @ 723),** click **Instrument Panel** (same as "instrument driver" in this context) in the **Instrument Type** menu, then click **Get Instr**.

   If you had chosen Direct I/O, you would have gotten a Direct I/O object with the same name talking to an instrument at the address specified.

3. Place the outline of the **Multimeter** panel where you want it and click to place it.

   You may now use the instrument driver in your program like any other HP VEE object.

Try the **On Your Own** example to make sure you understand the configuration process, then we'll do an exercise that configures an instrument for **Direct I/O**.

On Your Own

Configure an HP 54600 Oscilloscope without the instrument present, and call it **Digit_Scope**. Then put it in the work area, as though you were going to use it in a program.

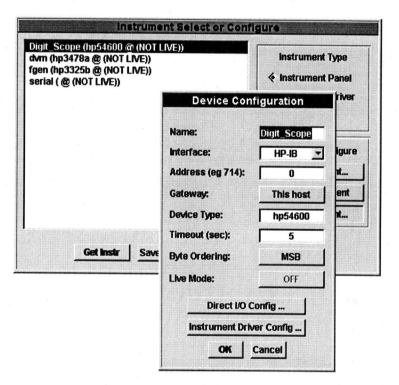

Fig. 3-5. The Device Configuration for Digit_Scope

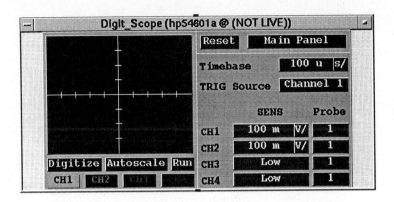

Fig. 3-6. The Digit_Scope Instrument Driver

Lab 3-2: Configuring a Function Generator for Direct I/O

When you don't have a driver for a particular instrument, or you want higher throughput, use the Direct I/O object. Let's configure a function generator (HP 3325B) using Direct I/O.

1. Select **I/O => Other Instruments...** to get the **Instrument Select or Configure** dialog box.

2. Click **Add Instrument...** to get the **Device Configuration** dialog box. Then edit the **Name** field to **FuncGen** and press the **Tab** key.

   Note: We are using the HP-IB interface here (IEEE488). To configure Serial, GPIO, or VXI instrumentation, see HP VEE documentation.

3. Click **Direct I/O Config...** to get the **Direct I/O Configuration** dialog box, as shown in Figure 3-7.

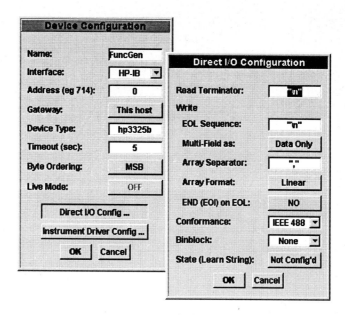

Fig. 3-7. The Direct I/O Configuration Dialog Box

HP VEE selects default values based on your previous selection of an interface. Edit these values, if necessary.

4. Click **OK** to return to the **Device Configuration** box, and notice that the **Device Type** field is not completed, because you're not configuring an instrument panel. Click **OK** to return to the **Instrument Select or Configure** box.

5. Notice that **FuncGen (@ (NOT LIVE))** is now highlighted. If you have an instrument, fill in the Address field. Click **Save Config** to preserve your new configuration and return to the work area.

6. Select **I/O => Other Instruments....** Highlight FuncGen and click Direct I/O for **Instrument Type.** Click **Get Instr** and place the **Direct I/O** object where you want it.

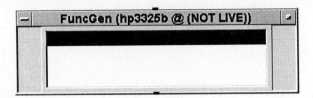

Fig. 3-8. The FuncGen Direct I/O Object

Of course, you have to configure I/O transactions, before the object above can do useful work in your program. We'll teach you how to do that in the Using Direct I/O section, but first try this On Your Own exercise to make sure you understand the configuration process.

On Your Own

Configure any HP-IB instrument you have for Direct I/O. You can experiment sending and receiving commands when we get to the Using Direct I/O exercises.

Using an Instrument Driver

We'll use the HP 3325B Function Generator for these exercises. The principles are the same in using any HP VEE instrument driver. You use an instrument driver instead of programming an instrument directly, because it saves you time in the development and modification of your programs. You change the settings on an instrument through menu selections or editing fields in dialog boxes. If the instrument is connected and Live Mode is on, the changes you make will register on the instrument.

To use an instrument driver in a program you simply add inputs and/or outputs as needed, and connect it to other objects to make a program. You can use several instances of the same driver in a program to set the instrument to different states. HP VEE allows you to iconize a driver to save space or to retain the open view for an easy reminder of instrument settings. You can even change settings while a program is running. We'll practice first, and then you can experiment using your own instruments.

To Change Settings on an Instrument Driver

1. Select **I/O => Other Instruments...**.

2. Double-click **fgen** to select the pre-configured HP 3325B and place it on the left. (This process would be the same regardless of the instrument, as long as the instrument had been configured and added to your list.)

   You are programming without the instrument attached, but, if it were attached, you would edit your configuration to the proper address.

3. Click **Sine** in the **Function** field to get a pop-up menu, then select **Triangle**. See Figure 3-9.

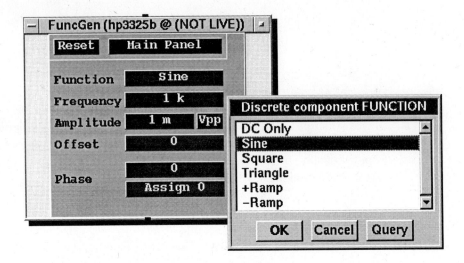

Fig. 3-9. The Function Pop-up Menu on the HP3325B

4. Click the field to the right of **Frequency**.

5. Type **100** in the **Continuous component FREQUENCY** dialog box that appears, and click **OK**.

   Note that your **Frequency** setting has now changed.

Employ the same methods to change the instrument settings on any driver. If the instrument is configured with an address and Live Mode is on, every change you make in the driver panel is reflected by the instrument.

To Move to Other Instrument Driver Panels

Most drivers have more than one panel to simplify the user interface. To move to a different panel you click Main Panel to get a menu of panels.

1. Click **Main Panel** and select **Sweep Panel** from the menu presented.

   Return to the **Main Panel**.

To Add Inputs and/or Outputs to an Instrument Panel

So far we've just interacted with the panel directly. You can also control settings or read data from an instrument in your program by adding data inputs and/or outputs to the driver. The input and output areas are shown in the figure below.

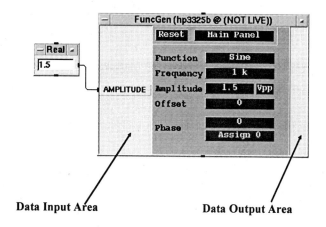

Data Input Area   Data Output Area

Fig. 3-10. The Data Input and Output Areas on a Driver

1. Place the mouse pointer over the data input area of the function generator instrument panel, and press **CTRL-a** to add a data input terminal.

   A list box of the instrument components appears.

2. Select the desired component from the menu presented.

   Note: You could also open the object menu and select Add Terminal by Component => Select Input Component. Then select the desired component field on the driver.

Follow the same process to add a data output, except you place the mouse pointer in the data output area instead of the input area.

To Delete Data Input or Output Terminals

1. Place the mouse pointer over the terminal and press **CTRL-d**.

   Note: You could also open the object menu and select Delete Terminal => Input... from the object menu and choose the appropriate input from the menu presented.

On Your Own

Set a state on the HP 3325B Function Generator (or any other function generator you have). Change the Function setting to a Square wave. Add input components for Amplitude and Frequency. Create input dialog boxes for the amplitude and frequency and modify the titles to user prompts. Enter different values for the amplitude and frequency, and run your program to see if the settings are changed after user inputs. (If an instrument is attached, then its settings will change if **Live Mode** is on.)

Using Direct I/O

Let's explore the most fundamental operations: writing text commands, reading data, and uploading/downloading instrument states.

To Write Text Commands to an Instrument

(a) Sending a Single Quoted String

Most HP-IB instruments use alphanumeric strings for commands sent to the instrument. Let's suppose you want to send a command to the HP3325B Function Generator to set the amplitude to 5 volts. The command string is "AM 5 VO". After configuring the instrument for Direct I/O and selecting it from the available devices, you would do the following:

1. Click the transaction bar to get the **I/O Transaction** dialog box, as shown below.

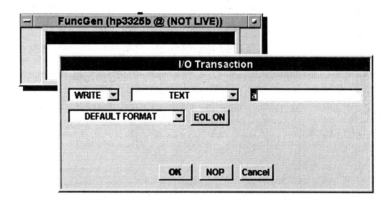

Fig. 3-11. The I/O Transaction Dialog Box

The button labeled WRITE holds a menu including the actions READ, WRITE, EXECUTE, and WAIT. In this context, you want to write data to an instrument, so use the default selection. Open the object menu and consult Help to find out what each action means.

You can also use three of the other default selections: TEXT, DEFAULT FORMAT, and EOL ON. However, the field containing "a" must be edited to our text command string.

WRITE TEXT transactions are of this form:

WRITE TEXT ExpressionList [Format]

ExpressionList is a single expression or a comma-separated list of expressions. When you edit **a**, you will be creating an ExpressionList in the form of a single quoted string of text. DEFAULT FORMAT means that HP VEE will automatically determine an appropriate text representation based on the data type of the item being written. For example, text strings are sent without conversion, but a variable containing a scalar integer such as 4427 in decimal notation would be converted to four text characters. EOL ON signifies that the end-of-line sequence specified during configuration will be sent.

2. The input field labeled **a** will be highlighted, so just type **"AM 5 VO"** (including the quotes), then click **OK**.

   You now see the transaction bar labeled with **WRITE TEXT "AM5VO" EOL**, as shown below. The text in quotation marks is the command that will be sent to the HP3325B when your program runs.

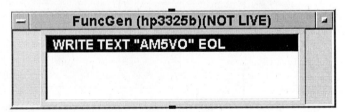

Fig. 3-12. A Direct I/O Transaction

In most cases this process will be the same for sending text commands to instruments. However, there are instruments that specify characters sent at the end of each command or at the end of a group of commands. You need to get this information from the instrument documentation, then include it in the Direct I/O Configuration dialog box.

(b) Sending an Expression List

Another variation of sending text command strings is brought out in the following exercise. Suppose you want to loop through a number of frequencies in the function generator. How would you do that using a single Direct I/O transaction? (Ans: Use a variable for the frequency as a part of an Expression List, and add a data input for that variable to the Direct I/O object.)

1. After putting the **Direct I/O** object for the HP3325B in the work area, click the transaction bar to get the **I/O Transaction** dialog box.

   You can use all of the defaults except for the command string. In this case, you need the format "FR", <frequency number>, "HZ". This is an Expression List, each expression being separated by commas. The frequency number will be signified by the variable A, which you'll add to the Direct I/O object as a data input.

2. The input field for command strings is highlighted, so type **"FR",A,"HZ"**.

   For example, if A were 100, HP VEE would send the "FR100HZ" string.

3. To add a data input pin, place the mouse pointer over the **Direct I/O** data input area and press **Ctrl-a**.

   HP VEE adds a data input pin labeled **A**.

4. Select **Flow => Repeat =>For Range** and place it to the left of the **Direct I/O** object.

5. Connect the **For Range** data output pin to the **Direct I/O** data input pin.

6. Edit the fields in **For Range** to: **From 10, Thru 1.8M**, and **Step 50k**.

   This means For Range will send out numbers ranging from 10 to 1.8 million in steps of 50,000. As those numbers are received by the Direct I/O object, the command string will tell the function generator to sweep those same frequencies. Your Direct I/O setup should look like Figure 3-13.

Fig. 3-13. Direct I/O Setup Using an Input Variable

7. (optional) Connect an HP3325B to your computer and edit the configuration of this **Direct I/O** object to include the address of the instrument. Run this program and you will see the instrument sweeping through these frequencies.

To Read Data From an Instrument

Instruments send data to a computer in many different formats. You must know what datatype you want to read, and whether the data is returned as a single value (scalar) or an array. You must also know if the instrument returns data as text (ASCII) or binary. You can find this information in the instrument documentation or you can use the HP VEE Bus I/O Monitor in the I/O menu to examine the data being returned. This information determines how you will configure the HP VEE transaction. Since READ TEXT transactions are the most common, we will discuss them here. Other encodings for READ besides TEXT are BINARY, BINBLOCK, and CONTAINER, which are discussed in detail in the HP VEE documentation.

(a) Reading Measurements from a Multimeter

Let's use the HP3478A Multimeter for an example. It's already configured at address 723 to be run with the HP VEE examples. Suppose the Multimeter is connected to the HP3325B Function Generator you used in the last exercise. When the generator sends out a certain frequency you would like the multimeter to trigger a reading and send the results back to HP VEE. Here's how you would configure the transactions for the multimeter:

1. Select **I/O => Other Instruments...**, highlight **dvm (hp3478a @ 723)**, click **Direct I/O**, then click **Get Instr**.

2. Double-click the blank transaction bar to get the **I/O Transaction** dialog box.

3. The input field is highlighted, so type **"T5"**, then click **OK**.

   T5 is the command for a single trigger to the multimeter.

4. Open the object menu and click **Add Trans...** to add another transaction bar and open the I/O Transaction dialog box.

   *Shortcut: Double-click the area immediately below the last transaction to add another transaction and display its **I/O Transaction** dialog box.*

5. Click the down arrow beside **WRITE** to get a drop-down menu, then select **READ**.

   You'll notice that there are new buttons appearing in the I/O Transaction box resulting from this selection.

6. Change the ExpressionList input field containing **x** to X. Press **Tab** to move to the next field.

   Data returned from an instrument is sent to data output pins. We will add one in a moment, and the default name of the pin is X, so we have labeled our variable by the same name. (Note: The names are not case sensitive.)

7. Leave the **REAL FORMAT** default.

   The multimeter returns single readings as real numbers.

8. Leave **DEFAULT NUM CHARS** as is.

The default for the number of characters is 20. If you want to change this number, click on **DEFAULT NUM CHARS** to toggle to **MAX NUM CHARS** and change the number **20** to the number of characters you want.

9. Leave **SCALAR** as is and click **OK**.

You will see your transaction displayed on the bar as:

READ TEXT X REAL

Note: *If the instrument is returning an array of values, just click on the SCALAR menu in the I/O Transaction dialog box to get the menu for different dimensions, as shown below. Once you've selected the array dimension, you will also have to specify a size for the array.*

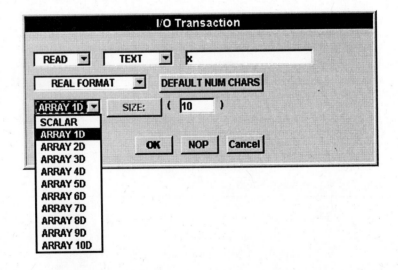

Fig. 3-14. The Select Read Dimension List Box

11. Place the mouse pointer over the data output area and press **Ctrl-a** to add a data output pin labeled **X** for the returned measurement.

Your two Direct I/O transactions should look like Figure 3-15.

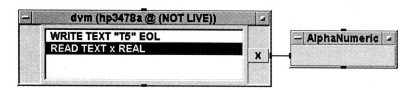

Fig. 3-15. Direct I/O Configured to Read a Measurement

The process we followed in the above exercise would be similar regardless of the data format for the **READ TEXT** transaction. The table below includes a brief description of the other data formats supported. For a more detailed discussion of each item refer to HP VEE documentation.

Table 3-1. Formats for READ TEXT Transactions

Format	Description
CHAR	Reads *any* 8-bit character.
TOKEN	Reads a contiguous list of characters as a unit called a token. Tokens are separated by specified delimiter characters that you specify such as a space or comma.
STRING	Reads a list of 8-bit characters as a unit. Most control characters are read and discarded. The end of the string is reached when the specified number of characters has been read, or when a newline character is encountered.
INTEGER	Reads a list of characters and interprets them as a decimal or non-decimal representation of an integer. The only characters considered to be part of a decimal INTEGER are 0123456789-+. VEE recognizes the prefix 0x (hex) and all Non-Decimal Numeric formats specified by IEEE 488.2: #H (hex), #Q (octal), #B (binary).
OCTAL	Reads a list of characters and interprets them as the octal representation of an integer. These characters include 01234567. VEE recognizes the IEEE 488.2 Non-Decimal Numeric prefix #Q for octal numbers.
HEX	Reads a list of characters and interprets them as the hexadecimal representation of an integer. These characters include 0123456789abcdefABCDEF. The character 0x is the default prefix; it is not part of the number and is read and ignored. VEE also recognizes the IEEE 488.2 Non-Decimal Numeric prefix #H for hexadecimal numbers.

Format	Description
REAL	Reads a list of characters and interprets them as the decimal representation of a Real (floating-point) number. All common notations are recognized including leading signs, signed exponents, and decimal points. The characters recognized to be part of a REAL are 0123456789-+.Ee. VEE also recognizes certain characters as suffix multipliers: P for 10^{15}, T for 10^{12}, G for 10^{9}, M for 10^{6}, k or K for 10^{3}, m for 10^{-3}, u for 10^{-6}, n for 10^{-9}, p for 10^{-12}, f for 10^{-15}.
COMPLEX	Reads the equivalent of two REALs and interprets them as a complex number. The first number read is the real part, and the second number is the imaginary part.
PCOMPLEX	Reads the equivalent of two REALs and interprets them as a complex number in polar form (phasor notation). The first number is the magnitude and the second is the angle. You may specify units of measure for phase in the transaction.
COORD	Reads the equivalent of two or more REALs and interprets them as rectangular coordinates.
TIME STAMP	Reads one of the specified HP VEE time stamp formats which represent the calendar data and/or time of day.

To Upload and Download Instrument States

Some instruments offer a learn string capability. The learn string embodies all the function settings that compose an instrument state. Direct I/O will upload this learn string, save it with that particular Direct I/O object, and later download it to the instrument in your program. The procedure to follow is a simple one.

1. Set your instrument to the desired state manually.

2. Open the **Direct I/O** object menu and click **Upload State**.

   Now this state is associated with this particular instance of the **Direct I/O** object.

3. Open an **I/O Transaction** dialog box by clicking a blank transaction bar.

4. Click **TEXT**, highlight **STATE (LEARN STRING)** from the **Select Write Encoding** list box, and click **OK**. Then click **OK** to close the I/O **Transaction** box.

Uploading and downloading are controlled by your settings in the Direct I/O Configuration dialog box. If Conformance is IEEE 488.2, then HP VEE will automatically handle learn strings using the 488.2 *LRN? definition. If Conformance is IEEE 488, then Upload String specifies the command used to query the state, and Download String specifies the command that precedes the state string when downloaded. Look at the example in Figure 3-16.

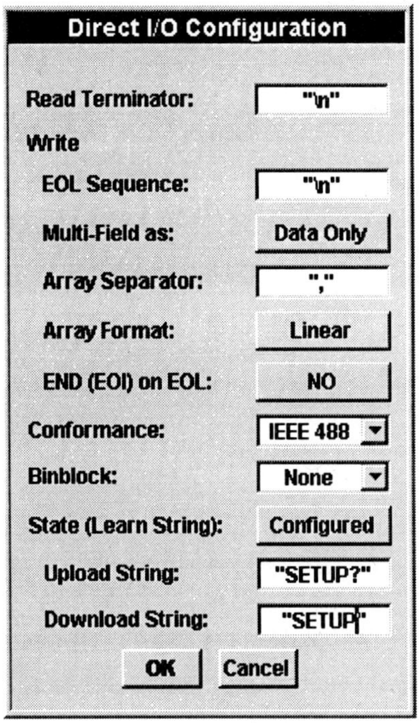

Direct I/O Configuration	
Read Terminator:	"\n"
Write	
EOL Sequence:	"\n"
Multi-Field as:	Data Only
Array Separator:	","
Array Format:	Linear
END (EOI) on EOL:	NO
Conformance:	IEEE 488 ▼
Binblock:	None ▼
State (Learn String):	Configured
Upload String:	"SETUP?"
Download String:	"SETUP"
OK	Cancel

**Fig. 3-16. Configuring for
Learn Strings**

Conformance can support IEEE 488 or IEEE 488.2. Here we're using the
HP 54100A Digitizing Oscilloscope, which conforms to IEEE 488 and
requires a "SETUP?" to query the learn string and "SETUP " to precede the
learn string when downloading. When you select Configured for State
(Learn String) two more fields appear, Upload String and Download String.
The proper strings have been entered in their input fields.

VXIplug&play Drivers

To quote the **VXIplug&play Systems Alliance VPP-1: Charter Document, June 21, 1995**:

"The VXIplug&play Systems Alliance is an organization whose members share a common commitment to end-user success with open, multivendor VXI systems. The alliance will accomplish major improvements in ease of use by endorsing and implementing common standards and practices in both hardware and software, beyond the scope of the VXIbus specifications."

What this means in terms of drivers is that the Alliance has endorsed a unique type of VXI instrument driver in the WIN, WIN95, WIN-NT, and HP-UX frameworks that can be used with different application development environments such as HP VEE, C, C++, Visual Basic, and LabVIEW.

The drivers are issued and supported by the various instrument vendors. These are C-based drivers and are designed for the maximum performance and ease of use. See the next two figures for an example using the HPE1410 VXIplug&play driver.

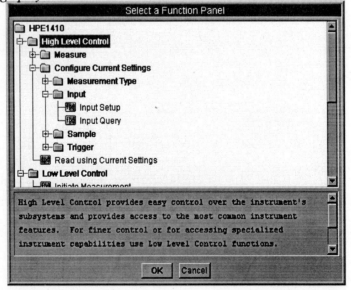

Fig. 3-17. Clear Organization in a VXIplug&play Driver

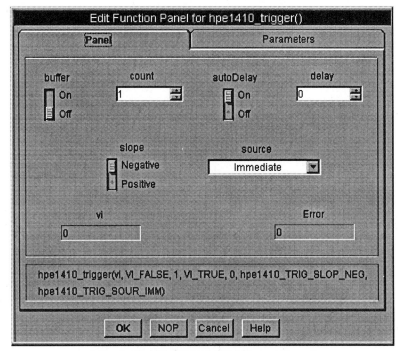

Fig. 3-18. The HPE1410 Front Panel

HP VEE 3.1 for Windows 3.1 and HP VEE 3.2 for Windows 95 and Windows NT are fully VXI*plug&play* compatible. All available VXIplug&play drivers from HP will ship in the near future as a separate product (contact HP's WWW page, http://WWW.hp.com, or the BBS for information). For more information about VXI*plug&play*, please call HP Test & Measurement's FaxBack service with a touch-tone phone at 970-679-3031. Enter the following responses when requested: 1, 1, 1080#, #, your FAX number, 1, your voice telephone number, and #. See HP VEE documentation for more information.

The HP VEE team intends to exceed the Alliance's standards and deliver the most effective implementation of these drivers. They also view HP VEE as one of the software components of an integrated test system, so other languages such as C, C++, or Visual Basic are viewed as logical extensions to HP VEE systems, not as competitive languages.

The Instrument Driver Monitor

The ID Monitor in the I/O menu is used to monitor the current states of instruments in your system. It can be used within HP VEE and as a separate utility. It also supports instument state store/recall capability. This is particularly useful in manufacturing functional test when you want to check your instruments at a glance. (At this point, the monitor may only be used with HP VEE instrument drivers, not the Direct I/O object or VXI*plug&play* drivers.)

Other I/O Features

- Explore the full power of HP VEE's I/O capabilities in the I/O => Advanced I/O submenu: Interface Operations, Device Event, Interface Event, and MultiDevice Direct I/O.

- You can display, print, or store your bus activity for careful debugging with the Bus I/O Monitor in the I/O menu.

- You can also change I/O configurations in your program. Consult HP VEE documentation for further details.

PC Plug-in Boards/Cards

HP VEE provides two ways to control PC plug-in boards or cards:

(1) Data Translation's Visual Programming Interface (Order the VPI application directly through Data Translation. See Appendix A.)

(2) Dynamic link libraries supplied by the PC board manufacturer (See chapter 12 for information on using dynamic link libraries.)

Data Translation's Visual Programming Interface (VPI)

Data Translation's VPI works with HP VEE 3.2 to create the most seamless data acquisition performance for PC plug-ins. By leveraging the flexibility of Data Translation's Open Layers standards, you have access to over 50 data acquisition boards.

The method works with plug-in ISA and PCI of PCMCIA-based data acquisition applications that require low channel or single point counts. The VPI adds a menu selection and specific PC plug-in data acquisition icons to HP VEE. These drive the Data Translation hardware functionality.

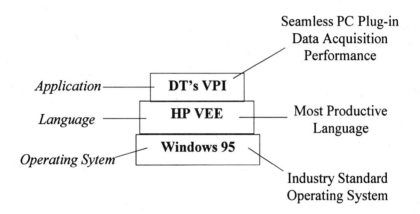

Fig. 2-19. Data Translation's VPI Application

Chapter 3 Checklist

You should now be able to perform the following tasks. Review the appropriate topics, if necessary, before moving on to the next chapter.

- Explain the benefits of using instrument drivers and Direct I/O.

- Explain the process for controlling instruments.

- Configure an instrument for a state driver.

- Configure an instrument for Direct I/O.

- Change settings on an instrument driver.

- Add and delete component inputs and outputs.

- Move to different panels on an instrument driver.

- Use Direct I/O to write commands to an instrument.

- Use Direct I/O to read data from an instrument.

- Upload and download instrument states using learn strings.

- Explain VXI*plug&play* drivers conceptually and how HP VEE supports them.

- Explain two methods for controlling PC plug-in boards.

Analyzing and Displaying Test Data

4

Overview

This chapter gives you the basics on HP VEE analytical and display capabilities. You'll find out where to locate the right math objects for your applications, and how to display your test results, so that you can turn data into useful information easily and quickly.

In this chapter you'll learn about:

- HP VEE data types

- HP VEE analysis capabilities

- Using math objects

- Using the Formula object

- HP VEE display capabilities

- Customizing your displays

- The PV-WAVE option

HP VEE Data Types

The following are brief descriptions of HP VEE data types. Just read
through them quickly. More important issues involving the usage of these
data types will be explained in the coming chapters. HP VEE packages data
in containers, which carry data between objects. Each container has data of a
specific type and shape. The types are explained in the table below. Shape
is expressed as a Scalar or an Array. (A Scalar is a single number including
numbers expressed as two or more components such as Complex numbers.)
The dimension may be specified for an Array, such as Array 1D for a
one-dimensional array, Array 2D for a two-dimensional array, and so on.

In general, you won't be concerned with data types or shapes, because most
objects operate on any HP VEE data type and will automatically convert data
to the type required for that object. For example, if a Magnitude Spectrum
display receives a Waveform data type, HP VEE automatically performs a
Fast Fourier Transform to convert it from the time domain into the frequency
domain. Occasionally, however, an object will only take a particular data
type, so it's good to be aware of them.

Data Type	Description
Int32	A 32-bit two's complement integer (-2147483648 to 2147483647).
Real (or REAL64)	A 64-bit real that conforms to the IEEE 754 standard (+/- 1.797693138623157 E308).
PComplex	A magnitude and phase component in the form (mag, @phase). Phase is set by default to degrees, but can be set to radians or gradians with the **File => Edit Default Preferences => Trig Mode** setting.

Data Type	Description
Complex	A rectangular or Cartesian complex number having a real and imaginary component in the form (real, imag). Each component is Real. For example, the complex number 1 + 2i is represented as (1,2).
Waveform	A composite data type of time domain values that contains the Real values of evenly-spaced, linear points and the total time span of the waveform. The data shape of a Waveform must be a one-dimensional array (Array 1D).
Spectrum	A composite data type of frequency domain values that contains the PComplex values of points and the minimum and maximum frequency values. The domain data can be mapped as log or linear. The data shape of a Spectrum must be a one-dimensional array (Array 1D).
Coord	A composite data type that contains at least two components in the form (x,y,...). Each component is Real. The data shape of a coord must be a Scalar or an Array 1D.
Enum	A text string that has an associated integer value. You can access the integer value with the ordinal(x) function.
Text	A string of alphanumeric characters.
Record	A composite data type with a field for each data type. Each field has a name and a container, which can be of any type and shape (including Record).

In addition to the ten data types above, HP VEE has three more data types used *only* for instrument I/O. All integer values are stored and manipulated internally by HP VEE as Int32 data types, and all real numbers are stored and manipulated by HP VEE as Real64 data types. However, instruments generally support 16-bit integers or 8-bit bytes, and some instruments support 32-bit reals. To accomodate these situations, HP VEE also supports the following data types for instrument I/O:

Instrument I/O Data Type	Description
Byte	An 8-bit two's complement byte (-128 to 127). (Byte is used in **READ BINARY**, **WRITE BINARY**, and **WRITE BYTE** instrument I/O transactions.)
Int16	A 16-bit two's complement integer (-32768 to 32767).
Real32	A 32-bit real that conforms to the IEEE 754 standard (+/-3.40282347E+/-38.

HP VEE will automatically convert these data types into the appropriate internal data type. For rules on those converstions, consult HP VEE documentation.

Note: *Investigate I/O => To/From Socket for sharing data in mixed environments.*

HP VEE Analysis Capabilities

The following list of mathematical functions comes from the cascading menus in the Math and AdvMath menus. We've also listed functions that are not explicity included in the menus. This list will give you an overview of the analysis capabilities available. If HP VEE does not have a math function you need, you still have several options available. You can create the function with the Formula object, which we'll discuss later in this chapter; you can write the function in a compiled language such as C and link it to HP VEE; or you can communicate with another software application from HP VEE.

You will immediately understand what many of the objects in the following list do; however, some of them will look confusing at first. To get an explanation for a particular object, just select the object and consult Help in its object menu.

Math Menu

+ - * /

a+b, a-b, a*b, a/b, a^b, a mod b, a div b

Relational

a= =b, a~ =b, a! =b, a<b, a>b , a< =b, a> =b

Logical

a AND b, a OR b, a XOR b, a NOT b

Bitwise

bit(x,n), bits(str), setBit(x,n), clearBit(x,n), bitAnd(x,y), bitOr(x,y), bitXor(x,y), bitCmpl(x), bitShift(x,y)

Real Parts

abs(x), signof(x), ordinal(x), round(x), floor(x), ceil(x), intPart(x), fracPart(x)

Complex Parts

j(x), re(x), im(x), mag(x), phase(x), conj(x)

String

strUp(str), strDown(str), strRev(str), strTrim(str), strLen(str), strFromThru(str,from,thru), strFromLen(str,from,len), strPosChar(str,char), strPosStr(str1,str2), intToChar(a), charToInt(a)

Generate

ramp(numElem,from,thru), logRamp(numElem,from,thru), xramp(numElem, from,thru), xlogRamp(numElem,from,thru)

Power

sq(x), sqrt(x), cubert(x), recip(x), log(x), log10(x), exp(x), exp10(x)

Polynomial

1: poly(x, [a0 a1]), 2: poly(x, [a0 a1 a2]), 3: poly(x, [a0 a1 a2 a3]),
N: poly(x, [a0 a1 ... aN])

Trig

sin(x), cos(x), tan(x), cot(x), asin(x), acos(x), atan(x), acot(x), atan2(y,x)

Hyper Trig

sinh(x), cosh(x), tanh(x), coth(x), asinh(x), acosh(x), atanh(x), acoth(x)

Time & Date

now(), wday(aDate), mday(aDate), month(aDate), year(aDate), dmyToDate(d,m,y), hmsToSec(h,m,s), hmsToHour(h,m,s)

AdvMath Menu

Array

init(x, value), totSize(x), rotate(x, numElem), concat(x,y), sum(x), prod(x), sort(x)

Matrix

det(x), inverse(x), transpose(x), identity(x), minor(x, row, col), cofactor(x, row, col), matMultiply(A,B), matDivide(number, denom)

Probability

random(low, high), randomize(x, low, high), randomSeed(seed), perm(n, r), comb(n, r), gamma(x), beta(x, y), factorial(n), binomial(a, b), erf(x), erfc(x)

Statistics

min(x), max(x), median(x), mode(x), mean(x), sdev(x), vari(x), rms(x)

Frequency Distribution

magDist(x, from, thru, step), logMagDist(x, from, thru, logStep)

Calculus

integral(x), deriv(x, 1), deriv(x, 2), deriv(x, order), defIntegral(x, a, b), derivAt(x, 1, pt), derivAt(x, 2, pt), derivAt(x, order, pt)

Regression

linear, logarithmic, exponential, power curve, polynomial

Data Filtering

polySmooth(x), meanSmooth(x, numPts), movingAvg(x, numPts), clipUpper(x, a), clipLower(x, a), minIndex(x), maxIndex(x), minX(x), maxX(x)

Bessel

j0(x), j1(x), jn(x, n), y0(x), y1(x), yn(x, n), Ai(x), Bi(x)

Hyper Bessel

i0(x), i1(x), k0(x), k1(x)

Signal Processing

fft(x), ifft(x), convolve(a, b), xcorrelate(a, b), bartlet(x), hamming(x), hanning(x), blackman(x), rect(x)

Other Functions Not Explicitly in the Math Menus

- WhichOS( ), whichPlatform( ), whichVersion(), and errorInfo() functions. (As objects in the Data => System Info submenu.)

- The triadic operator: *(condition ? expression1 : expression2)*. If the *condition* is true, the result of *expression1* is returned; otherwise, the result of *expression2* is returned.

- Subarray syntax: A[2:4], for example, returns the third through fifth elements of the array A. (All HP VEE arrays have zero-based indexing.)

- Build array syntax: [1, 3, 6], for example, builds a 3 element array with the values 1,3, and 6.

- Global variables: You can use any global variable's name in an expression instead of the Get Global object.

  Note: All functions can be nested.

- Record Syntax: Records use a dot syntax to identify fields. For example, *rec.b* indicates the *b* field in the Record called *rec*.

- showPanel(UFname), showPanel(UFname,x,y), showPanel(UFname,x,y,width,height), hidePanel(UFname), lockPosition(UFname), unlockPosition(UFname), panelOrigin(UFname), panelSize(UFname). (All objects are in the Device => Panel submenu.)

Using Math Objects

These principles will be the same using any object from the math menus.

Lab 4-1: Calculating Standard Deviation

Generate a cosine waveform of at a frequency of 1 kHz, amplitude of 1 V, a time span of 20 ms, represented by 256 points. Calculate its standard deviation and display it.

1. Select **Device => Virtual Source => Function Generator**.

2. Select **AdvMath => Statistics => sdev(x)**.

3. Double-click **sdev(x)** to get to the open view and open the object menu to consult **Help**.

   Note: The sdev(x) object is defined as the square root of the variance of x, and x may be of the type Int32, Real, Coord, or Waveform.

Since the Function Generator outputs a Waveform data type, this program will run without error.

4. Connect the **Function Generator** to **sdev(x)**.

5. Select **Display => AlphaNumeric** and connect it to the **sdev(x)** data output pin.

6. Run your program. It should look like Figure 4-1.

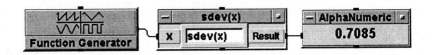

Fig. 4-1. Calculating Standard Deviation

On Your Own

Generate a cosine wave. Calculate its variance and the root mean square. Display your results.

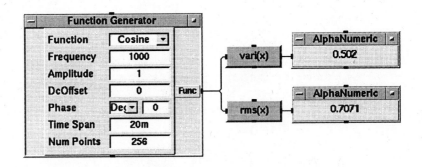

Fig. 4-2. On Your Own Solution: Variance and RMS

Using the Formula Object

The Formula object can be used to write mathematical expressions in HP VEE. The variables in the expression are the data input pin names. The result of the evaluation of the expression will be put on the data output pin. Examine the figure below. The input field for the expression is in the center of the object. A default expression (2*A+3) simply indicates where your formula should go. Just double-click this field and input your own expression.

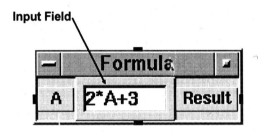

Fig. 4-3. The Formula Object

To Evaluate a Simple Expression with the Formula Object

Let's evaluate the expression, 2*A^4-B, where A=2 and B=1. (Notice the ^ sign for exponentiation.)

Note: The variable names are not case-sensitive.

1. Select **Math => Formula**. Click the **Formula** input field and type **2*A^4-B**.

2. Place the mouse pointer over the data input area and press **Ctrl-a** to add an input pin.

   It will be labeled B by default, but you could rename it to suit your expression.

3. Select **Data => Constant=>Integer,** clone it by selecting **Clone** from the object menu, and connect the two **Integer** objects to the **Formula** inputs **A** and **B.**

4. Enter **2** in the **A** input box and **1** in the **B** input box.

5. Select **Display => AlphaNumeric** and connect it to the output of **Formula,** and run your program.

You should get **31** for an answer, as shown in the figure below.

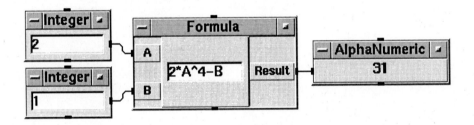

Fig. 4-4. Evaluating an Expression

To Use an HP VEE Function in the Formula Object

Let's generate a cosine wave and calculate the standard deviation and root mean square using the Formula object.

1. Select the **Function Generator, Formula,** and **AlphaNumeric** objects and connect them together using their data pins.

2. Clone the **Formula** object by opening the object menu and selecting **Clone**, and place it just below the first one. Connect the **Function Generator** data output pin to the second **Formula** object.

3. Clone another **AlphaNumeric** display and connect it to the second **Formula** object.

4. Enter **sdev(A)** in the first **Formula** object, and rms(A) **in the second one.**

You'll recall that these are the two math functions we used from the Statistics submenu in the AdvMath menu. Notice that they can be called as functions or independent objects.

5. Run your program.

You'll see the same answers putting these functions into the Formula object as you did when you used them as independent objects, as shown below.

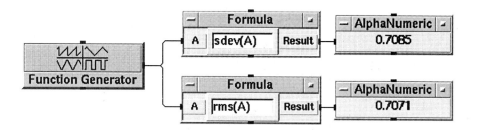

Fig. 4-5. Formula Examples Using HP VEE Functions

On Your Own

1. Use the **ramp** object in the **Math => Generate** submenu to create an array of numbers from **1** to **4096**. Calculate the standard deviation of this array and display it.

2. Do the same thing described in number one, but do it using the **ramp( )** function.

3. Do the same tasks as described in number two, but nest functions and use only two objects.

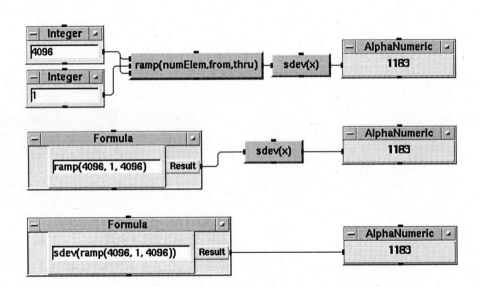

Fig. 4-6. On Your Own Solution: Ramp and SDEV

You have to delete the input terminal on the Formula object to avoid an error message, because all data input pins must be connected and have data before an object can operate. However, connecting the sequence input/output pins or the data output pin is optional.

Display Capabilities

Display	Description
AlphaNumeric	Display values as text or numbers. Requires SCALAR, ARRAY 1D, or ARRAY 2D.
Logging AlphaNumeric	Displays values as text or numbers when repeatedly logged. Requires SCALAR or ARRAY 1D.
Indicator=> Meter, Thermometer, Fill Bar, Tank, Color Alarm	All of these indicators display numbers with a graphical representation suggested by their names. They all have color-coded ranges - usually three, but the meter has five. The Color Alarm can simulate an LED with a text message flashing up on the alarm in each range.
XY Trace	Graphically displays mapped arrays or a set of values when y data is generated with evenly-spaced x values. The x value that is automatically generated depends on the data type of the trace data. For example, a Real trace would generate evenly-spaced Real x values; whereas, a Waveform trace would generate x values for time.
Strip Chart	Graphically displays the recent history of data that is continuously generated while the program runs. For each y input value, the x value is incremented by a specified Step size. When new data runs off the right side of the display, the display automatically scrolls to show you the latest data.
Complex Plane	Displays Complex, Polar Complex (PComplex), or Coord data values on a Real vs. Imaginary axis.

Display	Description
X vs Y Plot	Graphically displays values when separate data information is available for X and Y data.
Polar Plot	Graphically displays data on a polar scale when separate information is available for radius and angle data.
Waveform (Time)	Graphically displays Waveforms or Spectrums in the real time domain. Spectrums are automatically converted to the time domain using an Inverse Fast Fourier Transform (ifft). The x axis is the sampling units of the input waveform.
Spectrum (Freq)	A menu that contains frequency domain displays: Magnitude Spectrum, Phase Spectrum, Magnitude vs Phase (Polar), and Magnitude vs Phase (Smith). Inputs must be Waveform, Spectrum, or an array of Coords. Waveform inputs are automatically changed to the frequency domain with a Fast Fourier Transform (fft).
Picture	An object used to put a graphic image on the Panel View. The formats supported are: *.BMP (bitmaps), *.ICN (X11 bitmap), *.GIF (GIF87a), on MS Windows and UNIX; and *.xwd (X11 Window Dump) on UNIX only.
Label	An object used to put a text label on the Panel View. The colors and fonts may be easily adjusted through Edit Properties... in the object menu while in the Panel View.
Beep	Gives an audible tone to highlight a place in your program.
Note Pad	Uses a text note to clarify your program.

Customizing Displays

Displays may be customized in a variety of ways. Not only can you label, move and size them like all HP VEE objects, but you can also change the x/y scales, modify the traces, add markers, or zoom in on parts of the graphical display. Let's work through an example to illustrate some of these features. You'll use the Noise Generator to generate a waveform, and then display it with the Waveform (Time) display. You'll change the X scale, zoom in on a wave segment, and use the markers to measure the distances between points on the waveform. The same principles may be applied to all the graphical displays.

To Display a Waveform

1. Select **Device => Virtual Source => Noise Generator**.

2. Select **Display => Waveform (Time)**.

3. Connect the data output of the Noise Generator to the data input of **Waveform (Time)** and run your program.

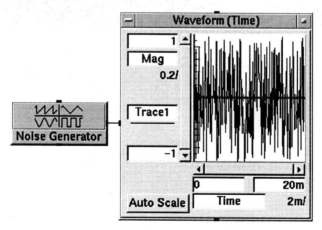

Fig. 4-7. Displaying a Waveform

To Change the X and Y Scales

1. Click the right input field below the **x** axis where it says **20m** and enter **1m**.

   This alters the time span of the display from 20 milliseconds to 1 millisecond.

2. Click the lower input field on the **y** axis where it says **-1**, and enter **- .5**.

   You'll see the display immediately adjust to the new y scale of -0.5 to 1 for Mag. You could also alter any of the other scales in the same way.

To Zoom In on Part of the Waveform

1. Open the **Waveform (Time)** object menu and click **Zoom => In**.

   The cursor becomes a small right angle. By clicking and dragging you can draw a square on the graph outlining the area you want to enlarge.

2. Outline an area of the waveform including several peaks, and release the mouse button.

   The display zooms in to this selected area of the waveform. Notice the x and y scales change automatically.

To Add Delta Markers to the Display

1. Open the **Waveform (Time)** object menu and select **Edit Properties...** (or just double-click on the title bar), then under **Markers**, click **Delta**. Then click **OK**.

You will see two white arrows pointing up and down at one of the data points on the waveform. Also, notice that the display records the x and y coordinates of these markers at the bottom of the display. To measure the x or y distance between two peaks, just click one of the other peaks. You'll see one of the markers jump to that new peak with the new coordinates recorded at the bottom of the display, as shown in the figure below.

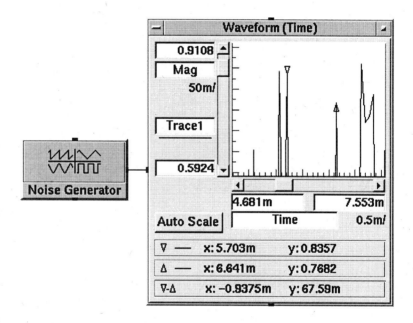

Fig. 4-8. Delta Markers on a Waveform Display

HP VEE will automatically interpolate between waveform data points, if you open the object menu and select Edit Properties..., then under Markers, click Interpolate.

To Change the Color of the Trace

1. Open the object menu and click **Edit Properties...**, then under **Layout** select **Traces & Scales....** Then click **OK**.

   A Traces and Scales dialog box appears that allows you to change the name(s) of the trace(s), the color, the type of line, and how points are displayed. You can also change the scale names, ranges, log or linear mappings, and colors.

   > **Note:** *You can also change these values at run time by using the Traces and Scales control inputs. See HP VEE documentation for more information.*

2. Click the button next to **Color** near the top of the dialog box, select the color you want, then click **OK**. Click **OK** to exit the **Traces and Scales** dialog box. Then click **OK** to exit the **Y Plot Properties** box.

   The trace will now be displayed in the new color.

Other display characteristics such as Panel Layout, Grid Type, Clear Control, and Add Right Scale may be customized in a similar fashion as the features in the exercise above.

   > **Note:** *HP VEE also includes Plot in the display object menus, which allows you to plot test results on the display without printing out the rest of the program.*

For Additional Practice

To learn about other HP VEE objects and gain more practice do some of the exercises in *Appendix B: Additional Lab Exercises* in the *General Programming Techniques* section. Solutions are provided with a discussion of key points.

PV Wave from Visual Numerics

HP's alliance with Visual Numerics, Inc. connects the power and productivity advantages of HP VEE 3.2 with the world-class graphics package, PV-WAVE. The HP VEE and PV-WAVE combination helps turn complex data into usable information. This new graphics toolkit option (Opt. VIS) imports an HP VEE 3.2 file and creates 2D, 3D, and 4D plots, surfaces, and projections for applications such as waterfall diagrams. HP VEE already supplies display capabilities for most programming needs. The PV-WAVE option should be purchased for applications with advanced display requirements, such as 3D plots.

Order PV-WAVE through HP. You can order other languages and support for PV-WAVE as well as mathematical and statistical libraries directly through Visual Numerics (see Appendix A).

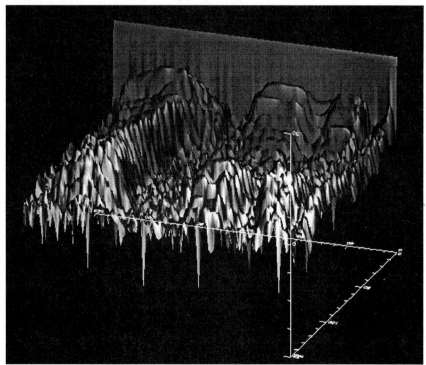

Fig. 4-9. A PV-WAVE 3D Display

Chapter 4 Checklist

Use the following checklist to determine whether there are topics you need to review before going to Chapter 5.

- Describe the main data types in HP VEE, and the three data types that are used for instrument I/O only.

- Describe some of the main areas of analytical capabilities in HP VEE.

- Find an online Help explanation for any object in the Math or AdvMath menus.

- Describe the relationship between input pins and variables in an HP VEE math object.

- Evaluate a mathematical expression using the Formula object.

- Use an HP VEE function in a mathematical expression in the Formula object.

- Describe major display capabilities in HP VEE.

- Customize a graphical display in terms of the scales used, the part of the waveform seen, the markers used, and the color of the trace.

Storing and Retrieving
Test Results

Average Time to Complete: 2 hrs.

Overview

This chapter will teach you the fundamentals of storing and retrieving test data. You'll learn how easy it is to create arrays of the right data type and size to hold your test results, and then how to access any part of that data for analysis or display. Getting data to and from files was introduced in a Chapter 2 exercise. Now we'll go into greater detail on the flexibility and power of the To/From File objects. For more elaborate tests, developers usually need to store several types of data in a single structure.

HP VEE satisfies this need with the Record data type. One or more Records may be stored in a file called a Dataset. You can easily perform sort or search operations on datasets. In effect, this provides you with a simple, customized test database that is easy to create and maintain.

*In this chapter
you'll learn about:*

- Putting test data into arrays

- Using the Collector object

- Using the To/From File objects

- Creating mixed data types using Records

- Performing search and sort operations using DataSets

- Creating simple test databases using the Dataset objects

Using Arrays to Store Test Results

In Chapter 4 you had an overview of the HP VEE data types, which can be stored as scalar values (that is, a single number such as 9 or (32, @10)) or as arrays from 1 to 10 dimensions. Indexing for arrays is zero-based in HP VEE, and brackets are used to indicate the position of the array element. For example, if the array A holds the elements [4, 5, 6], then A[0] = 4, A[1] = 5, and A[2] = 6. The colon is used to indicate a range of elements. For instance, A[0:2] = [4, 5, 6] in the array above. The asterisk, *, is a wildcard to specify all elements from a particular array dimension. A[*] returns all elements of array A. In the subarray syntax, commas are used to separate array dimensions. If B is a two-dimensional array with three elements in each dimension, B[1,0] returns the first element in the second row of B. This syntax to access elements of an array can be used in the Formula or any expression field, such as in the To/From File box object.

To Create an Array for Your Test Results

The easiest way to create an array is to use the Collector object. Let's use the For Count object to simulate 4 readings from an instrument, which you will put into an array and then print the results. The principles will be the same regardless of the data type or the size of the array, since the Collector will take any data type and create the array size automatically depending on the number of elements sent.

1. Select **Flow => Repeat => For Count, Data => Collector**, and **Display => AlphaNumeric**.

   Double-click the **Collector** to get the open view, and read through Help in the object menu to understand the object.

   For Count outputs increasing integer values starting at 0 depending on the number of iterations you specify in the input field. Highlight the default number **10** by double-clicking, then type **4**. For Count will output 0, 1, 2, and 3.

The Collector receives data values through its Data input terminal. When you're finished collecting data, you "ping" the XEQ terminal to tell the Collector to construct the array and output it. You can use the For Count sequence output pin to ping the Collector XEQ pin. The Collector displays a button that toggles between a 1 Dim Array and and n+1 Dim Array.

2. Click **n+1 Dim** in the **Collector** to change the selection to **1 Dim Array**.

3. Connect the **For Count** data output pin to the Data input pin on the Collector.

4. Connect the **For Count** sequence output pin to the **XEQ** input pin on the **Collector**.

   The XEQ pin is a control pin that exists on several different objects, that tells HP VEE when you want that object to execute. In this case, you want the object to fire after all of the data for the array has been collected.

5. Connect the **Collector** data output pin to the **AlphaNumeric** data input pin.

   You should enlarge **AlphaNumeric** to accomodate the array, so click-and-drag on the lower right corner of the object to do this. (Recall that you could also enlarge AlphaNumeric when you first selected it by using "click and drag" on the object outline.)

6. Run your program. It should look like the one below.

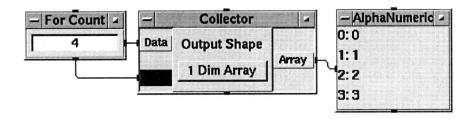

Fig. 5-1. The Collector Creating an Array

To Extract Values from an Array

You could do this in one of two ways: use the bracket notation in an expression, or use the Access Array => Get Values object. We'll use expressions in the Formula object for the following example. You'll add several objects to the program in the first exercise.

1. Delete the data line between the **Collector** and **AlphaNumeric** by placing the mouse pointer over the line, pressing **Shift-Ctrl**, and then clicking the left mouse button. Then iconize the **Collector**.

2. Select **Math => Formula** and clone it. Move **AlphaNumeric** to the right, and put both **Formula** objects to the right of the **Collector**.

3. Connect the **Collector** data output to the data inputs of the **Formula** objects. Enter **A[2]** in the upper **Formula** input field, and **A[1:3]** in the lower **Formula** input field.

    A[2] will extract the third element of the array as a Scalar; A[1:3] will return a sub-array of three elements holding the second, third, and fourth elements of A (meaning the array on the A input terminal).

4. Clone **AlphaNumeric** and connect a display to each **Formula** object.

5. Run your program. It should look like the one below.

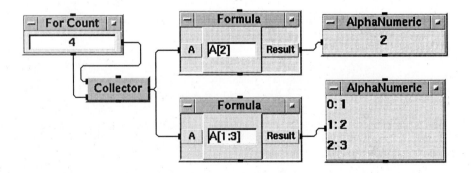

Fig. 5-2. Extracting Array Elements with Expressions

Using the To/From File Objects

We've used the To File and From File objects in Chapter 2. Now we'll discuss them in more detail. Before working on an exercise, there are some basic concepts you should understand about these objects:

- A data file is opened on the first READ or WRITE transaction after the program begins. When the program ends, HP VEE closes any open files automatically.

- HP VEE maintains one read pointer and one write pointer per file regardless of how many objects are accessing the file. The read pointer identifies the next data item to be read, and the write pointer indicates where the next data item should be written.

- You can append data to existing files or overwrite them. If the Clear File at PreRun & Open setting is checked in the open view of the To File object, then the write pointer starts at the beginning of the file; if not, the pointer is positioned at the end of the existing file. Each WRITE transaction appends information to the file at the location of the write pointer. If an EXECUTE CLEAR transaction is performed, the write pointer moves to the beginning of the file and erases its contents.

- A read pointer starts at the beginning of a file, and advances through the data depending on the READ transactions. You may perform an EXECUTE REWIND in the From File object to move the pointer back to the beginning of the file without affecting any data.

Understanding I/O Transactions

Before we do the lab exercise on the To/From File objects, let's look at "I/O transactions" in more detail. I/O transactions are used by HP VEE to communicate with instruments, files, strings, the operating system, interfaces, other programs, HP BASIC/UX, and printers. For example, look at the To File object in Figure 5-3.

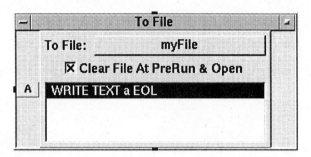

Fig. 5-3. The To File Object

You are sending data to the specified file, myFile. You can add inputs to accept data from your program. The highlighted line is called a transaction. It contains the default transaction statement: WRITE TEXT a EOL . When you click it, an I/O Transaction dialog box appears, which configures your specific transaction statement.

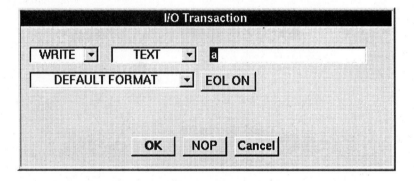

Fig. 5-4. An I/O Transaction Dialog Box

There are different forms of this dialog box depending on which object you're using, but there are certain common elements we want to stress: the "actions", the "encodings", the "expression list", the "format", and the "end-of-line" (EOL) sequence. An I/O transaction to write data is usually in the following format:

<action> <encoding> <expression list><format><EOL>.

The tables and comments that follow will give you a basic understanding of these elements.

The most common actions available are **READ, WRITE, EXECUTE,** and **WAIT**.

Action	Explanation
READ	Reads data from the specified source using the specified encoding and format.
WRITE	Writes data to the specified target using the specified encoding and format.
EXECUTE	Executes a specific command. For example, EXECUTE REWIND repositions a file's read or write pointer to the beginning of the file without erasing the contents. EXECUTE CLOSE closes an open file.
WAIT	Waits the specified number of seconds before the next transaction.

> *Note:* *There are also a number of actions for I/O => Advanced I/O Operations that you can examine by exploring the objects in that menu.*

Encodings and formats refer to the way data is packaged and sent. For instance, a TEXT encoding sends data as ASCII characters. The TEXT encoding could be formatted in a number of ways. For example, let's say you want to send a string of letters and numbers to a file. A WRITE TEXT STRING transaction would send the entire string represented by ASCII characters. A WRITE TEXT REAL transaction would only extract the Real numbers from the same string and send them using ASCII characters for the individual digits. The following table provides brief explanations of encodings:

Encodings	Explanations
TEXT	Reads or writes all data types in a human-readable form (ASCII) that can easily be edited or ported to other software applications. HP VEE numeric data is automatically converted to text.
BYTE	Converts numeric data to binary integer and sends or receives the least significant byte.
CASE	Maps an enumerated value or an integer to a string and reads/writes that string. For example, you could use CASE to accept error numbers and write error messages.
BINARY	Handles all data types in a machine-specific binary format.
BINBLOCK	Uses IEEE488.2 definite length block headers with all HP VEE data types in binary files.
CONTAINER	Uses HP VEE specific text format with all data types.

In a write transaction, an "expression list" is simply a comma-separated list of expressions that need to be evaluated to yield the data sent. The expression may be composed of a mathematical expression, a pin name, a string constant, an HP VEE function, a user function, or a global variable. In a read transaction, the expression list should consist of a comma-separated list of output terminal names indicating the data to be read in.

Data formats were presented in Chapter 3 in conjunction with reading data from instruments. Most of these formats apply to all I/O transactions.

EOL (end-of-line sequence of characters) may be turned on or off, and you can specify the EOL sequence by opening the object menu of most of the I/O => To objects and selecting Edit Properties..., then select Data Format, and make your changes under Separator Sequence.

Let's do the lab, so these abstractions are rooted in something more concrete.

Lab 5-1: Using the To/From File Objects

The purpose of this lab exercise is to teach the process of getting test data to and from files. Let's store and retrieve three common test result items: a test name, a time stamp, and a one-dimensional array of Real values. The same process will apply to all HP VEE data types.

To Send a Text String to a File

1. Select **I/O => To => File**.

   The default file is myFile, which can easily be changed by clicking the To File input field to get a list box of files in your home directory. You can leave this default. Click the box next to Clear File At PreRun & Open. By default HP VEE appends new data to the end of an existing file. You need to check this box to be certain the file is cleared before you write new data. WRITE TEXT a EOL is the default transaction. It means that you will write the data on pin a using TEXT encoding and a specified end-of-line sequence. HP VEE is not case-sensitive; you can use lower-case or upper-case strings for pin names.

2. Double-click the transaction line to get the **I/O Transaction** dialog box. (Refer to Figures 5-3 and 5-4, if necessary.)

3. The expression list field is highlighted, so type **"Test1"**, then click **OK**. (You need the quotation marks to indicate a Text string.)

If you typed Test1 without the quotation marks, HP VEE would interpret this as a pin name or global variable name. You can leave the other defaults, since you want the action WRITE. The encoding TEXT will send the data using ASCII characters. The DEFAULT FORMAT will choose an appropriate HP VEE format such as STRING. And finally, the default EOL sequence is the escape character for a new line \n.

You should now have WRITE TEST "Test1" EOL in the transaction line. This transaction means you will send the string Test1 to the specified file. If this were the only transaction, you would delete the input terminal A, but we will use it in a moment, so leave it there for now.

To Send a Time Stamp to a File

The object now( ) in the Math => Time & Date menu gives the current time expressed as a Real Scalar. The value of the Real is the number of seconds since 00:00 hours on Jan. 1, 0001 AD. Therefore, now( ) returns a value about 62.89G. HP VEE provides this format, because it's easier to manipulate mathematically and conserves storage space. If you want to store the time stamp in a more readable format, use the TIME STAMP FORMAT in the To File object.

1. Double-click just below the first transaction line in the **To File** object to get a new **I/O Transaction** box.

2. Double-click the expression list input field to highlight the **a** and type **now( )**.

   The now( ) function will send the current time from the computer clock in a Real format, but let's change that to the Time Stamp Format.

3. Click the arrow next to **DEFAULT FORMAT** to get a menu, select **TIME STAMP FORMAT.** HP VEE now adds some additional buttons to I/O Transaction dialog box.

   Click the down arrow next to **Date & Time**, select **Time**, then click **OK**.

Click **HH:MM:SS** (hour, minute, and second format) to toggle to **HH:MM** (hour and minute format).

Click **24 HOUR** (military time format) to toggle to **12 HOUR** (am or pm format).

Your box should look like Figure 5-5.

Click **OK**.

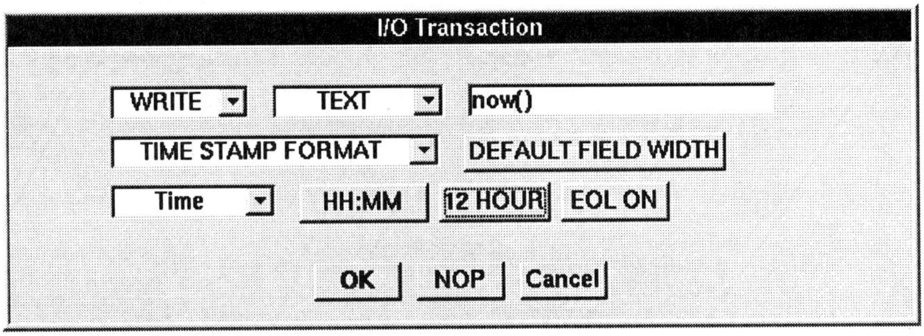

Fig. 5-5. The TIME STAMP I/O Transaction Box

Your second transaction bar should now have the statement:
WRITE TEXT now( ) TIME:HM:H12 EOL.

To Send a Real Array to a File

Let's create a one-dimensional array of four elements using the For Count and Collector objects. Then we'll append this to myFile.

1. Select **Flow => Repeat => For Count** and **Data => Collector**. Change the default value in **For Count** to **4**. Connect the data output of **For Count** to the data input of the **Collector**. Connect the **For Count** sequence output pin to the **XEQ** pin on the **Collector**. Iconize the **Collector**.

The Collector will now create the array [0 1 2 3], which you can send to your data file.

2. Connect the **Collector** data output to the **A** terminal.

3. Double-click below the second transaction bar in the **To File** object.

4. Open the **DEFAULT FORMAT** menu, select **REAL FORMAT**.

You now have new buttons in the box regarding your REAL FORMAT selection. You can leave all of the default choices, but you might want to investigate the options for future reference. Click **OK** to close the **I/O Transaction** box. You'll now see WRITE TEXT a REAL STD EOL on the third transaction bar, as shown below. (The configured I/O Transaction box is also displayed.)

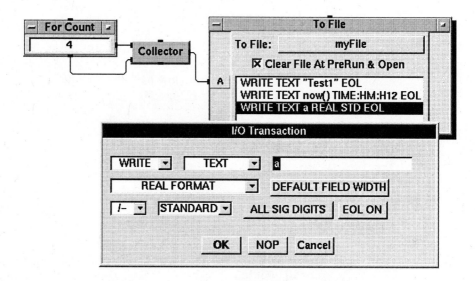

Fig. 5-6. Storing Data Using the To File Object

To Retrieve Data Using the From File Object

When you're using From File, you need to know how the data was stored. You will see later in this chapter that you can store and retrieve data using To DataSet or From DataSet, in which case you don't have to know what kind of data is in the file. In this example, you know that you stored the name of a test in a String Format, followed by a time stamp in Time Stamp Format, and finally an array of Real numbers. You will now create three transactions in From File to read that data back into HP VEE.

1. Select **I/O => From => File** and place it below the **To File** object.

2. Connect the sequence output pin of the **To File** object to the sequence input pin of the **From File** object.

   This sequence connection assures you that To File has completed sending data to myFile, before From File begins to extract data.

3. Leave the default data file, **myFile**, since you sent data to this file. Then click the transaction bar to get the **I/O Transaction** dialog box. Click **REAL FORMAT** and change it to **STRING FORMAT**. See Fig. 5-7.

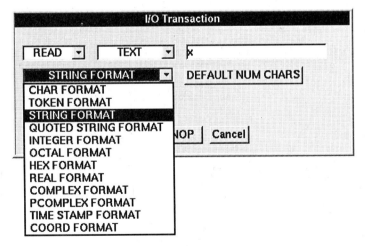

Fig. 5-7. Selecting String Format

All of the other defaults are correct, so click **OK** to close the **I/O Transaction** box.

You should now see the transaction statement: **READ TEXT x STR**.

You now need to add two more transactions to read back the time stamp and the real array.

4. Add a data output by moving the mouse pointer over the data output area and pressing **Ctrl-a**. A dialog box appears labeled **Select output to add**. Select **Y** and click **OK**. HP VEE adds the data output terminal **Y**. To add a third terminal, repeat the same procedure. Since the label **Y** is being used, HP VEE will offer you a data output terminal labeled **Z**. Select **Z** and click **OK**. You now have three outputs labeled **X**, **Y**, and **Z**.

5. Double-click below the first transaction bar. The **I/O Transaction** dialog box appears. Double-click on the expression list input field to highlight **x** and type **y**. This means that you want the second transaction to read data back to pin **y**. Change **REAL FORMAT** to **STRING FORMAT**, then click **OK**.

   Note: If you want to read the time stamp back as a text string, then use the STRING FORMAT. The TIME STAMP FORMAT converts the time stamp data back to a Real number.

6. Double-click below the second transaction bar to go directly to the **I/O Transaction** dialog box. Edit **x** to **z**, so that the **Real** array is read back to the **Z** output terminal. **REAL FORMAT** is correct in this case, but you need to change SCALAR to **ARRAY 1D**.

   Now the **I/O Transaction** box adds a **SIZE** button. In this case, we know the array has four elements, so edit **10** to **4** and click **OK**.

   Note: If you don't know or remember the size of an array, you may toggle SIZE to TO END. This will read data to the end of the file without HP VEE knowing its exact size. You could use this feature to read the entire contents of a file as a string array to examine the file contents.

You will now see **READ TEXT y STR** on the second transaction bar and **READ TEXT z REAL ARRAY:4** on the third. Iconize **From File**.

7. Select **Display => AlphaNumeric** and clone it twice to get three displays. Connect them to the three data output pins on **From File**. Size the second display to be wider to hold the time stamp, and the third one to be higher for the array.

   Note: Recall that you can size the AlphaNumeric displays as you clone them, just as you could with any object by clicking and dragging the object outline when you first select it from the menu.

8. Run your program. It should look like the one below.

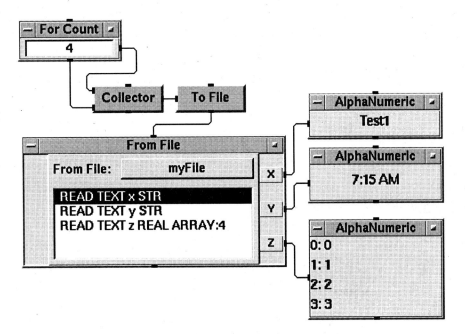

Fig. 5-8. Retrieving Data Using the From File Object

Using Records to Store Mixed Data Types

The Record data type can store different data types in a single data container. Any HP VEE data type including Record could be used. The data can be be in the shape of a Scalar or an Array. So you could store the test name, the time stamp, and the real array in the preceding example in a single data structure. The individual elements in a Record are stored as fields and are accessed using a dot notation. For example, Rec.Name would access the field, Name, within a Record called Rec. If you created an array of records then Rec[2].Name would signify the Name field in the third record in the array. (Recall that all arrays start their indexing at 0.)

There are several benefits to structuring your test data using the Record data type. First, you can create logical groupings of mixed data types in a single container, which makes a program easier to develop and maintain. For example, you might use the following fields for a record storing test data: test name, value returned, pass or fail indicator, time stamp, nominal value expected, upper pass limit, lower pass limit, and a description of the test. Secondly, manipulating a single data container rather than eight separate ones in the example above would greatly simplify your program and make it much more readable. Finally, records may be stored and retrieved from DataSets in HP VEE. A DataSet is a special file created to store records. When you retrieve records from a DataSet, you don't have to know what data types are inside. HP VEE provides you objects to retrieve, sort, and search the information stored in DataSets. So, in effect, you have a simple, customized database for your test results.

Lab 5-2: Using Records

This section teaches you the fundamentals of using the Record datatype. You'll learn how to build a record, retrieve a particular field in that record, set a chosen field, and unbuild the entire record in one step. Along the way you'll use the time stamp function, now(), in a different way. The last two sections in the chapter will show you how to use DataSets to simplify common test development tasks.

To Build a Record

You'll build a Record with three fields: the name of a test stored as a String, a time stamp stored as a Real Scalar, and simulated test results stored as a four element Array of Reals. When you retrieve these fields in the next exercise, you'll see that you can convert the time stamp into a number of different formats for display.

1. Create your test name by selecting **Data => Constant => Text** and entering **Test1** in the input field. Rename the object, **Text Constant**. Iconize **Text Constant**.

2. Select **Math => Time & Date => now( )** and place it below **Text Constant**.

3. Select **Data => Constant => Real** and place it below **now( )**.

   You can turn this Scalar Real into an Array 1D by clicking Edit Properties... in the Real object menu and choosing 1D Array.

4. Open the **Constant Properties** box by double-clicking on the **Real** title bar. Select **1D Array** under **Configuration**, change the **Size** to **4**, then click **OK**. Enter four values into this array by double-clicking next to element **0000** to highlight the first entry, then input the values **2.2**, **3.3**, **4.4**, **5.5** using the **Tab** key between each entry. Iconize **Real**.

5. Select **Data => Build Data => Record** and place it to the right of the three other objects. Add a third data input terminal, so you can input three fields. Open each terminal by double-clicking over the terminal and rename the three input terminals to **testname**, **time**, and **data**.

   The Output Shape on the Build Record object toggles between Scalar and Array. The Scalar default will be the correct choice for the majority of situations. For a discussion of the Array selection, see HP VEE documentation.

6. Connect the **Text Constant** object to the **testname** terminal, **now()** to the **time** terminal, and **Real** to the **data** terminal on the **Build Record** object.

7. Run your program in this stage of development. Double-click on the **Record** data output terminal to examine your record. It should look like the figure below.

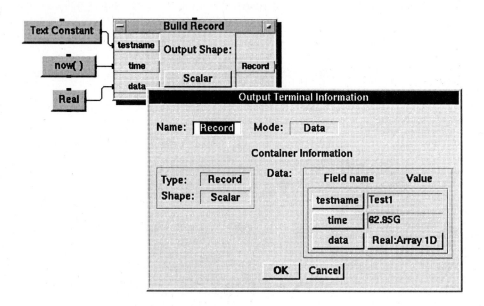

Fig. 5-9. Output Terminal Information on a Record

You can clearly see the three fields and their values. If you click on the **Real: Array 1D** button, a list box will show you the actual values. Notice that the time stamp has been stored as a Real Scalar. We'll show you how to convert that to a more readable form in the following exercise. Click **OK** to close the **Output Terminal Information** dialog box.

To Get a Field From a Record

Let's add to the program you already have. You'll use the Get Field object to extract each of the three fields from the record, then display the values for each.

1. Select **Data => Access Record => Get Field**.

   The data input labeled Rec will take any record regardless of the number and type of fields. Rec.A is the default selection in the input field, but this can edited to retrieve any field. Rec refers to the record at the data input terminal by the same name.

2. Clone **Get Field** twice and place the objects to the right of **Build Record**.

3. Connect **Build Record** data output to all three **Get Field** objects.

Since the three fields were stored as testname, time, and data, you'll have to edit the Get Field objects to get the appropriate field.

4. Edit the three **Get Field** object input fields to **Rec.testname**, **Rec.time**, and **Rec.data**.

5. Select **Display => AlphaNumeric** and clone it twice. Connect the three displays to the three **Get Field** objects. Size the third display to be about three times higher than the other displays to accomodate the real array.

Now you'll reconfigure the second display to present the time stamp using hours, minutes, and seconds in a 24 hour time format.

6. Open the second **AlphaNumeric** display object menu and select **Edit Properties...**, then select the **Number** folder. Click to the left of **Global Format** to remove the check mark.

   You can now set your own display format for this particular display. Open the **Standard** menu and in the **Real:** section. Select **Time Stamp** and click **OK**.

7. Click **HH:MM:SS** to toggle to **HH:MM**. Click **24 HOUR** to toggle to **12 HOUR**. See the figure below.

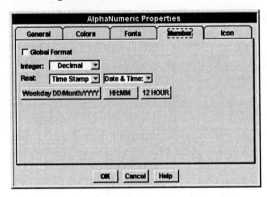

Fig. 5-10. The AlphaNumeric Properties Box

8. Run your program and save it as **getfield.vee**. See Fig. 5-11 below.

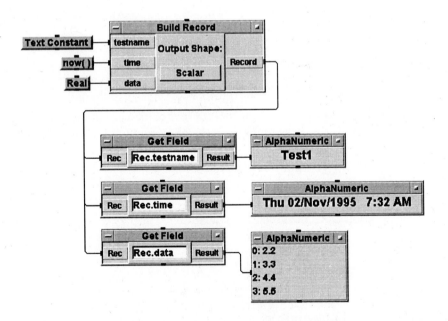

Fig. 5-11. Using the Get Field Object

Notice that the second display will now give you the weekday, the date, and the time expressed in hours, minutes, and an am or pm designation.

Now that you know the basics of using records, we'll show you how to change the value in a field using the Set Field object.

To Set A Field in a Record

You might want to use the same Record several times with different tests, so this exercise teaches you how to alter data in specific fields. We'll modify getfield.vee. Delete all objects after Build Record. Recall that pressing Ctrl-d with the mouse pointer over the desired object will delete it.

1. Select **Data => Access Record => Set Field** and place it to the right of **Build Record.** Connect their data pins together.

   Set Field works by setting the field specified in the box labeled Rec.Field to the value specified in the box labeled 2*A+3. You simply edit those labels to the names appropriate to your program. You connect the incoming record to Rec and the incoming new value to A. The modified record will be put on the data output terminal labeled Rec.

2. Edit **Rec.Field** to **Rec.data**, since you will change the value of the four element array in the **data** field. Also, edit **2*A+3** to **A**, since you will put the new values for the array on the input terminal, **A**.

3. Select **Data => Constant => Real**, open the object menu, and select **Edit Properties....** Select **1D Array** under **Configuration**, then edit the **Size** to **4**, and click **OK**.

   If the new values for the record field are contained in an array, it must have the same size as the current array.

   Enter the values **1, 2, 3, 4** into **Real** and connect it to the **Set Field** input labeled **A**. (Remember to highlight the first entry and use the **Tab** key when creating the new array.)

Now let's use Get Field to extract the field Rec.data from the record and display the results.

4. Select **Data** => **Access Record** => **Get Field** and edit the field specified from **Rec.A** to**Rec.data**. Connect the data output of **Set Field** to the data input of **Get Field**.

   Note: You could also have used a Formula object with A.data in the expression field.

5. Select an **AlphaNumeric** display, size it to accomodate an array, and connect it to the **Get Field** output pin.

6. Run your program and save it as **setfield.vee**. See the figure below.

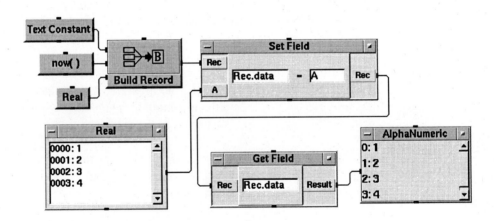

Fig. 5-12. Using the Set Field Object

To Unbuild a Record in a Single Step

If you would like to extract all record fields and get a list of the field names and their types, then use the UnBuild Record object. Let's modify setfield.vee. Delete all objects after Build Record.

1. Select **Data => UnBuild Data => Record**, get the open view, and connect it to **Build Record**. Add another data output pin to **UnBuild Record** and rename the **A, B,** and **C** outputs to the field names: **testname, time,** and **data.**

2. Select an **AlphaNumeric** display and clone it four times. Connect the five displays to the five output terminals on **UnBuild Record.** You will have to enlarge the displays for **Name List, Type List,** and **data** to accomodate arrays. Also, reconfigure the **time** display to present time in hours, minutes, and seconds using a 24 hour format.

3. Run your program and save it as **unbuild.vee.** It should look like the one below.

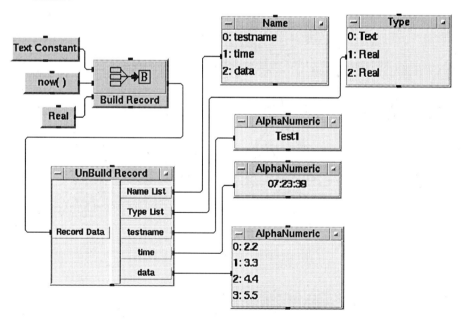

Fig. 5-13. Using the UnBuild Record Object

Notice that the Name List pin gives the names testname, time, and data of the three fields in your record, just as the Type List identifies testname as Text, time and data as Real types.

Using DataSets to Store and Retrieve Records

The advantage of storing records to DataSets instead of files is that you do not have to remember the specific types of the data you saved. With a DataSet you retrieve one or more records, and then HP VEE has objects that will unpack those records. You can also perform sort and search operations on that data creating your own customized test database.

Lab 5-3: Using DataSets

A DataSet is simply an array of Records stored in a file. The purpose of this exercise is to teach you how to get data into and out of a DataSet.

To Store and Retrieve a Record from a DataSet:

First, we'll create an array of ten Records, each containing three fields with a test name, a Real Scalar that could be a time stamp, and an array of Reals. We'll store this array of Records in a DataSet. Then we'll retrieve all ten records and display them.

1. Select **Flow => Start, Flow => Repeat => For Count**, and **Math => Formula**. Connect **Start** to the sequence input pin on **For Count**; connect the **For Count** data output pin to **Formula's** data input pin.

   Double-click the **Formula** expression field to highlight the default expression, and then type **"test" + a**.

When you click Start, For Count will output integers zero through nine sequentially to the A pin of Formula. Formula will add these integers to the word "test" and output the result, so you'll get the Text Scalars: test0, test1, test2,...,test9. These values will fill the first fields in the ten Records.

2. Select **Data => Build Data => Record**. Add a data input pin. Connect the data output of **Formula** to the **A** input of **Build Record**.

3. Select **Device => Random Number** and connect its data output to the **B** terminal of **Build Record**. Also, connect the **Formula** sequence output pin to the sequence input pin of **Random Number**.

   Connecting the sequence pins will assure you that on each of the ten iterations of this program a new random number will be put into the B field of that particular record.

4. Select **Data => Constant => Real**. Open its object menu, click **Edit Properties**, under **Configuration** click **1D Array**, and change the **Size** to **3**, then click **OK**. Highlight each entry in the array (by double-clicking), and type in the numbers **1,2**, and **3**. Open the object menu, click **Edit Properties ...**, type **Real Array** for the title, and click **OK**.. Connect the **Real Array** data output to the **C** terminal on **Build Record**.

5. Select **I/O => To => DataSet** and connect the data output of **Build Record** to its data input. Leave the default file, and make sure **Clear File At PreRun** is selected.

   Your program should now put an array of ten records into the DataSet called myFile. See Figure 5-14.

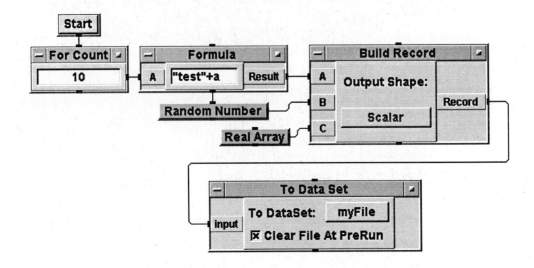

Fig. 5-14. Storing an Array of Records in a DataSet

Now you'll retrieve the array of records and display using the From DataSet and Record Constant objects.

6. Select **I/O => From => DataSet**. Leave the default file name, **myFile**. Click the **Get Records** field to toggle from **One** to **All**. Finally, leave the default of **1** in the expression field at the bottom.

   Your configuration means that HP VEE will look at the DataSet in myFile, find "All" the records that fit the criterion in the expression field. If you set Get Records to One, HP VEE would output the first record that met the criterion in the expression field. The 1 signifies a TRUE condition meaning that all of the records fit the criterion, so the entire array of records in that file will be put on the output pin labeled Rec. We will explain other uses of the expression field in later exercises. Consult Help in the object menu for more information.

   Connect the **For Count** sequence output pin to the sequence input on the **From Data Set** object. This assures you that the part of the program that sends data to **myFile** is done executing *before* you try to read data from the file.

7. Select **Data => Constant => Record**. Open the object menu and select **Add Terminal => Control Input**. Click **Default Value** from the list box presented, then click **OK**.

The record received will become the default value. In this case, Record Constant will receive an array of records from the From Data Set object, and it will format itself to display that array of records.

Connect the **From Data Set** output pin, **Rec**, to the **Default Value** pin on **Record Constant**. If you would like to see this terminal, open the object menu and select **Edit Properties...**, then **Show Terminals**, then **OK**. A dotted line between the two objects indicates a control line. See the figure below.

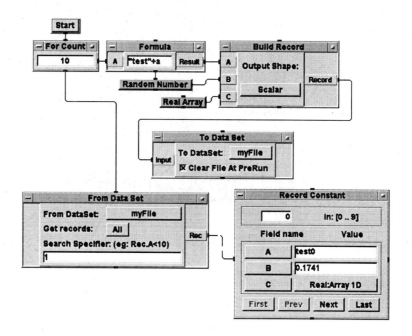

Fig. 5-15. Storing and Retrieving Data Using DataSets

8. Run your program and save it as **dataset1.vee**.

> *Note: When using the From Data Set object, if HP VEE doesn't find a record that meets your criterion, you get an error message. A more elegant way to handle this situation is to add an EOF (end-of-file) output pin to the object, which will fire if no records meet your criterion. You can then take whatever action you want programmatically.*

Customizing a Simple Test Database

You could store a number of records in a DataSet. Each record could contain different data types describing a particular test: the name, time stamp, test parameters, test values, pass or fail indicator, description of the test, and so on. You could create your own test database, if you could search and sort that data. The expression field in the From Data Set object is used for search operations. And the function sort( ) can be used to sort records using a specified field. First, you'll learn how to search a DataSet for information. Next, you'll create an operator interface for that search operation giving you a simple database. And finally, you'll program a sort operation.

Lab 5-4: Using Search and Sort Operations With DataSets

Let's modify the dataset1.vee program.

To Perform a Search Operation With DataSets

1. Double-click on the expression field at the bottom of the **From Data Set** object to highlight the current expression, **1.** Enter **Rec.B>=0.5**.

The object will now output all records, whose second field is greater or equal to 0.5. Let's also add an EOF pin. We won't connect it to anything to avoid making the program too complex. This pin will fire if no records match our criterion in the expression field.

2. Place your mouse pointer over the data output area of the **From Data Set** object, and press **Ctrl-a**. An **EOF** pin will appear. See Figure 5-16.

   Note: *You could also open the object menu, and click Add Terminal => Data Output... .*

3. Run your program and save it as **dataset2.vee**.

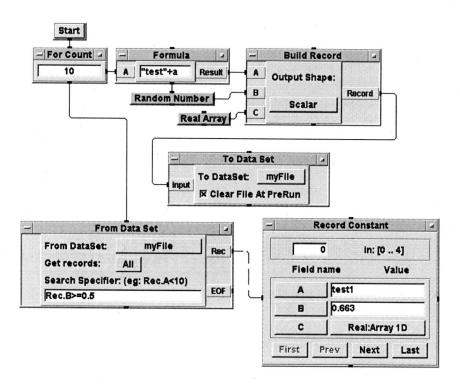

Fig. 5-16. A Search Operation With DataSets

To Create an Operator Interface for your Search Operation

Let's modify dataset2.vee. In this exercise you'll create a menu for extracting data from your test results database. You'll also create a very simple operator interface that can be secured to avoid unwanted modifications to your program.

The specifications of the program are:

- Provide a test menu that will allow the user to select a particular test from test0 through test9, from which they want all related test data.

- The specified test results will be displayed with the fields and values labeled. The user should be able to interact with the display to gain more detailed information.

- The program should give clear instructions for operation.

With dataset2.vee in your work area, you first need to add a control input that will allow you to input the expression in the From Data Set object programmatically.

1. Open the **From Data Set** object menu and select **Add Terminal... => Control Input...**. Select **Formula** from the menu presented. A **Formula** input terminal appears. Click the **Get records** field to toggle from **All** to **One**, since you only want one test record at a time.

You want the user to select a particular test name. The test names are located in field A of all records. So you need the expression:
$$\text{Rec.A}==\text{<test name in quotation marks>}.$$
This statement means that the object should output the record whose first field matches the test name the user has selected. For example, if the user selects test3, your expression should read: Rec.A=="test3". The object would then extract the test record for that test, which you could display.

Let's create a menu next. The Data => Selection Control => Radio Buttons object is used for this purpose. We'll discuss this in more detail in a later chapter. For now, we'll create a menu that allows the user to make selections by clicking a button next to the desired selection.

2. Select **Data => Selection Control => Radio Buttons**. Open the object menu and select **Edit Enum Values...**. **Item 1** will be highlighted, so type the values **test0, test1, test2,...,test9** using the **Tab** key after each one, except for **test9**. Click **OK** and you will see your first entry, **test0**, on a button.

   Using the **Edit Properties...** selection in the object menu, change the object name to **Test Menu**. Next, select **Auto Execute** under **Execution**, then click **OK**. Now your program can execute whenever the operator makes a menu selection, so you can delete the **Start** object.

   Place the mouse pointer over the **Start** object, and press **Ctrl-d**.

   But you only want the program to execute after you make a menu selection, so connect the **Test Menu** sequence output pin to the **For Count** sequence input pin. Refer to Fig. 5-17 on the next page.

As you can see in the figure, the output of your Test Menu goes into a Formula object, which then sends the correct formula to the From Data Set object. Let's create that formula now.

3. Select **Math => Formula**, and enter the following expression: "Rec.A==" + "\"" + A + "\"". Connect the data input pin on the **Formula** object to the **Test Menu** data output pin. Connect the **Formula** data output pin to the control input pin on the **From Data Set** object (labeled Formula). Iconize the **Formula** object. To assure yourself that you don't use old data from **Formula**, delete the sequence line between **For Count** and **From Data Set**, and instead connect the **For Count** sequence output pin to the **Formula** sequence input pin. Then connect the **Formula** sequence output pin to the **From Data Set** sequence input pin. This will make sure the right data from Formula is being used.

   This probably seems very confusing, so let's break down what you're doing. First of all, you need a Text data type to send to the From Data Set object, which means you want your formula in quotation marks. So, you start with "Rec.A==" in the Formula object. This tells HP VEE to look at the first field (labeled A) of all the records in your DataSet file, and to select the first one (Get records: One) that equals (note the double-equal sign, ==) the <selected test name>. The test name comes from the Test Menu as an Enum data type without quotes, so you need to put quotes around it. A quotation mark is indicated by the escape character \", so you need to add one before and after the input on terminal A of the Formula object. Thus, the final expression in the Formula object is:

$$\text{``Rec.A=='' + ``\verb|\|''' + A + ``\verb|\|'''.}$$

This will put the right formula into the From Data Set object. For example, if test3 is selected, then your final formula will read: '

$$\text{Rec.A==``test3''.}$$

The From Data Set object then outputs the first record it finds, whose "a"

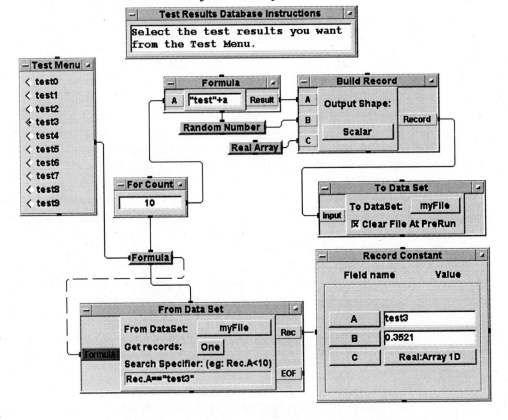

Fig. 5-17. Adding a Menu to the Search Operation

field is equal to "test3".

Now you need to create a box displaying instructions for the user. We'll use the Note Pad object for this. Refer to Figure 5-17.

4. Select **Display => Note Pad**. Change the title to **Test Results Database Instructions**.

The Note Pad should expand in size to accomodate the new size. Click on the Note Pad input area below the title to get a cursor. Type:
> **Select the test results you want from the**
> **Test Menu.**

(You might want to use the Size command in the object menu to reduce the size of the object.)

You now have the detail view, as shown in Figure 5-17. Run the program a few times to verify that it works.

Now, you'll create an operator interface in a couple of minutes. When you understand the process, which you'll go over more thoroughly in a later chapter, it will take only a few seconds.

5. By pressing **Ctrl** and clicking these objects, select the **Test Menu**, **Test Results Database Instructions**, and **Test Results** objects.

All objects selected show a shadow. Verify no other objects are selected.

Then select **Edit => Add to Panel**, and your operator interface appears as a panel view. You can then move and size the objects to your taste. One layout is shown in Figure 5-18 on the next page.

Note: If the Add to Panel selection is grayed out, it means that you do not have any objects selected in the work area.

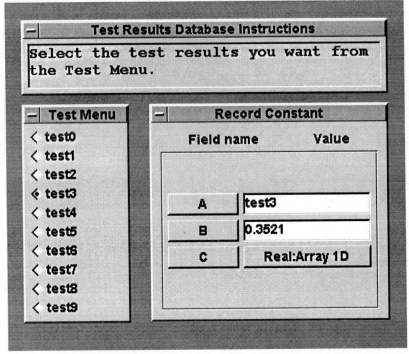

Fig. 5-18. The Operator Interface for Your Database

6. Run your program a few times simply by making selections in your **Test Menu** to be sure it runs properly. Save it as **database.vee**.

Notice that you can get more detailed information on any given record simply by clicking the field names or the values in the Record Constant object (named Test Results).

To Perform a Sort Operation on a Record Field

Open your **dataset2.vee** program, and let's modify the end of it. Scroll your work area up for more room. This is the program that sets some condition in the From Data Set object such as Rec.B>=0.5, then HP VEE will extract all of the records that meet that requirement. The array of records that meet the criterion are displayed in the Record Constant object. Now suppose you wanted to sort the resulting records by the second field in ascending order, so that you could tell which tests were failing by the greatest margin. This exercise shows you how to do that.

1. Select **Math => Formula** and connect the **From Data Set** data output pin **Rec** to the **Formula** object data input pin. Double-click the **Formula** expression field to highlight the default formula, then enter **sort(a, 1, "B")**.

   The Sort object is found in the AdvMath => Array menu, and you can read detailed information on its capabilities in the object menu Help entry. Here, we are calling the sort( ) function from the Formula object. Briefly, the first parameter tells HP VEE to sort the data on Formula's A pin - an array of records in this case. The second parameter indicates the direction of the sort: any non-zero number indicates an ascending direction, a zero indicates descending. The default direction is ascending. The third parameter, in the case of a Record data type, indicates the name of the field you want to sort. Therefore, we are performing an ascending sort on the B field in our array of records.

2. Select **Display => AlphaNumeric** and connect it to the data output pin of the **Formula** object.

3. Run your program a few times, and notice how the program sorts all of the records returned from the DataSet file in ascending order by field **B**.

   In Figure 5-19 we have just shown the modified part of the program.

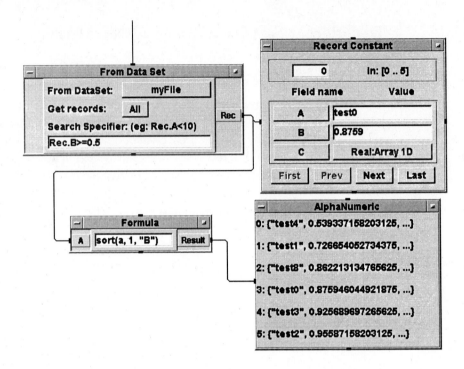

Fig. 5-19. A Sort Operation on a Record Field

Chapter 5 Checklist

You should now be able to perform the following tasks. Review topics, if necessary, before proceeding to the next chapter.

- Explain the basic notation for using arrays.

- Create an array using the Collector object.

- Extract elements from an array using the Formula object.

- Send a string, time stamp, and real array to a file.

- Retrieve a string, time stamp, and real array from a file.

- Use the function now( ) for a time stamp.

- Format time stamps in a variety of ways for display.

- Build and unbuild a record.

- Get and set fields in a record.

- Store a record to a DataSet.

- Retrieve a record from a DataSet.

- Perform a search operation on a DataSet.

- Perform a sort operation on a Record field.

- Combine HP VEE tools to create a simple test database.

Part II: Common Tasks Using HP VEE

Creating Reports Easily

Average time to complete: 1.5 hrs.

Overview

In the first lab exercise, we'll show you how to send data to an MS Excel spreadsheet automatically using Dynamic Data Exchange(DDE). DDE allows applications to pass data and commands back and forth. In MS Word, you can then integrate HP VEE's generated documentation file, your spreadsheet, and screen bitmaps of your programs that are correlated to your text description.

This is a very fast process for detailed, effective reports on your programs. The principles will be the same even when using another spreadsheet and word processing program.

In this chapter you'll learn about:

- Using MS Excel to capture HP VEE data

- Using MS Word with HP VEE

Lab 6-1: Using MS Excel To Capture HP VEE Data

We'll use the To/From DDE object to send HP VEE data to specific rows and columns of an MS Excel spreadsheet automatically. You can get more information on DDE in chapter 12. Here we'll just focus on how you would use DDE to create a report. (If you don't have MS Excel, you can use the same principles with another spreadsheet program.) The steps will be given in a shorter form, since many of you won't have access to these particular packages and just need to understand the process.

1. Create the following program in HP VEE to simulate sending five rows of data with eight elements in each row.

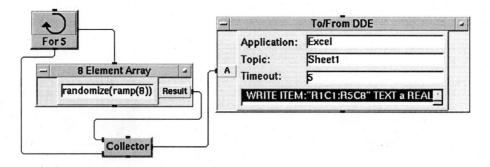

Fig. 6-1. Sending Simulated Data To MS Excel

- **For Count:** (in Flow =>Repeat) Set to **5**, rename to **For 5**, and iconize.

- **Formula:** (in Math) Use embedded functions to generate an 8-element array. The **ramp** function generates an array of **8** elements stepping from 0 to 1 in equal increments (using the default). **Randomize** takes this array and changes the values in a random way.

- **Collector:** (in Data) Keep the default setting for an **n+1 Dim Array**, so the five 1-dimension arrays received on the input will be turned into a single 2-dimension array with five rows and eight columns.

- **To/From DDE:** (in I/O) The default settings initiate a conversation with **MS Excel** and direct your transactions to **Sheet1**.

  Configure the transaction as:
  WRITE ITEM:"R1C1:R5C8" TEXT a REAL STD EOL
  See the figure below.

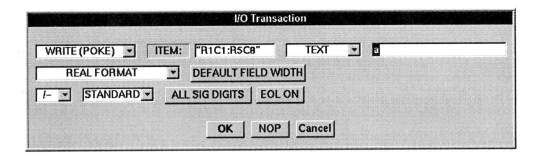

Fig. 6-2. Configuring the To/From DDE Transaction

An Excel row number is specified by R<number> and a column number by C<number>. You could therefore read or write to a particular cell. The colon is used to specify a range, so "R1C1:R5C8" signifies the cells that will hold our two-dimension (2D) array of data.

Using the **Edit Properties** box and the **Data Format** tab, change the array separator from a blank space to a tab ("\t"), since this is the default separator between columns in MS Excel. "\n" signifies an End-Of-Line (EOL) in Excel, so you can use the HP VEE default here. See the figure on the next page.

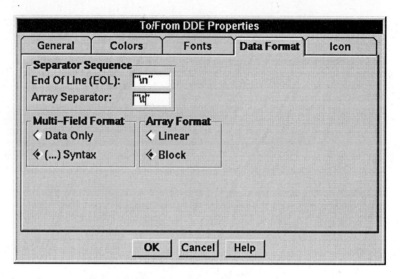

Fig. 6-3. Setting the Array Separator

2. Launch **MS Excel**, then run your program. (Make sure the MS Excel directory is in your PATH.) You will see the data appear immediately in **Sheet1**. See the figure below.

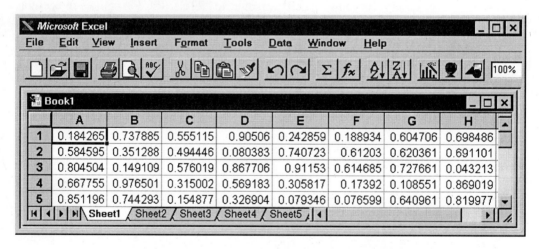

Fig. 6-4. The HP VEE Data Appearing in MS Excel

Lab 6 - 2: Using MS Word With HP VEE

We'll now show you how you can use the Edit Description, Save
Documentation, and Print All commands with your spreadsheet to generate a
fast, detailed, effective report. (Once again, the instructions will be brief,
since many may not have MS Word or MS Excel. The principles will be the
same regardless of the word processing or spreadsheet application you use.

1. Using the program from the first lab, click **File => Edit Description...**
   and type in the documentation shown in the following figure. (We'll save
   this program as Report.vee in a moment.)

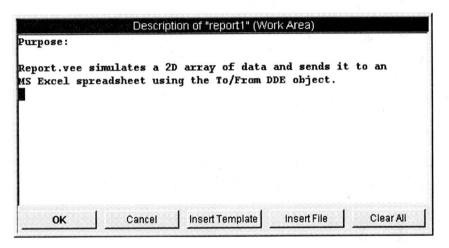

Fig. 6-5. The Edit Description Dialog Box

2. Click **File => Save Documentation...**, name the file **Report.txt**, put it in
   the directory of your choice, and click **OK**.

   This command automatically documents your program, as we
   demonstrated in chapter 2, and stores it in a text file.

3. Save your program as **Report.vee**, and save your spreadsheet as
   Report.xls. (Select the number of significant digits you would like in the
   data before saving.)

4. Launch **MS Word** and open **Report.txt**. Reformat it to your taste. See the figure below with formatting done to emphasize the titles and description of the program purpose as well as removing some things we didn't need.

Example Report

Source file: "C:\\CH6\\report1.vee"
File last revised: Fri Nov 10 11:11:38 1995
Date documented: Fri Nov 10 11:17:33 1995
VEE revision: 3.2

Purpose:

Report.vee simulates a 2D array of data and sends it to an MS Excel spreadsheet automatically using the To/From DDE object.

HP VEE Objects

0: Formula: "8 Element Array"
Formula: randomize(ramp(8))

1: For Count: "For 5"
Count: 5

2: Collector: "Collector"
Output shape: n+1 Dim Array

3: To/From DDE: "To/From DDE"
Transactions:
 1: WRITE ITEM:"R1C1:R5C8" TEXT a REAL STD EOL
Application: Excel

Topic: Sheet1
Timeout: 5

Fig. 6-6. Report.txt Formatted In MS Word

You not only have a thorough description of the objects and their nesting in the program (there's only one level of nesting in this program), but also any Edit Description or NotePad entries. HP VEE gives you the object name and any new title.

5. Putting the **MS Word** cursor at the bottom of your report, click **Insert =>** **File...,** and select your spreadsheet file. Once **MS Word** inserts it, you can format using **Table Autoformat...** in the **Table** menu. See the figure below for our formatting choices.

Data Spreadsheet

0.00125	0.56357	0.19330	0.80872	0.58499	0.47986	0.35028	0.89594
0.82281	0.74658	0.17410	0.85892	0.71048	0.51352	0.30399	0.01498
0.09140	0.36444	0.14731	0.16589	0.98849	0.44568	0.11908	0.00467
0.00891	0.37787	0.53165	0.57117	0.60175	0.60715	0.16623	0.66302
0.45078	0.35211	0.05704	0.60767	0.78329	0.80258	0.51987	0.30194

6. In HP VEE, click **File => Print All...,** select from the options presented (we just chose the "network" view), and click **OK**. See the figure below for the printed output.

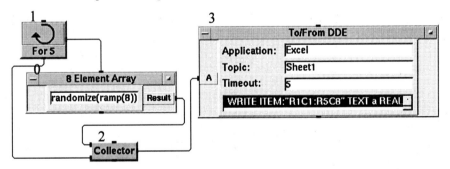

Fig. 6-7. Using the Print All Command On Report.vee

Notice the numbers on the objects correlate to the object numbers in your report. (The numbers are assigned in the order you programmed the objects.) Simply attach this printout to your report, or some printer drivers allow you to route this output to a file, which could be inserted into your MS Word document.

Chapter 6 Checklist

You should now be able to perform the following tasks. Review topics, if necessary, before moving on to the next chapter.

- Pass HP VEE data to an MS Excel spreadsheet using the To/From DDE object.

- Explain the general principles of passing HP VEE data to a spreadsheet program, such as the escape sequences used to separate rows and columns.

- Use the Edit Description, Save Documentation, and Print All commands with an HP VEE program.

- Use MS Word to integrate a program documentation file and a spreadsheet.

- Explain how the Print All output correlates to the program documentation file generated by HP VEE.

Integrating Programs
In Other Languages

7

Overview

One of the great advantages of HP VEE is that it integrates well with other applications and programs. In this chapter you'll learn the easiest way to integrate compiled programs and operating system commands with HP VEE.

First, there is a conceptual discussion about the Execute Program object: how it specifies programs and parameters, how it uses the operating system commands, and the distinctions between the UNIX and PC versions of the object. Then you'll do three lab exercises - one for PC users and two for UNIX users.

- The Execute Program object

- Using operating system commands from HP VEE

- Calling compiled programs from HP VEE (UNIX)

Understanding the Execute Program Object

There are three major ways to run programs in other languages from HP VEE. The first method uses the Execute Program object to escape HP VEE and run another program, application, or operating system command. This method is the most versatile and easy to use. The second method links compiled functions in other languages to HP VEE, either through Shared Libraries in UNIX operating systems or Dynamic Link Libraries on the PC. Although this way is slightly more difficult to execute, it will give you significant performance gains. Refer to Chapter 11 for more information on Shared Libraries and Chapter 12 for a discussion of Dynamic Link Libraries. The third method is specifically designed for HP BASIC/UX programs and will also be discussed in Chapter 12.

The Execute Program object is located in the I/O menu and looks like the next two figures. Notice that in the PC version the Execute Program object does not use transaction I/O to communicate with programs, so you don't add data input and output pins to pass data to your compiled program. The UNIX version does use transaction I/O, so we've added input and output pins and created a ficticious program to better illustrate how the object would be used.

Execute Program (PC)	
Run Style:	Normal ▾
Wait for prog exit:	Yes
Prog with params:	cprog –param1
Working directory:	c:\progs\cprogs

Fig. 7-1. The Execute Program Object (PC)

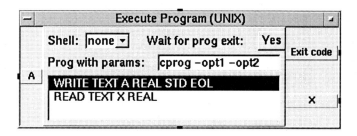

Fig. 7-2. The Execute Program Object (UNIX)

Using the Execute Program Object (PC)

You use this object to run the following from HP VEE:

- Compiled programs written in other languages

- ***.BAT** or ***.COM** files

- MS DOS system commands, such as **dir**

The *Prog with params* (program with parameters) field will hold the same words you would type at a DOS prompt. If you were running a program in C, you would enter the executable file name - myprog.exe, for example. (You can omit the .exe extension.) If the program has parameters, they would follow the executable file name preceded by a hyphen: myprog -param1 -param2, for instance. If you want to run a DOS system command, you first need to run the DOS command interpreter with the /c option (i.e., *command.com /c <system command>* for Windows 95, or *cmd /c <system command>* for Windows NT). This option tells the command interpreter to read the string following the /c as a system command.

The *Wait for prog exit* field, when set to Yes, will not fire the sequence out pin until the program is done executing. When set to No, the sequence out pin fires before the specified program is done executing. *Run Style* gives you a choice of Normal for a standard window, Minimized for running in an icon, and Maximized for the maximum window size. The *Working directory* is simply the directory that holds any files related to the program.

Using the Execute Program Object (UNIX)

UNIX is designed to run a number of programs called processes concurrently. If HP VEE initiates another program, HP VEE is called the parent process and the program initiated is called the child process. The Execute Program object spawns a child process, either directly or through a command shell. The Shell field opens a menu with the following choices: none, sh, csh, and ksh. If the Shell field is set to none, the first token in the *Prog with params* field is interpreted as the name of an executable program, and the following tokens are assumed to be parameters. If you have shell-dependent features in the *Prog with params* field, such as standard input and output redirection (< and >), wildcards (*, ?, [a-z]), or pipes (|), you need to specify a shell; otherwise, select none because it yields a faster execution speed.

The *Wait for prog exit* field toggles between Yes and No. Regardless of the setting, HP VEE spawns a child process, if one is not already active. All transactions specified in the Execute Program object are completed.

When set to Yes:

The child process must terminate before the data output pins are fired.

When set to No:

The child process fires the data output pins and remains active. The performance of your program is greater with this setting.

Prog with params accepts:

- The name of an executable program file and command line parameters

- A command that will be sent to a shell for interpretation

You may add input or output terminals to the Execute Program object. Data is received from an HP VEE program on an input pin, and then you perform a WRITE TEXT transaction to send the data to the child process. A READ

TEXT transaction reads data from the child process, and places it on a data output pin for use by your HP VEE program.

You may also send the name of your program or shell command to the Execute Program object by adding the data input terminal labeled Command, which is available by adding data inputs.

Now that you understand the fundamentals of this object, let's try some lab exercises.

Lab 7-1: Using a System Command (PC)

Calling a compiled program in another language is straightforward. You just type the executable file and any parameters into the Execute Program (PC) object. On the other hand, executing an MS DOS system command is a little tricky, so this exercise clarifies this process. For example, if you want your HP VEE program to execute a *dir* command, you first need to run the DOS command interpreter, as this example will show.

1. Create a subdirectory in your root directory called **ch7**.

2. Select **I/O => Execute Program (PC)**. Click the **Prog with params** field to get a cursor, then type:

   command.com /c dir > c:\ch7\tmp

   > **Note:** *Replace "command.com" with "cmd" for Windows NT.*

   (You may need to include the complete path of the command.com executable.) This will run the DOS command interpreter, which will run the system command to display the current directory, and redirect the output (>)to the tmp file instead of the computer screen. Leave **Yes** for the **Wait for prog exit** selection. Leave **Normal** for **Run Style**, and enter **c:\ch7** for the **Working directory**.

3. Select **I/O => From => File** and place it below **Execute Program**. Connect the sequence out pin of **Execute Program** to the sequence in pin of the **From File** object.

   Click the **From File:** input field labeled **myFile** to get a list box, double-click the input field to highlight **myFile**, type **\ch7\tmp**, then click **OK**.

   Click the transaction bar to get the **I/O Transaction** box, change **REAL FORMAT** to **STRING FORMAT**, change **SCALAR** to **ARRAY 1D**, change **SIZE: (10)** to **TO END: (*)**, then click **OK**.

   The transaction bar should now read: **READ TEXT x STR ARRAY:*** .

   This transaction will read the contents of the tmp file.

4. Select **Display => Logging AlphaNumeric** and connect its data input pin to the **From File** data output.

5. Run your program. It should look like the figure below.

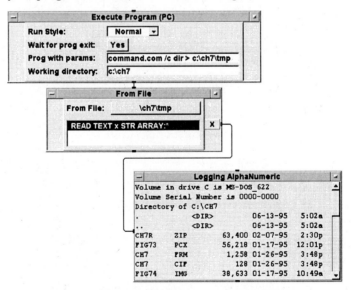

Fig. 7-3. Using Execute Program (PC)

Lab 7-2: Using a System Command (UNIX)

In this exercise you'll use the operating system command ls, which lists the filenames in a directory. Since this is not a shell-dependent command, you can set Shell to *none*. Then you'll program a variation of this exercise using a shell-dependent feature, the pipe (|).

To List the Files in a Directory

You'll use the UNIX operating system command *ls*, to list the files. In this case, you want *ls* to terminate before HP VEE continues with your program, so you set the *Wait forprog exit* field to Yes. To read the output of *ls*, you use a READ TEXT transaction with a STRING FORMAT in the shape of a one-dimensional array. Since you don't know how many files are in the directory, you choose the TO END: (*) option when configuring the I/O transaction.

1. Select **I/O => Execute Program (UNIX)** and place it in the upper-left work area.

2. Make sure the **Shell** field is set to **none** and the **Wait for prog exit** field is set to **Yes**.

3. Click the **Prog with params** field and enter: **ls /tmp**.

   You could specify any directory. We're using **/tmp** as an example.

4. Add a data output terminal. The default will be named **X**.

   Since you are not using an exit code from the program, you may disregard the terminal labeled Exit code.

5. Double-lick the transaction bar to get the **I/O Transaction** box. Edit the default variable **a** to an **X**, since data from the program will be read into that output terminal.

7 - 7

Change **WRITE** to **READ**. Change **REAL FORMAT** to **STRING FORMAT**. Change the shape of the data from **SCALAR** to **ARRAY 1D**. And finally, toggle the **SIZE:** button to **TO END: (*)**. Click **OK**.

Your transaction bar should now read: **READ TEXT X STR ARRAY:*.**

6. Select **Display => Logging AlphaNumeric** and connect its data input pin to the **X** terminal on the **Execute Program** object.

7. Run your program. It should look like the one below.

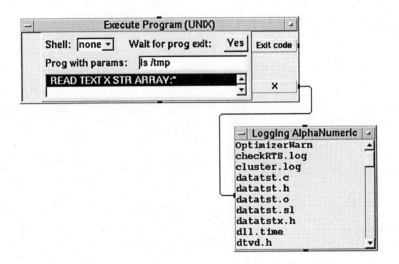

Fig. 7-4. Listing the Files in a Directory (UNIX)

To List the Files in a Directory Using a Shell

This variation of the last exercise is for instructional purposes. You'll use a shell-dependent feature, a pipe (|), which sends the output of one operating system command to another. The second command will be *wc*, which stands for word count. The *wc* command counts lines, words, and characters in the named files. The command *wc -l filename* counts the number of lines in the specified file. You'll count the number of lines in a directory, then display the number and the files.

1. Select **I/O => Execute Program (UNIX)**. Set the **Shell** field to **sh,** which is needed to use the shell features, "**|**" and "**;**". Enter the command, **ls /tmp|wc -l;ls /tmp**, in the **Shell command** field. Add two data output terminals, one labeled **X** and the other labeled **Lines**.

    Configure your first transaction to: **READ TEXT Lines INT**. **Lines** replaces the default variable **a**.

    Configure a second transaction to: **READ TEXT X STR ARRAY:Lines**. **Lines** should be entered in the **SIZE** field, when specifying the length of the array.

2. Select **Display => AlphaNumeric** and **Display => Logging AlphaNumeric**. Connect **AlphaNumeric** to the **Lines** output and **Logging AlphaNumeric** to the **X** output pin.

3. Run your program. It should look like the Figure 7-5.

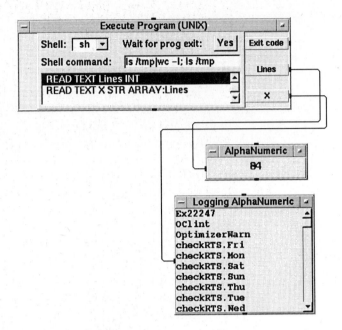

Fig. 7-5. Using a Shell Command with a Pipe

Now that you understand the basic process for using operating system commands, let's call a program written in C using input and output pins on the Execute Program object.

Lab 7-3: Using Compiled Programs (UNIX)

Although you'll use a program written in C for this exercise, the same principles apply to any compiled programs in other languages. First, use your favorite editor to write the following program and save it in AddOne.c. Then compile it using the following command: *cc AddOne.c -o AddOne*.

```
#include <stdio.h>

main ( )

{

  int c;

  double val;

  setbuf(stdout,NULL);        /* turn stdout buffering off */


  while (((c=scanf("%lf",&val)) != EOF) && c > 0) {

    fprintf(stdout,"%g\n",val + 1);

    fflush(stdout);           /* force output back to VEE */

}

  exit(0);
```

Fig. 7-6. The C Program Listing for AddOne.c

Note: *You might want to just read through this exercise, if you're not familiar with programming in C.*

HP VEE uses *stdin* and *stdout* of the C program to transfer data. The program simply reads a Real number from standard input, which will be your HP VEE program, in this case. Then AddOne adds one to the value and sends the result back to HP VEE. The program in the figure below uses two standard C routines, *setbuf* and *fflush* to force data through *stdout* of the C program. In practice, either *setbuf* or *fflush* is sufficient. Using *setbuf(file,NULL)* turns off buffering for all output to file, which will be stdout in this case. Using *fflush(file)* flushes any already buffered data to file.

For those of you who don't know C, here's a simple explanation of the program. The #include attaches a standard library of I/O routines to your program. The main body of the program first declares an integer variable c, and a real (double) variable *val*. The buffering is turned off in the *stdout* file.

The *while* loop reads one value at a time. If the value is not the EOF character and it is greater than 0, the value is incremented by one and printed to the *stdout* file. The *fflush* routine forces the output back to HP VEE.

The *exit(0)* sends no exit code back to HP VEE. You could send a number back using *exit( )* and it would appear at the Exit code terminal. You could use this routine to flag a particular condition in your C program.

After you have compiled this program, put the executable file AddOne, in any directory you want. Here we'll assume it's in the root directory. Now you can create your HP VEE program.

1. Select **Data => Real Slider** and place it to the left side of the work area. Rename it **Number**.

   You use the Real Slider by placing the mouse pointer over the slider bar, pressing the left mouse button, and dragging it up or down. You can select a range of real values using the input fields on the slider. The value selected is displayed at the top of the slider.

   Change the upper range from **1** to **100.**

2. Select **I/O => Execute Program (UNIX)** and place it to the right of the **Real Slider**. Add an input terminal and connect it to the **Real Slider** object. Make sure **Shell** is set to **sh** and **Wait for prog exit** is set to **Yes**. Add a data output terminal. Enter the executable file **<pathname>AddOne**, in the **Shell command** field. (I will enter my entire pathname here. You enter yours.)

   Configure two transactions: **WRITE TEXT a EOL** and **READ TEXT X REAL**.

   This will write the value at terminal **A** to your **AddOne** program, the program will increment the value, and return it to terminal **X**.

3. Select **Display => AlphaNumeric**, rename it **Result**, and connect it to the **X** terminal on the **Execute Program** object.

4. Select an input value with the **Real Slider (Number)** and run your program. It should look like the figure below.

> *Tip:* *If you would like your program to run automatically after selecting a number on the slider, open the Real Slider object menu, click Edit Properties, then click the Auto Execute box under Execution.*

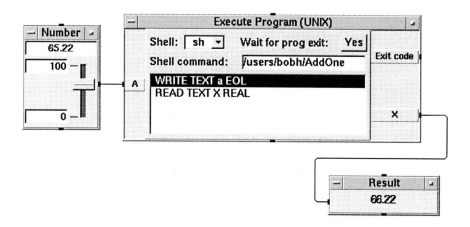

Fig. 7-7. Running a C Program Using Execute Program

You now understand the fundamentals of running a compiled program in another language. When you use a different compiled language, you will still need to turn buffering off to standard output or flush already buffered data. Refer to Chapters 11 and 14 for other methods of integrating other programs with HP VEE.

Writing Programs That Port Easily

When you're integrating programs in other languages, you might want to write your HP VEE program so that it ports easily between platforms. So HP VEE includes the following three objects (which can also be used as functions) in the Data => System Info submenu:

- **whichOS( )** This object (or function) determines your operating system, then sends out one of the following strings:

  Windows
  Windows_95
  Windows_NT
  HP-UX
  Su nOS

  Your program can then branch based on these results when incorporating programs in other languages. For example, look at the program, <home dir.>\examples\manual\manual49.vee to see a program that uses whichOS() to make sure it's importing the right type of library - a shared library on HP-UX or a Dynamic Link Library on a PC operating sytem.

- **whichPlatform( )** This object (or function) is used to determine the hardware system on which HP VEE is running, then returns one of the following strings:

  PC
  HP9000s300
  HP9000s700
  SPARCstation

- **whichVersion( )** This object (or function) will tell you which version of HP VEE is running, which is useful for program maintenance and debugging.

Chapter 7 Checklist

You should now be able to perform the following tasks. Review topics, if necessary, before moving on to the next chapter.

- Explain the purpose of the Execute Program object.

- Give an overview of the configuration settings on the Execute Program object.

- Explain the general process of how the Execute Program object sends data to/from a program on a UNIX platform. Explain how the PC platform differs.

- Run operating system commands from HP VEE.

- Run programs in other languages from HP VEE using the Execute Program object.

- Create a program that will use the whichOS( ), whichPlatform( ), or whichVersion( ) object so that it will run perfectly regardless of the operating system or platform.

Using HP VEE Functions

8

Average Time to Complete: 1 hr.

- Merging existing HP VEE programs with your tests

- Defining a user function

Overview

- Creating, calling, and editing functions

In the last chapter, you learned how to combine programs written in other languages with your HP VEE programs. This is especially important for test development today because of the strong pressures to reduce time to market. Test developers need to leverage their past work and to program in such a way that their tests will be easy to modify in the future.

- Creating, merging, importing, and deleting function libraries

Part of the solution is creating well-documented, modular programs, that use functions that could be merged into other programs. Another part is learning how to incorporate past HP VEE programs into your current tests. Let's see how easy this is using HP VEE.

Merging HP VEE Programs

The easiest way to leverage your programming is to merge a past program with your current test. This is done using the Merge... command in the File menu. You are presented with a list box displaying the *lib* subdirectory from the HP VEE home directory. This directory contains many useful programs, which expand your power. For example, you could merge a program that gives you a bar chart display or one that provides a data entry keypad for accepting numeric user input such as ID numbers. You could also switch to another directory and merge a program that you've written. Once the program has been merged, it can be edited to suit your current needs.

Lab 8-1: Merging a Bar Chart Display Program

This is a very simple exercise to show you how to merge an existing program with your present one. Although you'll use a program from the HP VEE *lib* directory, you could do the same thing with one of your own programs. You'll create an array with five values from 1 to 5 using the ramp( ) function. Instead of displaying the array with one of the internal HP VEE displays, you'll merge the BarChart program with the program you're creating.

1. Select **Math => Formula** and place it in your left work area.

2. Delete the data input terminal.

3. Change the default formula to **ramp(5,1,5)**.

   The first parameter is the number of elements desired in the ramp array. The second parameter is the starting number, and the third is the last number. For more information on this function select Math => Generate => ramp(numElem,from,thru), and examine Help in its object menu.

4. Click on **File => Merge...** to get the **Merge File** list box. Select **BarChart**.vee and place it to the right of the **Formula** object. Connect the two objects.

5. Run your program. It should look like the figure below.

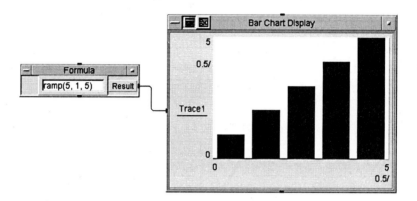

Fig. 8-1. Merging the BarChart Program

Notice that the Bar Chart Display takes a one-dimensional array and displays the values as vertical bars. It uses the number of bars necessary to display the values in the array. If you want to examine how it's programmed, open the detail view of the display. By searching through this library directory you can get some ideas on programs you might like to create to make your job easier.

Using Functions

Most programming languages use functions to create subprograms that perform specific tasks. First, we'll define an HP VEE function. Then you'll have some lab exercises to show you how to create, call, and edit HP VEE user-defined functions. Once you understand the basics, you'll learn how to create libraries of functions, which can be merged into your programs in the development phase or imported at runtime.

Defining an HP VEE User Function

There are three types of user-defined functions in HP VEE:

(1) **User Function**

- Created by selecting Make UserFunction in the object menu of a UserObject.

- You can call the User Function from different places in your program by using the Call Function (Device => Function => Call) or an expression (from the Formula object, for example).

- You edit the User Function by clicking on Edit => Edit UserFunction ... and selecting the appropriate User Function from the list box presented.

- All changes made to one User Function will be inherited by other User Functions of the same name in your program.

- You can easily transfer User Functions from one program to another either by merging them in during program development or by importing them at runtime (Device => Function => Import Library).

(2) Compiled Functions

- Created outside of HP VEE using a compiled language. These functions are then put in a library, which is linked to HP VEE at run time (refer to Chapters 11 and 13 for a more detailed discussion).

- To call these functions, you first have use the Import Library object to link them to your program. Then you may call them using the Call Function object or an expression.

(3) Remote Functions

- Similar to a User Function except that it runs on a remote host computer connected by your Local Area Network.

Lab 8-2: User Function Operations

To Create a User Function

In this exercise you'll create a UserObject named ArrayStats, which will accept an array, calculate its maximum value, minimum value, mean, and standard deviation, and put the results on its output pins. Then you'll convert the UserObject to a UserFunction. In the next exercise, we'll discuss moving UserFunctions between programs.

1. Select **Math => Formula**, change its title to **ramp(10,1,10)**, delete its default input pin, then change its default expression to **ramp(10,1,10)**.

   This will create a 10 element array with values from 1 to 10.

2. Select **Device => UserObject** and place it to the right of the **Formula** object. Rename it **ArrayStats**, add one data input terminal for the array, and add four data ouput terminals for the results.

Rename the output terminals: **Max**, **Min**, **Mean**, and **Sdev**. Select **max(x)**, **min(x)**, **mean(x)**, and **sdev(x)** from the **AdvMath => Statistics** menu, place them in the UserObject, and connect their data inputs to **A** and their data outputs to the appropriate output terminals. Also, connect the **Formula** object to the **UserObject**.

3. Select Display => AlphaNumeric, clone it three times, and connect the displays to the **UserObject** output pins. Rename the displays.

4. Run your program. It should look like the one below.

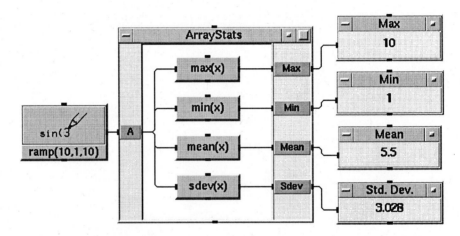

Fig. 8-2. ArrayStats Before Creating a User Function

5. Open the **ArrayStats** UserObject menu and click **Make UserFunction**. See Figure 8-3.

You see the UserObject named ArrayStats replaced by a Call Function object calling a User Function named ArrayStats. It will produce the same functionality as the UserObject ArrayStats. Also, you can call it from different places in the program. Any new edits to the UserFunction only have to be made once, and they'll be carried out whenever it's called.

If you wanted to use ArrayStats elsewhere in your program, you would click on Device => Function => Call, change the default expression name to ArrayStats, and the necessary input and output terminals will be added for you.

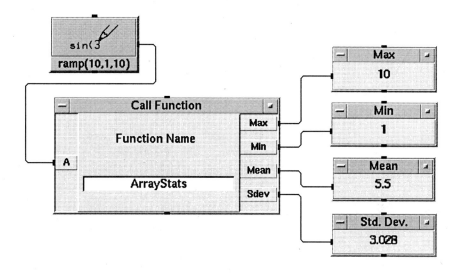

Fig. 8-3. Calling the User Function ArrayStats

To Edit a User Function

Let's suppose you wanted to edit ArrayStats to deliver a record with four fields giving the array statistics. Notice how quickly you can do that in the following exercise.

1. Delete the four **AlphaNumeric** displays.

2. Select **Edit => Edit UserFunction...** and select **ArrayStats** from the **Edit UserFunction** list box.

   All of the User Functions in your program will be displayed here.

3. Open the UserFunction: ArrayStats menu, click on **size**, and enlarge the editing window. (Click-and-drag the lower-right corner to size an object.)

4. Delete the four lines going to the output terminals. (Press **Ctrl-Shift** and click on the line you want to delete.)

5. Select **Data** => **Build Data** => **Record** and place it to the right side of the **UserFunction: ArrayStats** editing window. Add two data input terminals. Label the four terminals after the statistical functions: **max, min, mean**, and **sdev**. Connect the four inputs with the appropriate objects. Rename the **Max** output terminal **X** (Double-click **Max**, type the new name, click **OK**). Delete the other **UserFunction** data output terminals. Connect the **Build Record** output to the X output terminal on the **User Function** editing window. Click **Close**.

Before you click Close, your editing should look like the figure below.

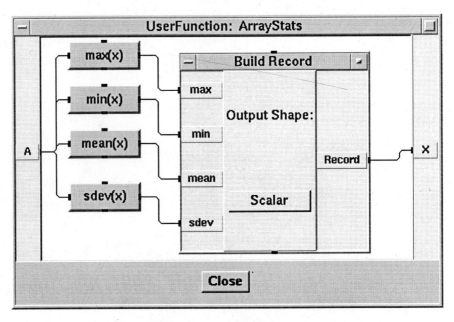

Fig. 8-4. Editing the UserFunction ArrayStats

6. Open the **Call Function** object menu and click **Configure Pinout**.

> *Note:* *This will adjust the number of pins to match your recent edits. You must do this any time you change the number of inputs or outputs in a User Function.*

An excellent way to display a record is by using the Record Constant object. You use the Default Value control input to accept a record from ArrayStats. HP VEE will automatically configure the Record Constant to hold the incoming record. It sounds confusing, so let's do it to clarify what we mean.

7. Select **Data => Constant => Record** and place it to the right of the **Call Function** object. Open the **Record Constant** object menu and click Add Terminal => Control Input.... Select **Default Value** from the list box presented. Now connect the **Call Function** data output to the control input pin on the **Record Constant** object.

   Notice that control lines are indicated by dotted lines to differentiate them from data lines.

8. Run your program. It should look like the figure below.

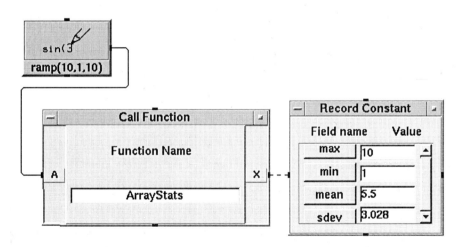

Fig. 8-5. After Editing ArrayStats Output to a Record

To Call a User Function from an Expression

Now you'll learn how to call ArrayStats from an expression in the Formula object.

1. Delete the **Call Function** object from the previous exercise.

2. Select **Math => Formula** and replace the default formula with **ArrayStats(A)**.

   Now the Formula object will take the input at terminal A, feed it to the User Function ArrayStats, which will deliver the record of statistics to its terminal X. The first output value from the UserFunction (X) will be returned to the Formula object and delivered to its Result output.

   Connect the **ArrayStats Formula** object to the **ramp(10,1,10) Formula** object and the **Record Constant**.

3. Run your program. It should look like the figure below.

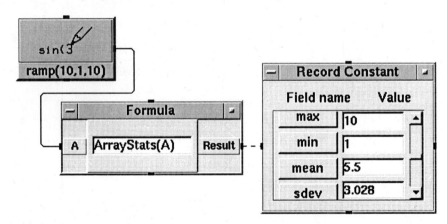

Fig. 8-6. Calling the ArrayStats User Function

Notice that the functionality of ArrayStats in the Formula object is exactly the same as it was in the Call Function object. We have used a Formula object in this example, but you could call ArrayStats from any input field that accepts expressions.

Note: *When you are calling a User Function from an expression, the User Function will only deliver a single output (the uppermost data output pin). If you need all of the outputs, or they cannot be put into a Record, then you will have to use the Call Function object.*

Reminder: *When calling a User Function from an expression, input terminals are used as function parameters to pass to your function. If no data is passed to your function, you must still include empty parentheses after the function name; otherwise, HP VEE will think you're referring to a Global variable or input terminal. For example, if the User Function called MyFunction has no input parameters, you must write MyFunction( ) in an expression. The Call Function object does not require the parentheses, because HP VEE knows you are referring to a function.*

Using Libraries With HP VEE User Functions

When you save a program, the User Functions you created are automatically saved as well. You have already learned how to merge a past program into your current program with the Merge... command. You can also use the Merge Library... command in the File menu to merge User Functions from a particular file. That file might hold an HP VEE program, or you might have created a group of logically related User Functions to use as a library. The merged User Functions can be edited and used exactly like the ones you created locally. This is an effective way to leverage your HP VEE test programs.

There is another way to bring outside User Functions into your active program using the Import Library and Delete Library objects in the Device => Function menu. With the Merge... command the User Functions are copied into your active program; whereas, the Import Library object accesses the original functions in another file without making a copy. The functions are imported at runtime at the point in the program when they're needed.

You can then delete them programmatically. This spreads out the load times and conserves disk space. If you use this technique, you may not edit the functions imported. Instead you can modify them in their original files, or use the Merge... command. You can view the imported UserFunctions for debugging purposes, but you cannot change them. So, you *import* when you want a single source for your function or want to save space, and you *merge* when you want a new copy of the function to modify or want a standalone program. Let's work through two examples to clarify these concepts.

Lab 8 - 3: Creating and Merging a Library of User Functions

When you save any program you automatically save the User Functions within the program. The Merge Library... command in the File menu will merge the User Functions from the specified file into your active program. You can think of this group of functions as a library. In this exercise you'll use the report generation program from Chapter 6, change the four UserObjects to User Functions, creating a library within that program. You'll resave the report program, then create a new program that merges your newly created library of User Functions.

1. Use the **File => Open...** command to recall the report generation program from Chapter 6, *repgen.vee*. It should look like the figure below. (If you're using the Evaluation software, you'll have to re-program it.)

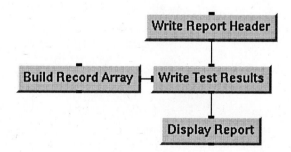

Fig. 8-7. Report Generation With UserObjects

2. Open the **UserObject** menus with the right mouse button, change their names to **BuildRecAry**, **ReportHeader**, **ReportBody**, and **ReportDisplay**, then open the menu again and select **Make UserFunction**.

You are creating names that will have no spaces, because this is a requirement of a User Function. Underscores may be used to make the name more readable. Double-click each Call object to go to the open view.

Each UserObject is replaced by a Call Function object that calls that particular User Function. From the open view, notice that the Call Function object does not require parentheses when referring to a User Function. If you were calling the function from a Formula object, you would need to include parentheses whether or not the function used parameters.

Run your program and note the functionality is exactly the same as before. Use the **File => Save As...** command and name it **Report1.vee**.

Your program should look like the figure below.

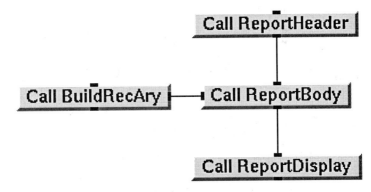

Fig. 8-8. Report Generation With User Functions

4. You have now created a library of four functions. You can see them listed by clicking **Edit => Edit UserFunction...** , as shown in the figure below. Click **Cancel** to close the list box.

Fig. 8-9. Your Library of User Functions

You're now going to create a new program and merge this library into it. Let's suppose you want to build a library of functions for generating reports, and you want to start it using these four functions. The new program will simply contain a Note Pad object explaining each function in the library. You could then create new report generation User Functions, merge them with this program, and update the Note Pad object to keep track of them. Whenever you had to create a new report, you could simply use the Merge Library... command to leverage all the functions from this program, which you'll call RepGen.

5. Select **File => New**. Since you've already saved your program, you can select **No** from the **Save changes first?** prompt that appears.

6. Select **File => Merge Library...** . Select **Report1.vee** from the **Merge Library** list box.

   Select **Edit => Edit UserFunction** to make sure your library from **Report1.vee** transferred to your new program. When you use the Merge Library... command, you can edit the merged functions just like functions you created locally.

7. Select **Display => Note Pad** and type the **User Function** descriptions similar to the ones shown in the figure below. Then save your new program as **libmerge**.

   Note: *You can save a "program" of User Functions for the purpose of creating a library, even though there is no actual HP VEE program calling these functions.*

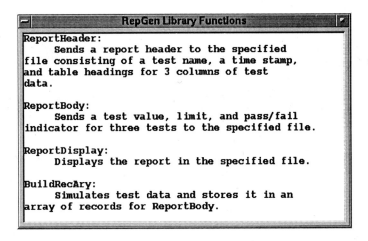

```
RepGen Library Functions
ReportHeader:
     Sends a report header to the specified
file consisting of a test name, a time stamp,
and table headings for 3 columns of test
data.

ReportBody:
     Sends a test value, limit, and pass/fail
indicator for three tests to the specified file.

ReportDisplay:
     Displays the report in the specified file.

BuildRecAry:
     Simulates test data and stores it in an
array of records for ReportBody.
```

Fig. 8-10. The RepGen Library of UserFunctions

Lab 8 - 4: Importing and Deleting Libraries

Once you've created a library of UserFunctions, you may not want to merge them into every program. You might like to bring in the library at runtime, use some of the functions, then delete it. The Import Library and Delete Library objects were designed for this situation. In the following exercise, you'll import functions from your libmerge program. Then you'll call the BuildRecAry function to simulate some test data, display it, and finally delete the library to free up memory and swap space.

1. Select **Device => Function => Import Library** and place it in the upper-left work area.

   The menu in the Library Type field allows you to select a User Function, a Compiled Function, or a Remote Function(UX only). In this case you want a User Function library, so leave the default. The Library Name shows myLibrary as a default. This name is used as a "handle" by your HP VEE program to distinguish between different libraries being imported. The Delete Library object uses this name to identify the library to be deleted. You can use the default name.

   The File Name field will show you a dialog box for the user program directory by default on a PC. (UNIX systems access whatever directory you were in when you started HP VEE.) You simply need to specify the file that holds the library of functions.

   Click the default name **myFile** to get the list box. Select **libmerge** (from Lab 8-3). This file will be in the directory you specified for your programs during installation.

   Open the object menu and select **Load Lib** to import the library immediately instead of waiting until runtime. This command is very useful in the development stage. Notice that when selecting Edit => Edit UserFunction... the functions are designated with the library handle first - myLibrary.BuildRecAry(View Only), and as the title suggests you can only view the UserFunction, not edit it. Recall that, if you want to edit a function, then use the Merge... command. You cannot edit imported functions.

2. Select **Device => Function => Call** and place it below the **Import Library** object. Connect their sequence pins to make sure **Import Library** executes first.

3. Open the **Call Function** object menu and click **Select Function** to show you a list of the functions you imported with your **Load Lib** command. Select **BuildRecAry**.

   HP VEE automatically inserts this function in the Function Name field and adds the required output terminal. You could also have entered myLibrary.BuildRecAry in the Function Name field to accomplish the same results. Use Select Function when you can't remember the names of the functions in the library.

4. Select an **AlphaNumeric** display, enlarge it, and connect it to the **Call Function** data output.

5. Select **Device => Function => Delete Library** and place it below the **Call Function** object. Connect the sequence pins, so the library is deleted after the BuildRecAry function has been called. You can leave the default **Library Name**, since this is the same one you used with the **Import Library** object.

6. Run your program. It should look like the one below.

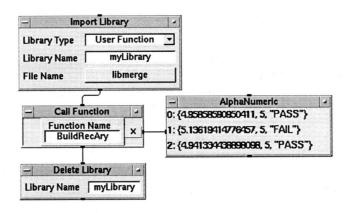

Fig. 8-11. Importing and Deleting a Library

Note: *What happens if merged or imported functions have the same names as local functions? With merged functions HP VEE will give you an error. With imported functions HP VEE will allow it, but will use the local functions. If two imported libraries have the same function names, the results will be indeterminate.*

Chapter 8 Checklist

You should now be able to perform the following tasks. Review topics, if necessary, before moving on to the next chapter.

- Merge an entire HP VEE program with your current program.

- Define a User Function and compare it to a Compiled Function and a Remote Function.

- Create, call, and edit a User Function.

- Create, merge, import, and delete User Function libraries.

9

Test Sequencing

Average time to complete: 2 hr.

Overview

This chapter teaches the fundamentals of using the Sequencer object, one of the most useful features of HP VEE. Some of the benefits of the Sequencer include:

- Easy development of a test plan

- Wide array of branching capabilities between tests

- Major component for building a customized test executive

- Ability to call tests in HP VEE and other languages

- Automatic logging of test results

- The Sequencer object

- Configuring a test for the Sequencer

- Creating a test execution order based on run time results

- Accessing data logged by the Sequencer

- Ways to pass data to or from Sequencer tests

- Performing analysis on logged data from the Sequencer

- Storing Sequencer test data

In this chapter you'll work through two lab exercises. The first one shows you how to configure a test for the Sequencer object, to add or insert or delete a test in your test execution flow, and to access the test data that's been logged by the Sequencer. To keep things simple, you'll simulate test results with the random( ) function. This way you can focus all your attention on the characteristics of the Sequencer.

The second lab will be more challenging. You'll learn how to structure data passed to tests using global variables, to call User Functions from the Sequencer, and to log Sequencer data to files. Performing analysis on parts of that data will complete your basic skills, and you'll begin to see the power at your disposal when developing test plans.

To use a status panel that updates through a sequence of tests, see chapter 10.

Using the Sequencer Object

The Sequencer object executes tests in a specified order based on runtime results. Each test may be an HP VEE User Function, a Compiled Function, or a Remote Function, which returns a single result. That result is compared to a test specification to determine whether or not it passes. The Sequencer then uses a pass or fail indicator to determine the next test it should perform. You have six different options for branching to the next test. These options include executing the next test, repeating the same test, or jumping back to an earlier test. We'll discuss these in detail in the following lab exercise. The Sequencer can even ask for user input to decide what course of action to take. After the specified tests have been executed, the Sequencer automatically logs the test data to an output terminal. From this point the data can be analyzed and displayed, or stored to a file for future investigation.

The Sequencer object is simple and powerful. Let's get started with an easy example, so that you can visualize what we're talking about.

Lab 9 - 1: Creating a Test Execution Order

In this lab you'll simulate test results using the random( ) function, establish a test execution order, learn how to modify that order, and retrieve specific data from the logged results. Fields in the Sequencer will be discussed as they arise in the exercise.

To Configure a Test

The steps will apply to the specific example of implementing the random( ) function with a certain range of test results expected, but the principles may be employed when configuring any test.

1. Select **Device => Sequencer** and place it in your upper-left work area.

2. Select **Display => AlphaNumeric** display, place it below the **Sequencer**, increase its width, and connect its data input to the **Log** output terminal on the **Sequencer** object.

3. Double-click the **Sequencer** transaction bar to get the **Sequence Transaction** dialog box.

   The TEST field has a default name of test1, which you can leave. This is just the label for the test in the Sequencer; it is not the test function itself. The FUNCTION field (testFunc(a) is the default) holds the actual function that performs the test. In this case, you'll replace the default field with the random( ) function. The random(low,high) object is located in the AdvMath => Probability menu. Recall that you can call this math function from an expression field without actually using the object in the menu. If you don't provide the parameters low and high, which is what we're going to do in this example, the function will use the default parameters 0 and 1.

4. Click the **FUNCTION** input field, which currently holds **testFunc(a)**, and type **random( )**.

Note: *Be sure not to press Enter after you type something, since that tells HP VEE that you're done editing the dialog box. Either click on new fields you want to modify or press Tab to move forward to different fields. Shift-Tab will move the cursor backward.*

Random( ) will return a Real value between 0 and 1 simulating a test result. This result will be compared to the test specification. **SPEC NOMINAL** represents the expected test value; the default is **.5**. Change this to **.25**, and then alter the upper **RANGE** field (on the far right) from **1** to **.5**. You can leave the other defaults as they are. This configuration will lead to a PASS result in approximately half of the runs. Your dialog box should look like the figure below.

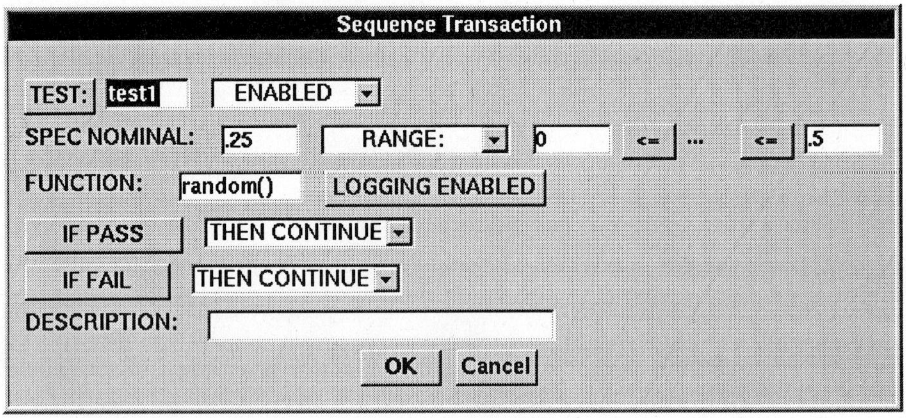

Fig. 9-1. The Sequence Transaction Dialog Box

Click **OK** to close the dialog box. You will now see the transaction **test1** **0 <= (.25) <= .5** on the first transaction bar. This means that test1 will pass if the returned value is in the range from 0 to .5 with the end points included. The expected result is about .25.

5. Run your program, and you will see the name of the test, the test result, and the pass-fail indicator (**1** for **PASS**, **0** for **FAIL**) in the display.

Before proceeding study the following table to understand the various choices in the Sequence Transaction dialog box. Open the dialog box again by double-clicking on the transaction bar. Open the various menus and make sure you understand the different options.

Sequence Transaction Field	Explanation
TEST:	The TEST: button toggles to EXEC:. The TEST: field holds the unique name used to reference this test in the Sequencer. The default names start with test1 and increment with each test. Choosing TEST: means that a test result will be compared to specifications and branching will occur to the next test based on your configuration. You may toggle TEST: to EXEC:, which means that the test will be executed without a comparison between a test result and specifications. For example, you might choose EXEC: when your User Function is setting up global variables. Selecting EXEC: will also disable logging for this test.
ENABLED	This button gives you four menu choices. ENABLED executes the test under all conditions. ENABLED IF: executes the test, if the stated expression evaluates to TRUE. For example, the test might be enabled if the input pin A holds the value 1 (A == 1). ENABLED IF: may be used for audit test control. You might want a particular test to execute every ten runs, for instance. DISABLED and DISABLED IF: are just the opposite of the first two menu choices.
SPEC NOMINAL:	The expected value from the test.

Sequence Transaction Field	Explanation
RANGE:	This menu includes RANGE:, LIMIT:, TOLERANCE:, and %TOLERANCE:. RANGE: fields signify the range of test values that signify a PASS condition. You may also choose from the usual comparisons: >, >=, <, <=, ==, !=. LIMIT: uses just one value for a comparison of test data. The TOLERANCE: selection states the passing range of values by adding or subtracting the specified tolerance to the SPEC NOMINAL: value. %TOLERANCE: states the passing range of values by adding and subtracting a percent tolerance of the SPEC NOMINAL: value to the nominal specification.
FUNCTION:	The FUNCTION: field specifies which test to run. You can call User Functions, Compiled Functions, Remote Functions, or you can write in an expression to be evaluated. The result of the function you call is tested against your specifications. If a User Function returns more than one value, HP VEE assumes the top output pin holds the result to be tested.
LOGGING ENABLED	This button toggles to LOGGING DISABLED. If logging is enabled, each test logs a record. By selecting the logging tab in the Edit Properties box, you can choose which fields you want from a list that includes: Name, Result, Nominal, High Limit, Low Limit, Pass, Time Stamp, and Description. Name, Result, and Pass are the default selections.
IF PASS	This button toggles to IF PASS CALL:. If your test passes, HP VEE goes to this line for branching instructions. IF PASS tells HP VEE to branch according to your selection in the following menu. See THEN CONTINUE. IF PASS CALL: tells HP VEE to call the stated function, then go to the branching menu selection.

Sequence Transaction Field	Explanation
THEN CONTINUE	This button holds a menu with six branching options. THEN CONTINUE simply executes the next test configured in the Sequencer. THEN RETURN: tells HP VEE to stop executing tests and put the specified expression on the Return output pin of the Sequencer. THEN GOTO: jumps to the test named in its field. THEN REPEAT repeats the current test up to the number of times specified in the MAX TIMES: field. If the PASS/FAIL condition still exists after the maximum number of repeats, then HP VEE continues with the next test. THEN ERROR: stops execution by generating an error condition with the given error number. An error can be trapped with the Error output pin on the Sequencer. No other output pins will send data. THEN EVALUATE: calls the specified User Function, which must return a string that states a branching menu option. Valid strings results from the User Function are: "Continue", "Return <expr>", "Goto <name>", "Repeat <expr>", "Error <expr>", where <expr> is any valid HP VEE expression and <name> is the name of a test in the sequence. This option allows you to ask the user what to do next.
IF FAIL	IF FAIL toggles to IF FAIL CALL:. If your test fails, HP VEE goes to this line for branching instructions. Options are the same as for IF PASS.
DESCRIPTION:	This field holds Text comments on your test. They will show on the Sequencer transaction bar and can be stored with your test record by using the Logging tab in the Edit Properties dialog box.

To Add or Insert or Delete a Test

In this section you'll add another test transaction to the Sequencer object. You can use the same random( ) function to simulate a test result, but this time you'll compare the result to a limit instead of a range of values.

1. Double-click below the first **Sequencer** transaction bar to get the **Sequence Transaction** dialog box.

   Notice that HP VEE gives you the default name **test2**. You can use that. Change **SPEC NOMINAL** from **.5** to **.25**. Click **RANGE:** to get the **Select Spec Type** dialog box. Select **LIMIT:**. Choose **<** for your operator. Change **1** to **.5** for your limit.

   Change the **FUNCTION** field from **testFunc(a)** to **random( )**. Leave the other default selections and click **OK** to return to the **Sequencer**.

   *Note: You could also add a transaction after the highlighted one by selecting **Add Trans...** from the object menu.*

You have just added a second transaction to your Sequencer test plan. The transaction bar should read: **test2 (.25) < .5**. Now let's suppose you want to insert a transaction between these two tests.

2. Make sure the second transaction bar is highlighted. Then open the object menu and select **Insert Trans...** .

   Change the **TEST** name field to **Insert**. Change the **FUNCTION** field to **random( )**. Then click **OK**. You will now see **Insert 0 <= (.5) <= 1** on the second transaction bar. Run your program to see the three records from your three tests. You may have to enlarge your display to see all the entries.

Now you'll delete **Insert**.

3. Click the **Insert** transaction bar, place the mouse pointer over the **Insert** transaction bar, and press **Ctrl-k** to delete **Insert**.

Note: *You could also click the target transaction bar and select Cut*
Trans from the object menu. You can also paste a transaction that
has been cut by choosing Paste Trans from the object menu
(Ctrl-y is the shortcut). And in a similar fashion you can copy a
transaction with the Copy Trans selection.

4. Run your program and note the two records of data from the two tests.
Save the program as **seq1.vee.**

Note: *The braces indicate a Record data type. The Sequencer outputs a*
Record of Records, as you can see in the AlphaNumeric display.
This means you could put the sequencer in a loop and run the
same sequence of tests several times yielding an array of Records
of Records.

Your program should look like the figure below.

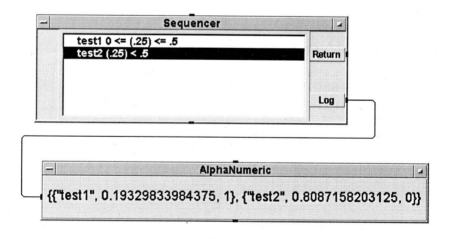

Fig. 9-2. A Simple Sequencer Example

To Access Logged Test Data

The Sequencer outputs a Record of Records. Each test uses the test name as its field name in the Sequencer record. The fields within each test are named according to your logging configuration. Using the default configuration with the fields Name, Result, and Pass you could access the result in test1 with the notation Log.Test1.Result, as shown below.

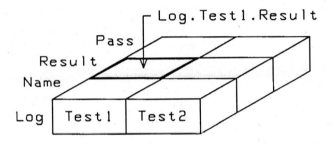

Fig. 9-3. A Logged Record of Records

Let's build on the last exercise to try this out. Open **seq1.vee**.

1. Select **Math => Formula** and place it below your display. Change the input terminal name from **A** to **Log** and connect it to the Sequencer **Log** terminal.

   Change the default formula to **Log.Test1.Result**. (Remember that HP VEE is not case sensitive and the capitals in the names are for clarity in documentation.)

   We have renamed the input pin; however, you could leave the default name A. Your formula would then read A.Test1.Result.

   Select an **AlphaNumeric** display and connect it to the **Formula** output.

2. Run your program and you will see that you have accessed the **Result** field in **Test1**. Save the program as **seq2.vee**.

Your program should look like the figure below.

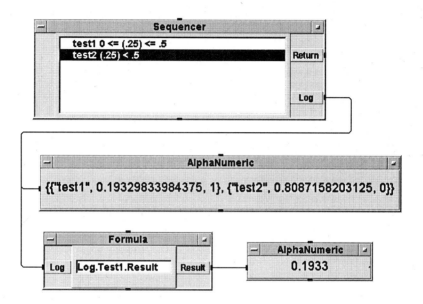

Fig. 9-4. Accessing Logged Data

Note: *Each test creates a record - named by the test name - as it executes within the Sequencer. This record can be used in subsequent tests. For example, you could enable test2 if test1 passed (ENABLED IF: test1.pass == 1). If you need to access test data in an expression field while the test is still running, test data is stored in the temporary record **thistest**.*

3. Change the formula to read **Log.test1** and run your program again.

You can now see that you have retrieved the entire record for test1 indicated by the braces around the three values in the display.

4. By changing the formula, try accessing the **result** and **pass** fields in both **test1** and **test2**. Select **Logging** tab in the **Edit Properties** box and add the **Nominal** and **Time Stamp** fields to your logged records. Access these new fields with the **Formula** object.

Lab 9 - 2: Passing Data in the Sequencer

In the first lab exercise you learned how to alter the test execution order and access the logged test data. In this lab you'll create a User Function and call it from three different tests. In the first part, you'll pass data to the User Functions through an input terminal on the Sequencer. In the second part, you'll modify the program to use a global variable instead of an input terminal. This will give you a chance to call a function in EXEC mode rather than TEST mode. In the third part, you'll learn how to test a waveform output against a mask.

To Pass Data Using an Input Terminal

First, you'll create the User Function Rand, which will simulate a measurement procedure. Rand( ) will simply add an input parameter to the output of the Random Number object, and put this result on the output pin. Rand( ) will be called from three different tests.

1. Select **Device => UserObject** and place it in the center of your work area. Change the name from **UserObject** to **Rand**.

2. Select **Device => Random Number** and place it in **Rand**. Select **Math => + - * / => a + b** and place it to the right of **Random Number**. Connect the output of **Random Number** to the upper left input of the **a + b** object.

3. Add a data input terminal to **Rand**. Connect the input terminal **A** to the lower left input terminal of the **a + b** object.

4. Add a data output terminal to **Rand**. Connect the output of the **a + b** object to the **Rand** output terminal.

Your UserObject Rand should look like the figure below.

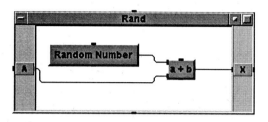

Fig. 9-5. The Rand UserObject

Note: The Rand UserFunction is obviously only for teaching purposes.

5. Open the **Rand** object menu and click on **Make UserFunction**. When the **Call Function** object appears calling **Rand**, delete it, since you'll be calling **Rand** from the **Sequencer** object.

Deleting the Call Function object does not remove the User Function. If you want to check this, just click on Edit => Edit UserFunction and you'll see Rand come up in a list box of User Functions to edit.

Now you'll set up three tests in the Sequencer to call Rand using a Sequencer input pin to feed the input parameter to Rand.

6. Select **Device => Sequencer** and place it in the upper-center work area. Add an input terminal to the **Sequencer**.

Click the transaction bar to get the **Sequence Transaction** dialog box. Change the **FUNCTION** field from **testFunc(a)** to **rand(a)**. (This will call the UserFunction Rand( ) and send it the value on the Sequencer input terminal A.) Click **OK** to get back to the **Sequencer** open view.

Note: *You could also use a Sequencer input terminal name, such as A, to pass data to any expression within the Sequence Transaction box.*

To reproduce this test two more times you'll have to cut or copy it to put it in a buffer, then paste it back in three times.

Make sure your transaction is highlighted, place the cursor on the transaction bar, press **Ctrl-k** to cut the test, then press **Ctrl-y** three times to paste the test back into the Sequencer. (You could also do the same thing with object menu selections.)

The default test names will be **test1x2**, **test1x1**, and **test1**. Open the three **Sequence Transaction** dialog boxes and change these names to **test1**, **test2**, and **test3** for clarity.

7. Select **Data => Continuous => Real Slider** and place it to the left of the Sequencer. Change the name to the prompt **Select Num:**, size the object to be smaller, and connect it to the **Sequencer** input terminal.

Tip: You can size an object as you place it by clicking and dragging using the left mouse button.

8. Select an **AlphaNumeric** display, place it below the **Sequencer**, enlarge it to be wider, and connect it to the **Log** output terminal on the **Sequencer**.

9. Save your program as **seqdat1**. Select a number on the **Real Slider** object and run **seqdat1**. It should look like the figure below.

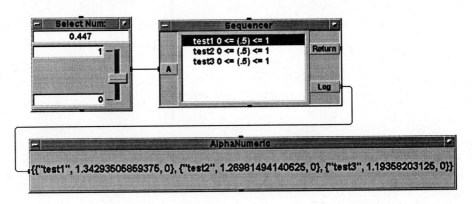

Fig. 9-6. Passing Data Using an Input Terminal

If you have a lot of tests, this method could get awkward with too many input pins. One way to reduce the number of input pins would be to pass records to input terminals, and then use individual fields within the records for the separate tests. Another solution is to use a separate User Function to set up global variables, which can then be called by other User Functions or any expression field within your program. That's exactly what you'll do in the following exercise.

To Pass Data Using a Global Variable

Let's modify the program in the first part to use a global variable to pass the parameter *a* to your User Function Rand.

1. Delete the **Real Slider** object labeled **Select Num**. Delete the **A** input terminal on the **Sequencer**.

2. Highlight the **test1** transaction bar, open the object menu, and click **Insert Trans...** . When the **Sequence Transaction** box appears, click **TEST** to toggle the selection to **EXEC** and change the name to **Setup**.

   You'll use EXEC mode, since the User Function will just set up a global variable and will not yield a result that needs to be tested against a specification.

3. Change the **FUNCTION** field to **global( )** and click **OK** to close the dialog box.

You'll now create the User Function global( ).

4. Select **Device => UserObject** and place it in the center of your work area. Change the name **UserObject** to **global**.

   Select **Data => Continuous => Real Slider** and put it in the **UserObject**, change the name to **Select Num:**, and size it to be smaller vertically.

Select **Data => Global => Set Global** and place it to the right of the **Real Slider**.

Change the global variable from **globalA** to **a**. Connect the **Real Slider** to the **Set Global** object.

You want this function to appear on the screen long enough for the user to select a number, so you need a pop-up panel view. You'll also need an OK button, so that the panel remains on the screen until the user has made a selection. (You could have also done the above tasks with a Real Input Dialog Box inside the global( ) UserFunction.)

5. Select **Flow => Confirm(OK)** and place it above the **Real Slider** object. Connect the **OK** data output pin to the **Real Slider** sequence input pin.

Note: Most people want to place the OK button below the Set Global object, which will lead to an error. That's because HP VEE will send the old value on the Slider to the Set Global object and pause until the OK button is pressed. Any new value you entered on the pop-up panel would be ignored. When OK is connected above the Real Slider, HP VEE waits to set the global variable until after the OK is pressed, so the new Slider value will definitely be used.

6. Select **Display => Note Pad** and place it to the right of the **OK** button. Enter the following user prompt in the **Note Pad**:

Please select a number for this run of tests 1, 2, and 3.

7. Select the **Note Pad**, the **Real Slider**, and the **OK** button by pressing **Ctrl** and clicking on those objects. Each object will now have a shadow indicating that it's been selected. Now open the object menu and click **Edit => Add To Panel**.

When you get the **Panel** view, size it to be smaller, and position the **Note Pad** on top, the **Real Slider** in the middle, and the **OK** button on the bottom. You can position the objects in any way you want without altering the Detail view.

Open the object menu, click **Edit Properties...**, then click next to **Show Panel on Execute**. See the following figures.

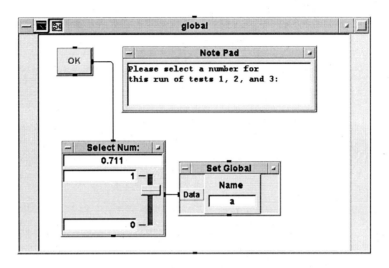

Fig. 9-7. The Global UserObject (Detail)

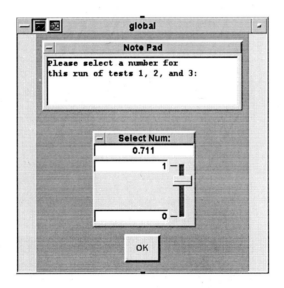

Fig. 9-8. The Global UserObject (Panel)

7. Open the object menu and click **Make UserFunction**. Delete the **Call Function** object that appears. You won't need it, because you've called the global function from the Sequencer.

8. Save your program as **seqdat2** and run it. When the pop-up panel appears, select a value and press **OK**. It should look like the figure below.

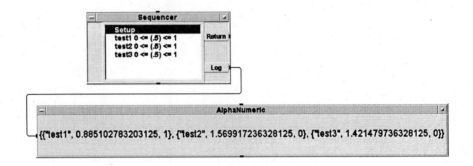

Fig. 9-9. Passing Data Using a Global Variable

Note: *The pop-up panel will appear in the center of the screen by default. To move it anywhere, double-click on the title bar to get the Edit Properties box, deselect Lock Panel Position under Pop-up Panel, and click OK. Then you can simply drag the panel to any new location on the screen.*

To Compare a Waveform Output with a Mask

In this exercise you'll create a User Function called noisyWv and call it from a single transaction bar in the Sequencer. The user will be able to vary the amplitude of the wave from 0 to 1. This function simulates a test result that returns a noisy waveform. You'll use the Coord object in the

Data => Constant menu to create a straight line mask at 0.6, which the Sequencer will use to test the noisy waveform.

1. Create the **UserObject** called **noisyWv,** as shown below in the **Detail** view.

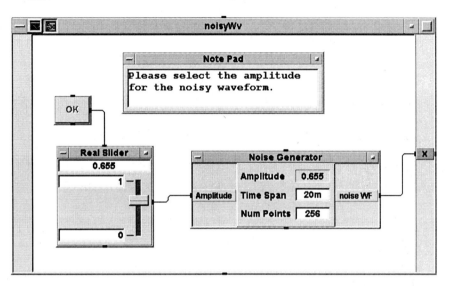

Fig. 9-10. The noisyWv UserObject (Detail)

2. Press **Ctrl** and click on the **OK** button, the **Real Slider**, and the **Note Pad** to highlight them for creating a Panel view. Open the object menu and select **Edit => Add To Panel**.

   When you get the **Panel** view, rearrange the objects to your taste, and size the window.

   Open the object menu, click **Edit Properties**, and click next to **Show Panel on Execute**.

   Your Panel view should look like Figure 9-11.

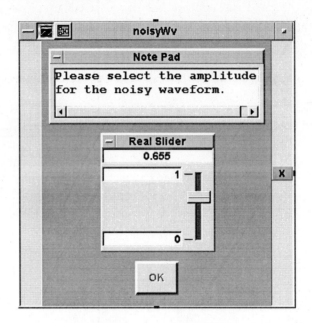

**Fig. 9-11. The noisyWv UserObject
(Panel)**

3. Open the object menu and click **Make UserFunction**. When the **Call
   Function** object appears, delete it, since you'll call this function from the
   Sequencer.

4. Select **Device => Sequencer** and place it left-center of the work area.

   Add a data input terminal and name it mask.

   Click the transaction bar to get the **Sequence Transaction** dialog box.
   Type **noisyWv( )** in the **FUNCTION** field. Click **RANGE** and select
   LIMIT from the pop-up menu. Type the terminal name **mask** in the
   LIMIT field. All of the other defaults are fine, so click **OK**.

   This means that test1 will get a result from noisyWv( ) and test it against
   the limit value at the input terminal named mask. If the noisy wave is less
   than or equal to the mask at all points, it will pass; otherwise, it will fail.

5. Select **Data => Constant => Coord** and place it above the **Sequencer**. Connect its output to the **Sequencer** input terminal **mask**.

   Open the **Coord** object menu, click **Edit Properties**, then **1D Array** under **Configuration**. Enter **2** in the **Size** field. (You'll only need two pairs of coordinates to specify a straight line.)

   You'll now see two indices for pairs of coordinates. Double-click the first index, **0000:** and a cursor will appear. You only need to type the coordinates separated by a comma, because HP VEE will add the parentheses automatically. Type **0, 0.6** <Tab> **20m, 0.6** then click on the work area outside the object.

   The x axis (time axis) for a default waveform in HP VEE goes from 0 to 20 milliseconds; hence, the two x values of 0 and 20m. The two y values are both 0.6, since you want a straight line mask. You can create any mask waveforms you like by configuring the proper number of coordinate pairs and filling them in. The Sequencer comparison mechanism operates just like the Comparator object, which accepts the Coord data type to test waveforms. Of course, you could also compare two Waveform data types. Notice that you should press Tab to move between coordinate pairs, and that clicking on the work area tells HP VEE you are done with your input.

6. Select an **AlphaNumeric** display, increase its width, and connect it to the **Log** output from the **Sequencer**.

7. Save your program as **seqdat3** and run it. It should look like Figure 9-12.

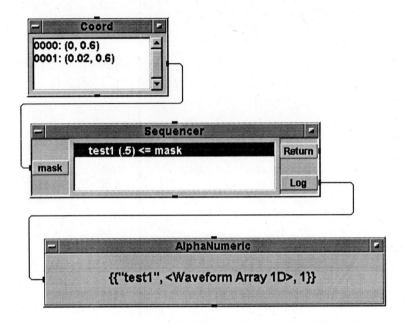

Fig. 9-12. Comparing a Waveform to a Mask

You have now done three exercises focused on passing data with the Sequencer. You used an input terminal and a global variable to pass scalar values, and then you learned how to work with waveform comparisons. In the next lab exercise, you'll focus on accessing and analyzing data from several iterations of the Sequencer object.

Lab 9 - 3: Analyzing Data from the Sequencer

As we mentioned earlier in the chapter, Sequencer data comes out as a record of records. In many cases, however, the Sequencer may run through a series of tests several times. This would generate an array of records. Each record would represent one run through the Sequencer and would hold other records representing each test within a run. The easiest way to visualize this is to imagine a cube of data in memory, as shown in the following figure.

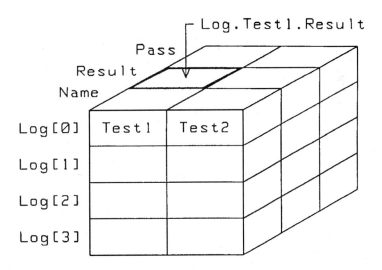

Fig. 9-13. A Logged Array of Records of Records

The array of records is called Log, because that's the name associated with the Sequencer output pin. To access a particular run you use array indexing with the bracket notation. So, Log[0] is the first run through the Sequencer, Log[1] is the second run, and so forth. The main record for each run has two fields, Test1 and Test2. Within the record Test1 there are three fields: Name, Result, and Pass. The same holds for the record Test2. Therefore, Log.Test1.Result gives an array of 4 values, each one representing one of the four runs. Log[0].Test1.Result outputs a scalar value, the Result of Test1 in the first run (Log[0]).

The implications for analysis are that you can think of your data in a simple manner, and you can investigate it in a number of ways. For example, you might want to know how many tests passed in a particular run. Or you might want to average the results of Test2 in all runs. Or you might want to see all of the data on Test1 in the fourth run. All of these are possible with this data structure. Let's perform some analysis operations on data from the seqdat1 program. Clear your screen and open this file.

To Analyze Several Runs of Data from the Sequencer

You'll modify the seqdat1 program to run through the Sequencer three times. Then you'll perform some analysis operations on the data.

1. Select **Flow => Repeat => For Count** and place it above the **Real Slider** object. Change the number of iterations to **3**, and connect the data output pin to the sequence input pin of the **Sequencer**.

2. Delete the data line between the **Sequencer Log** pin and the display. Select **Data => Collector** and place it to the right of the **Sequencer**. Connect its upper left data input pin to the **Sequencer Log** pin and its **XEQ** pin (lower left) to the sequence output pin on the **For Count** object. Connect the **Collector** data output pin to the **AlphaNumeric** display. Enlarge the display vertically somewhat to accomodate an array with three elements.

   The Sequencer will now run through test1 and test2 three times and collect the data into an array with three elements, each one holding a record of records for each run. (Refer to the cube of data in the figure above to visualize this.)

   Run your program at this point to see the display of the Sequencer data.

Now you'll use the Formula object to extract part of this data to analyze. We'll use the results of test1 for all three runs as an example, and find the mean of that array.

3. Select **Math => Formula** and place it below the display. Connect the **Formula** input pin to the output of the **Collector**. Change the **Formula** input field to read: **a.test1.result**. Connect an **AdvMath => Statistics => mean(x)** object to **Formula**, and an **AlphaNumeric** display to **mean(x)**.

The **a** refers to the array on the input terminal A. Test1.result accesses the proper field. All runs will be shown in an array, since no particular run was designated. (A[0].test1.result would refer to the first run only, for example.)

4. Run your program. It should look like the figure below.

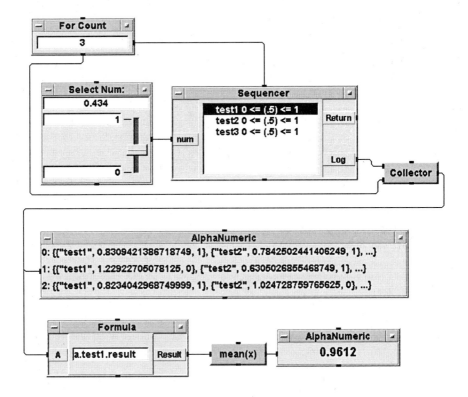

Fig. 9-14. Analyzing Several Runs of Sequencer Data

You have only accessed a single array, but the principle is the same for extracting other arrays of data from the Sequencer output. Note that you can easily change which fields are saved for each test with the Edit Properties => Logging selection in the Sequencer object menu.

Lab 9 - 4: Storing and Retrieving Logged Data

We'll modify your seqdat2 program for an example. The first part will use the To/From File objects for data storage, and the second part will use the To/From DataSet objects. First, open the **seqdat2** file and delete the data line to the display.

Using the To/From File Objects with Logged Data

1. Select **Flow => Repeat => For Count** and place it to the left of the **Sequencer**. Change the **For Count** number to **3**, and connect its data output pin to the sequence input pin on the **Sequencer**.

2. Enlarge your work area vertically and place the **AlphaNumeric** display near the bottom. Select **Data => Collector** and place it in the left work area. Connect the **Sequencer Log** pin to the **Collector** data input pin. Connect the **For Count** sequence output pin to the **Collector XEQ** pin.

The Collector will create an array of records of records from the Sequencer. Using the WRITE CONTAINER transaction in the To File object you can write any HP VEE data container to a file quite easily.

3. Select **I/O => To => File** and place it to the right of the **Collector**. Select **I/O => From => File** and place it below the **To File** object. Connect the **Collector** output to the **To File** input. Connect the **To File** sequence output to the **From File** sequence input pin. Connect the **From File** data output to the display.

Check **Clear File At PreRun & Open** in **To File**, and configure a **WRITE CONTAINER a** transaction. Configure a transaction in the **From File** object like the following: **READ CONTAINER x** .

You can use the default data file for storage.

4. Run your program. It should look like the figure below.

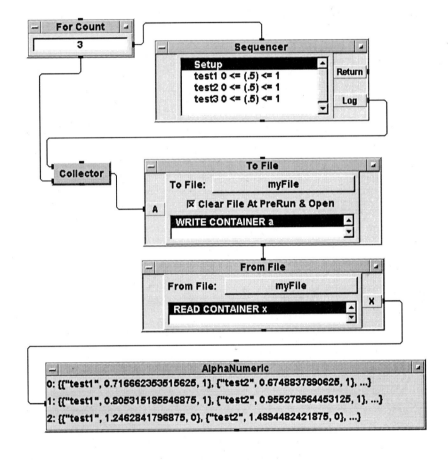

Fig. 9-15. Storing Logged Data with To/From File

Using the To/From DataSet Objects with Logged Data

Since you are storing test data as records, you may prefer to use the To/From DataSet objects. In this case you won't need a Collector, because you can append each run of the Sequencer to the end of the DataSet.

Modify the last program to look like the figure below. The **To/From DataSet** objects are in the **I/O** menu. Notice the sequence line going into From DataSet. Can you explain why? (Ans: You want to wait for all three runs to be appended to the DataSet, before you trigger From DataSet.) Did you remember to change the *Get records* field in From DataSet to *All*?

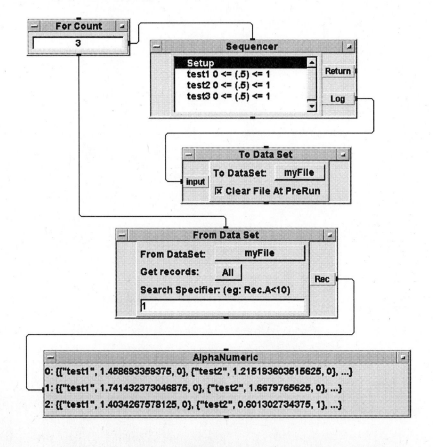

Fig. 9-16. Storing Logged Data with To/From DataSet

Do you know the best reason you would use the To/From DataSet objects to collect data instead of the To/From File objects?

You can easily turn your data into useful information with the Search Specifier feature in the From DataSet object.

Chapter 9 Checklist

Use the following checklist to determine whether there are topics you need to review before going to the next chapter.

- Describe the Sequencer object conceptually.

- Configure a test for the Sequencer.

- Add, insert, and delete operations for a Sequencer test.

- Access logged data from the Sequencer.

- Use Sequencer input terminals to pass data to tests.

- Use Global variables to pass data to tests.

- Compare a waveform output to a mask.

- Analyze several runs of data from the Sequencer.

- Store data using the To/From File objects.

- Store data using the To/From DataSet objects.

Using Operator Interfaces

10

Overview

You have already created a number of operator interfaces and pop-up panels. In this chapter we'll expand upon what you already know, and teach you how to add menus, customize interfaces, add warning signals, and import bitmaps.

Some benefits of using HP VEE operator interface features are:

- Maximum ease of use for the operator

- Improved program performance

- Security from unauthorized changes

- Clarity through visual aids

In this chapter you'll learn about:

- Building operator interfaces

- Using menus for your operator

- Importing bitmaps to add clarity

- Securing your test programs

- The many operator interface features available to you

Key Points Concerning Operator Interfaces

Process for Creating an Operator Interface

1. Select the object or objects that you want in the panel view (i.e., click each object to create a shadow).

2. Select **Edit => Add To Panel**.

Note: *While editing UserObjects or User Functions you can open the Edit menu in the work area by placing the mouse pointer on the background and clicking the right mouse button. You can also locate the Edit menu in the object menu as a submenu.*

Moving Between Panel and Detail Views

First, you have to create a "panel" view. Then click the panel or detail button on the title bar of the UserObject (or the tool bar, if the panel is for your main program).

Panel Button — Detail Button

Customizing

Once you have a panel view, you can change the size of objects, change their placement, and alter the features of display objects without affecting the same objects in the detail view. For example, you could remove the title bar and the scales from a Waveform (Time) display. However, if you delete an object in the detail view, it will also be deleted in the panel view. You have different colors and fonts to add emphasis; you have scalable bitmaps to clarify points. HP VEE gives you a wide range of selection controls (such as buttons, switches, check boxes, drop-down menus, list boxes), pop-up dialog boxes, indicators (such as tanks, thermometers, fill bars, vu meters, color alarms), and displays to achieve exactly the interface you'll need -and they only take minutes to create. The ID Monitor can show you the current states of your instruments. Programming in HP VEE can be fun as well as efficient.

Notice that there are less menu selections available in a panel view to prevent you from altering the program in any way. You can also document the panel view by editing title bars, using the Note Pad object, and the Edit Description option in the object menus.

Let's take a look at some of these options in the following figures.

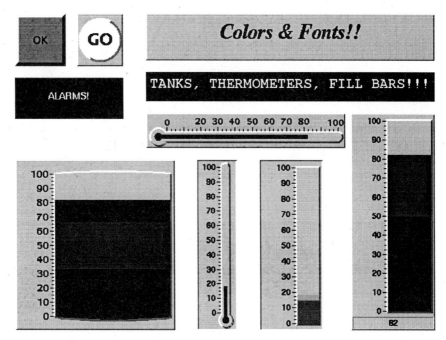

Fig. 10-1. A Selection of HP VEE Indicators

Colors, Fonts, and Indicators

- **Colors and Fonts**   You can configure colors and fonts in a global way through the File => Edit Default Preferences... selection, or through the Edit Properties... selection in each object menu. The choice of colors and fonts depends on your operating system.

- **Color Alarms**   These objects are available in the Display => Indicator submenu. They can be configured for three different ranges with color and a text message and with a square or circle format. They are often used to simulate an "LED" or for warning operators of some situation that demands their attention.

- **Tanks, Thermometers, Fill Bars, Meters**   All of these are in the Display => Indicator submenu. They can be customized with colors and labeling, come in horizontal or vertical formats, and have three default ranges, which can be easily configured under Edit Properties... in the object menus.

Graphic Images

Fig. 10-2. Scaling an Image to the Right Size

- **Importing Bitmaps**   You can import bitmaps into the panel view by setting the Background Picture in the Panel folder of the Edit Properties box. HP VEE imports *.xwd, *.GIF, *.bmp, and *.icn files to serve as the background for your UserObject or UserFunction Panel. (You can also change bitmaps for any icon using the Edit Properties => Icon tab.) There is a Picture object in the Display menu, if you just want to place a bitmap in your program, instead of using it for a background. Images may be scaled, tiled, cropped, or centered.

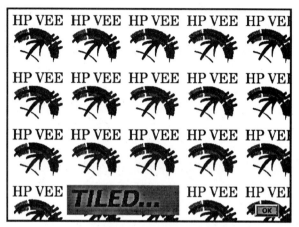

Fig. 10-3. HP VEE Tiles an Image

Fig. 10-4. A Cropped HP VEE Image

Controls

There are various ways to control a program, and you've already used some of them. You can get user input from pop-up dialog boxes, any data constant, sliders, or knobs. But let's look at a more complete collection of the objects you can use to simplify and clarify your programs for the operator.

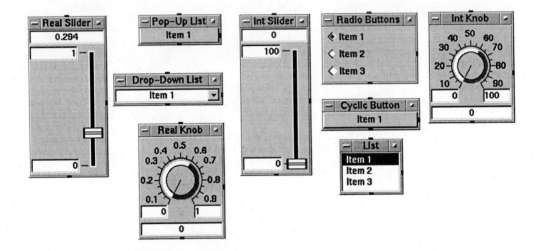

Fig. 10-5. Controls From Various Data Submenus

- **Controls**   You can see in the figure above that you have a variety of ways for operators to make selections when running your program. It's very easy to configure or customize the look and feel of all of these objects using the Edit Properties selection in the individual object menus. Let's take a look at an example of the Edit Properties selection for an X vs. Y Plot.

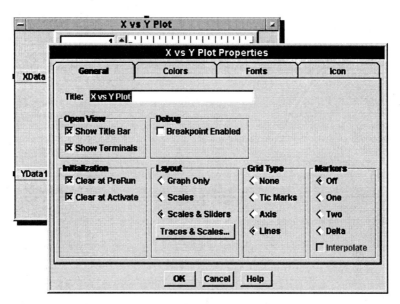

Fig. 10-6. The Edit Properties Dialog Box

- **Edit Properties Dialog Box**   You can see that configuring your object using this box is very intuitive. Categories such as Colors are chosen using a model that looks like folders in a file cabinet.

- **Dialog Boxes**   Built-in pop-up dialog boxes with automatic error checking, prompts, and error messages come in six different formats, as shown below. They are accessed in the Data => Dialog Box submenu.

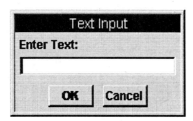

Fig. 10-7. A Pop-up Text Input Box

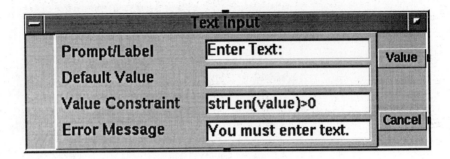

Fig. 10-8. Configuring a Text Input Box

Input boxes are very similar for text, integer, or real data types. You can see how easy it is to configure the prompt, range, and error message in the figure above.

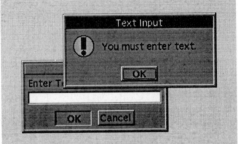

Fig. 10-9. An Example of Automatic Error Checking

Fig. 10-10. The Pop-up Message Box

Fig. 10-11. The List Selection Box

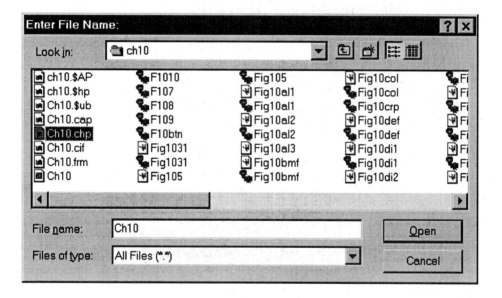

Fig. 10-12. A Pop-up File Selection Box

- **Toggles** As you can see in the following figure, you have a great variety of toggle controls. They all basically send out a 0 or a 1. Set the initial state, and you can use them to execute a subprogram when activated.

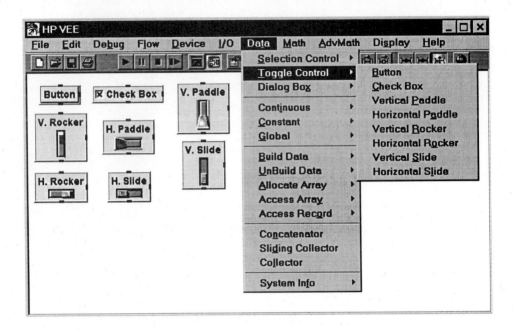

Fig. 10-13. Toggle Control Examples

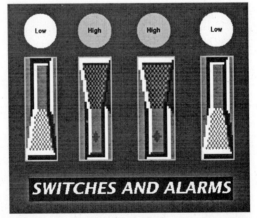

Fig. 10-14. Switches and Alarms Combined

- **Alignment of Objects**   In the panel view, you have a "snap-to-grid" feature to help you align objects. As you can see in the figure below, you can easily change the grid size from 10 to 1 (10 is the default) to make very accurate alignments. This will give your program a professional look. You'll find this in the Panel folder (you must have created a panel view) under the Edit Properties... selection of your UserObject menu.

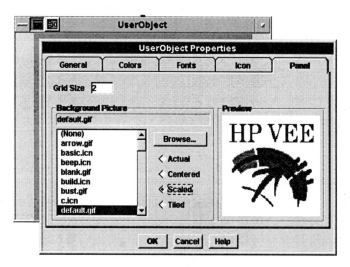

Fig. 10-15. Configuring Panel Properties

- **Softkeys**   You can configure the OK object to act as a softkey. Typically you configure it so that it's attached to one of the F-keys. It acts like a Start Button and can execute a UserFunction, as shown below.

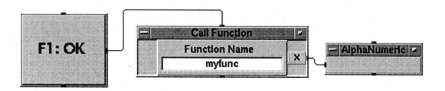

Fig. 10-16. A Softkey Example

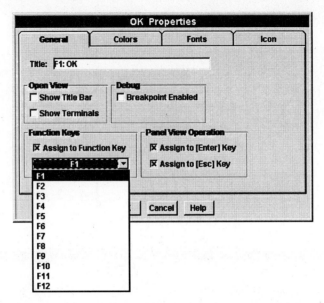

Fig. 10-17. Configuring the Confirm(OK) Object

- **Complete Keyboard Control**   The figure above shows how you would configure an OK object using the Edit Properties... dialog box to connect to a function key, Enter, or Esc keys. Furthermore, you can have full keyboard control of your program from your panel views. HP VEE will automatically highlight a button for your panel with a dotted outline. If you hit Enter, that button will be "pressed." If you are editing a text input area, pressing the Enter key accepts the edit, and pressing the Esc aborts the edit. The Tab key will move you forward through your various input object selections showing you which object is active. The Shift-Tab keys will move you backward. Use the following combinations for controlling program execution:

Ctrl-G	Run
Ctrl-C	Pause
Ctrl-T	Step
Ctrl-V	Continue

- **Selecting Your HP VEE Screen Colors**

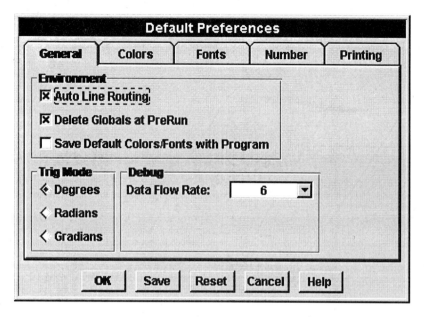

Fig. 10-18. The Default Preferences Dialog Box

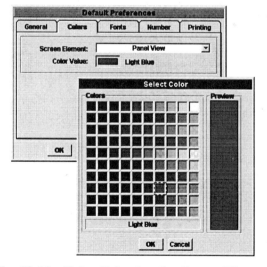

Fig. 10-19. Color Selection for Screen Elements

10 - 13

Use the File => Edit Default Preferences dialog boxes to set your HP VEE environment just the way you want it and Save the changes. You can see from the last two figures that it's very easy to alter particular particular screen elements to your desired color.

- **Securing Panel Views** Securing a panel view means that the user will not be able to access the detail view or be able to change the panel view. There is no "UnSecure" command, so you should save the original program and the secured program in separate files. To secure a program select File => Secure in the main work area. For UserObjects, open the object menu and select Secure.

- **Status Panels** You can implement status panels that will monitor the results of multiple tests or functions. We'll do an exercise in this chapter to illustrate how it's done. This feature is implemented with the ShowPanel and HidePanel functions, as shown below.

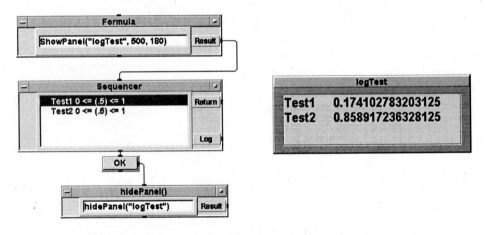

Fig. 10-20. Creating a Status Panel

- **Pop-up Panels** You can cause a panel to pop up at the execution of the UserObject or User Function by selecting Show Panel on Execute under Edit Properties... in the object menu. Since the panel will also disappear when the UserObject is done executing, you should also use the Confirm (OK) object in your panel to keep the panel on the screen until the user wants to proceed.

Common Tasks In Creating Operator Interfaces

The following examples will give you experience implementing the many features associated with panel views in HP VEE. Specifically we'll focus on creating menus, using effective warnings, creating status panels, and importing bitmaps to add more visual impact to your programs. All of the labs will give you a chance to customize the interfaces.

Lab 10 - 1. Using Menus

You'll create an operator interface that includes a menu with three choices: die1, die2, and die3. When the operator selects one, a function by the same name will be called that displays a die (dice is the plural) with one, two, or three dots on its top face. This program serves no practical purpose, but it does simulate a situation where the operator must choose which test to run from a menu. You'll also learn how to import a bitmap to change the appearance of an icon. We'll call it the Dice Program.

First, let's create the three User Functions.

1. Select **Device => UserObject** and place it in the center of your work area. Expand it to a full screen view.

Although we could use any icon to display the imported bitmap, we'll use the Picture object.

2. Select **Display => Picture**, place it in the **UserObject**.

3. Open the object menu, click **Edit Properties...**, then deselect **Show Title Bar** under **Open View**. Select **die1.gif** under **Picture**, click **Scaled**, then **OK**.

Although HP VEE automatically goes to the bitmaps subdirectory, you could get your bitmap from any directory. You should now have a colorful picture of a die with one dot on its top.

4. Select **Flow => Confirm (OK)** and place it below the die.

Select the **Picture** and the **OK** objects (press **Ctrl** and click the objects to create a shadow). Open the pop-up Edit menu by placing the mouse pointer on the background and pressing the right mouse button. Select **Add to Panel**.

5. Change the UserObject title to **die1**. Arrange the objects and size them to suit your taste. Select **Show Panel on Execute** from the **Edit Properties** dialog box. Also, deselect **Show Title Bar** and **Show Terminals**. Click the **Panel** folder and change the grid size to **2** for more accurate alignment. Then click **OK**.

Now open the object menu (mouse pointer over the object and click the right mouse button) and select **Make UserFunction**. Leave the **Call Function** object on the screen when it appears. You'll use it to call the function your user selects from the menu you'll create shortly.

6. Now create two more **User Functions** in the same way you did for **die1** called **die2** and **die3**. Make sure to select the **die2.gif** and **die3.gif** files for the appropriate bitmap.

In the process of creating these two additional User Functions for die2 and die3 a Call Function object will appear for each one. Just delete them when they appear. The new User Functions will still be available to you, and you only need one Call Function object for this program.

To check each User Function click Edit => Edit UserFunction and select the function you want from the list box presented.

Now you'll create a menu to select one of these three functions to call.

7. Select **Data => Selection Control => Radio Buttons** and place it to the left of **Call Function**.

Radio Buttons is an object that outputs an enumerated value (the Enum data type) from a user-defined list. For example, the user might define the list: Monday, Tuesday, Wednesday, Thursday, Friday. The user could then select one of these from a menu, and Radio Buttons would then output that day. The first item in the list is assigned the ordinal position 0; the nth item in the list is assigned ordinal position n-1. For instance, Monday in the list above has an ordinal position of 0, and Friday has an ordinal position of 4. The ordinal position can be extracted from an Enum value by using the ordinal( ) function in a Formula object.

Read the Help entry in the object menu for a more detailed explanation.

8. Open the **Radio Buttons** object menu and select **Edit Enum Values...** .

   Click the **Edit Enum Values** dialog box next to **0000:** to get a cursor. Then type in the names of your functions - **die1, die2, die3** - pressing the **Tab** key between each entry EXCEPT the last. When you're done click **OK**.

   There are six formats you can use for your menus. Radio Buttons will display your entries as buttons. The user's selection will be output in a text format as an Enum data type. A second format is Cyclic Button, which cycles through your enumerated values one at a time as you click the button. The third format is called List, which displays all of the enumerated values in a list; the selected item is highlighted. Drop-down list, pop-up list, and Slider list are self-evident.

9. Open the **Radio Buttons** object menu, click **Edit Properties...**, then deselect **Show Title Bar** and select **Auto Execute**.

Now you'll add the Function Name control pin to the Call Function object, which will accept an Enum value as input. Therefore, whatever value your user selects on the Radio Buttons object will become the function name that the Call Function object calls. This will become clear as you proceed.

10. Open the **Call Function** object menu and select **Add Terminal =>
    Control Input**. Select **Function Name** and click **OK**.

Connect the **Radio Buttons** data output pin to the **Function Name** input terminal on the **Call Function** object. Connect the **Radio Buttons** sequence out pin to the sequence in pin of **Call Function**.

Note: The Call Function input terminal requires a Text Scalar, so HP VEE converts the Enum Scalar to a Text Scalar.

Remember the dotted line indicates a control pin. When Auto Execute is turned on, Radio Buttons executes whenever you make a change to it and sends your selection to Call Function. The control pin on Call Function will replace the function name as soon as the pin receives data. But the Call Function object does not call the specified function until its sequence input pin is fired. (Using Auto Execute and the sequence pins means that the user doesn't have to click Run to begin the program.)

11. Select **Display => Label** and place it in the upper-left work area. From the object menu, select **Edit Properties...**, click **Center Justify**, and change the title to:

Select a Graphic:

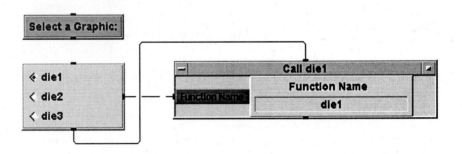

Fig. 10-21. The Dice Program (Detail View)

Now you need an operator interface that just shows the prompt, the menu, and the pop-up panels showing your graphic selections.

12. Select your prompt (**Label** object) and the **Radio Buttons** object by pressing **Ctrl** and clicking on the desired objects. Then select **Edit =>
    Add To Panel**. Arrange the icons and size them to suit your taste.

13. Open the **Label** object menu, select **Edit Properties...**, and adjust the colors and font to your taste. You can also adjust the size of the prompt automatically in the **Fonts** folder.

14. Run your program by making a selection. (Don't use the run button, because it will simply use the selection that's already made on the menu.)

    Your program should look like the figure below.

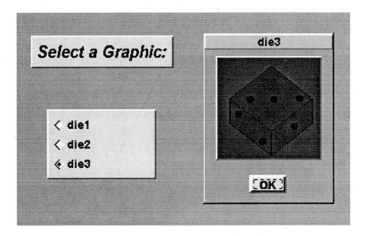

Fig. 10-22. The Dice Program (Panel View)

There are a few things to note, before we move on to the next lab exercise:

- You can use the same techniques in the exercise above to create menus for any program.

- Radio Buttons could also be used to select a compiled language program by using the Execute Program object with a control pin ("Command") that indicated which program to call. If you had imported a library of compiled functions, you could also use the Call Function object to run a function from your library.

- You could optimize this program by using the File Name data input pin on the Picture object inside a single UserFunction, and then sending the appropriate bitmap file to the object. If you're using a lot of different bitmaps, this would be a more efficient way to program.

Lab 10 - 2: Creating a Status Panel

Now we'll do a short exercise to familiarize you with the Hide/Show Panel functions, and how you would use them to create a status panel. Typically this would be used with the Sequencer object when you have a number of tests and you want to see the results as they are returned. You'll use the function, random( ), which returns a real value between 0 and 1.

1. Click **Device => Sequencer**. Double-click the transaction bar, and configure your test using the default name, **test1**, and replacing the **FUNCTION:** field with **random( )**. See the figure below.

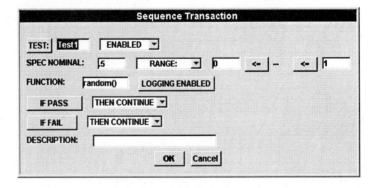

Fig. 10-23. Configuring Test1

Configure a second test the same way named **test2**.

2. Open the **Sequencer** object menu, click **Edit Properties**, choose the **Logging** tab, and under **Logging Mode** select **Log Each Transaction To: logTest(thisTest)**, then click **OK**.

As the Sequencer executes each transaction, it creates a record for each test called "thisTest," whose fields can be configured under the same tab. You can then create a UserFunction called "logTest" (or whatever you'd like to call it) and unbuild the record there to get the fields you want. In this way, you can update your status panel. The example should clear things up.

3. Click **Device => Panel => showPanel(UFname,x,y)** and place it above the **Sequencer**. Edit the parameters to **"logTest",500,180**.

LogTest is the name of the UserFunction you will create. The other two parameters are X and Y coordinates on your screen going from the upper left as origin. This tells HP VEE where to place the UserFunction panel when it's shown.

4. Create the **UserFunction** named **logTest**, as shown below. You can delete all but the **Name** and **Result** terminals on the **Unbuild Record** object. Put the **Logging AlphaNumeric** on the panel.

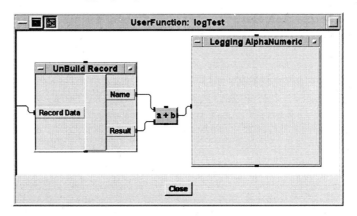

Fig. 10-24. The UserFunction LogTest (Detail)

10 - 21

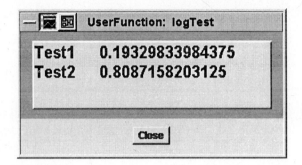

Fig. 10-25. The UserFunction LogTest (Panel)

5. Click **Device => Panel => hidePanel(UFname)** and **Flow => Confirm(OK)**, configure as shown in the next figure, and run your program. Remember to change the **hidePanel( )** parameter to **logTest**.

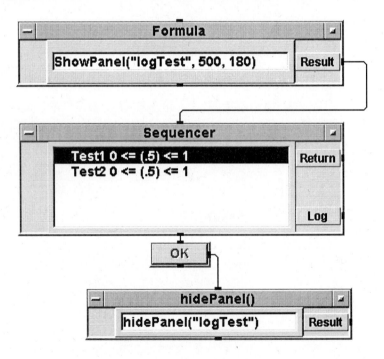

Fig. 10-26. Status Panel Program (before running)

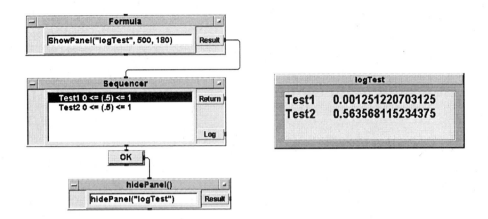

Fig. 10-27. The Status Panel Program (running)

In summary, the showPanel( ) puts the UserFunction panel up, but does not call the UserFunction. The Sequencer calls the UserFunction twice through its logging function, and each call updates the panel. Then, when the user is done, he or she can press OK and the panel is hidden.

Lab 10 - 3: Importing Bitmaps for Panel Backgrounds

Bitmaps are not essential to your programs, but they can add clarity and impact to your tests. For example, you might want to import a schematic to better illustrate what's being tested. In this exercise, we'll show you how to import bitmaps for panel backgrounds with standard HP VEE objects placed on top of them.

Bitmaps can only be imported for icons, the Picture object, or for the panel view backgrounds in UserObjects or User Functions. You'll create a pop-up User Function called Bitmap holding a few simple objects for demonstration purposes. We'll use the Label object and a simple Confirm (OK) to hold the graphic on the screen until you click the OK button.

1. Select **Device => UserObject** and place it in the work area.

2. Select **Flow => Confirm (OK)** and **Display => Label,** and place them in the work area of the **UserObject**.

3. Change the name of the **UserObject** to **Bitmap**.

4. Select the **OK** and the **Label** objects (highlight it with a shadow). Open the pop-up **Edit** menu by placing the pointer on the **UserObject** work area and clicking on the right mouse button. Select **Add to Panel**.

5. Open the **UserObject** menu, select **Edit Properties...,** then select **Show Panel on Execute**. (Remember to double-click on the title bar to get the Edit Properties box.) Deselect **Show Title Bar** and **Show Terminals** under **Open View**.

   Open the **Panel** folder, change the **Grid Size** to **2**, select **default.gif** and **Scaled** under **Background Picture,** then click **OK**.

6. Open the pop-up object menu on the **Label** object, click **Edit Properties...,** change the title to **Bitmap Function,** click **Center Justify**. Open the **Colors** folder and select **Light Gray** for the **Background** of the label. Click **OK**. Open the **Fonts** folder, choose a larger font with bold type, select **Automatically Resize Object on Font Change,** then click **OK**.

7. Open the **UserObject** menu and select **Make UserFunction**. When the **Call Function** appears, run your program. It should look like the figure on the next page.

   Note on Securing Program: *To secure this program from alteration: (1) create a panel view in the main work area for the program, (2) save it so that you have a copy you can alter, (3) select File => Secure from the panel view, and (4) save it again under another name for its secured form. Once a file is secured you cannot get to the Detail view to edit it! So be careful to save a version of your program before securing it.*

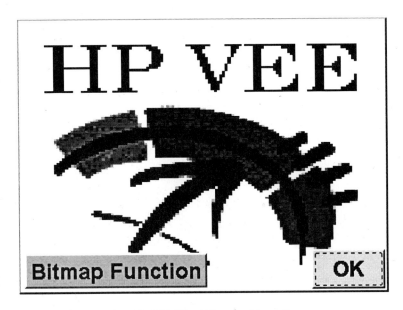

Fig. 10-28. The Bitmap Function

Lab 10 - 4: Creating a High Impact Warning

In this example we'll nest User Functions. One function will be the alarm itself, which will display a big red square and beep. The second function will call the alarm repeatedly creating a blinking light effect and a pulsing sound, until the user turns the alarm off.

First, you'll program the alarm function.

1. Select **Device => UserObject** and expand it to full screen. Change the name to **alarm**.

2. Select **Display => Beep** and place it in the upper-left of the **UserObject**. Adjust the settings so that you have a loud beep that lasts a second. Change the **Duration (sec)** field to **1**. Change the **Volume (0-100)** field to **100**. (These instructions assume your computer has the hardware to support a beep. Try running this now to verify this.)

   You don't need to attach the Beep object to anything. It will activate when the function executes.

3. Click **Display => Indicator => Color Alarm** and place it in the **UserObject**. Open the **Color Alarm** object menu, click **Edit Properties...**, deselect **Show Title Bar**, click **Rectangular** under **Layout**. Delete any text beside **High Text** under **Limits**.Then click **OK**.

4. Click **Data => Constant => Real**, change it to **1**, and connect it to the **Color Alarm** input pin. (This will always set the Alarm to its high range with the default color of red.)

You want the display to stay on the screen for one second to synchronize with the **Beep** object, so you'll use a **Delay** object set to **1** second.

5. Select **Flow => Delay**, set it to **1**, and connect its sequence input pin to the **Color Alarm** sequence out pin. The alarm will then last 1 second.

6. Select **Display => Note Pad** and add the message: **TURN OFF INSTRUMENTS!**. Size the **Note Pad** to your taste. Run the program.

Your detail view of the **UserObject alarm** should look like the figure below.

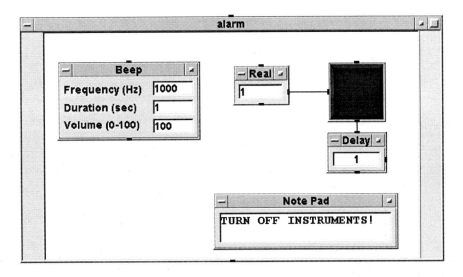

Fig. 10-29. The UserObject Alarm (Detail View)

7. Select the **Color Alarm** display and the **Note Pad**. Open the pop-up **Edit** menu and select **Add To Panel**. When you get the **Panel** view, size and arrange the objects to your taste. Open the **alarm** object menu and select **Move**. Move the panel view to the center of your work area. Open the **Note Pad** object menu, click **Edit Properties...**, and deselect **Show Title** and **Enabled** under **Editing**. Open the **Fonts** folder, enlarge the **Text** size and choose **Bold**, select **Automatically Resize Object on Font Change**, and click **OK** to close the **Edit Properties** dialog box.

8. Double-click on the UserObject title bar to get the **Edit Properties...** dialog box, and select **Show Panel on Execute**. Deselect **Show Terminals** and **Show Title Bar**.

9. Open the **alarm UserObject** menu again and select **Make UserFunction**. When the **Call Function** object appears, delete it. (HP VEE will still hold the function alarm in memory. If you want to edit the function again, select Edit => Edit UserFunction.)

You will now create the function that repeatedly calls the alarm function.

10. Select **Device => UserObject** and expand it to full screen size. Change the name of the **UserObject** to **warning**.

11. Select **Device => Panel => unlockPosition(UFname)**, replace **UFname** with **alarm**, and place in the upper-left work area. (This will enable you to position the alarm anywhere on the screen.) Select **Flow => Repeat => Until Break** and connect its sequence in pin to the **unlockPosition** data output pin.

12. Select **Device => Function => Call**, edit the **Function Name** field to **alarm**, and connect its sequence input pin to the **Until Break** data output pin.

You'll now use the Check Box object to ask the user, if he or she wants to turn off the alarm.

13. Select **Data => Toggle Control => Check Box**. Open the **Check Box** object menu, click **Edit Properties...**, change the name to **Turn off alarm?**, select **Scaled** under **Layout**, select **Initialize at PreRun**, and make sure the value is **0**, then click **OK**. Connect the **Call Function** sequence out pin to the **Check Box** sequence in pin.

This will give you an input object that uses a Check Box. If the user clicks the box an X will appear and the object outputs a 1; otherwise, the object outputs a 0. The output can be tested with an If/Then/Else object to tell HP VEE what to do next.

14. Select **Flow => If/Then/Else** and place it to the right of the **Toggle**. Connect the **Toggle** data output to the data input **A** of the **If/Then/Else** object. Edit the expression in the **If/Then/Else** object to: **a == 1**. (Recall that the symbol for "is equal to" is ==, not =.)

If the terminal A holds a 1, the Then output will fire; otherwise, the Else output fires.

15. Select **Flow => Repeat => Break** and connect it to the **Then** output on the **If/Then/Else** object. See the next figure.

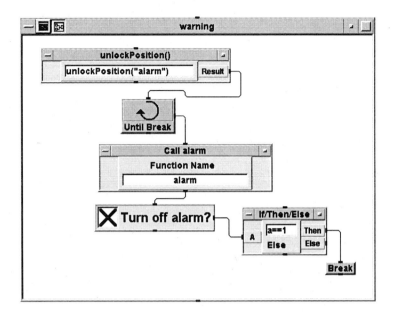

Fig. 10-30. The Warning UserObject (Detail View)

16. Select the **Check Box** object (**Turn off alarm?**). Open the pop-up **Edit** menu and select **Add To Panel**. **Size** the panel view to surround the **Check Box** .

17. Open the **warning UserObject** menu, click **Edit Properties...**, select **Show Panel on Execute**, deselect **Show Title** and **Show Terminals**, since the title serves no purpose to the operator.

18. Open the **warning UserObject** menu. Select **Make UserFunction**. Move the **Call Function** object to the top center of your screen. Click **Device => Panel => unlockPosition(UFname)**, replace **UFname** with **warning**, and connect the data output pin to the **Call warning** sequence input pin. (This allows you to position warning anywhere on the screen.)

19. Run your program. (Stop the program by clicking the box next to the **Turn off alarm?** prompt. It should look like the figure on the next page.

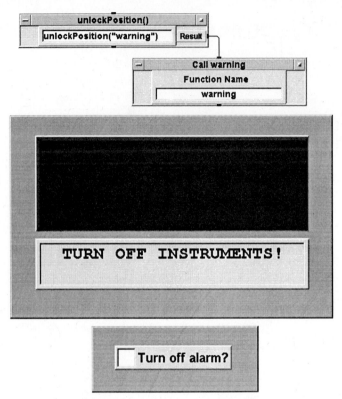

Fig. 10-31. The Warning Program

Note: *Position the pop-up panels to suit your taste. (The unlockPosition and Call warning objects are here for clarity. You could create a panel view for your program that would hide them in a detail view.)*

Chapter 10 Checklist

You should now be able to perform the following tasks. Review, if necessary, before moving on to the next chapter.

- Summarize the key points concerning operator interfaces.

- Use a menu to select tests on an operator interface.

- Import a bitmap for an operator interface.

- Create a status panel.

- List some of the operator interface features that HP VEE provides.

- Secure a program.

- Create a high impact warning.

Optimizing
HP VEE Programs

11

Overview

There are three basic components to performance in test programs: the speed of taking the measurement, the rate at which the data is transferred to the computer, and the speed at which your program processes the data. This chapter will focus solely on the execution speed of your HP VEE program, which can be improved as much as an order of magnitude by using the best programming techniques.

In the first section, you'll learn the basic principles for optimizing any HP VEE program. The second section will cover optimizing parts of your programs by linking compiled functions in other languages on UNIX platforms. (See chapter 12 for using compiled functions on a PC.)

In this chapter you'll learn about:

- Basic techniques for optimizing programs

- Using compiled functions in other languages on UNIX platforms (see chapter 12 for using compiled functions on a PC)

Basic Techniques for Optimizing Programs

This section covers the techniques that can improve program performance up by an order of magnitude.

Perform Math on Arrays Whenever Possible

Performing mathematical operations on arrays is not always the most intuitive approach, but it will improve program performance greatly. For example, suppose your test must find the square root of measurements you're taking. The most traditional way to program this would be to make a measurement and calculate the square root within a loop. The optimized technique in HP VEE would store all the measurements in an array, and then calculate the square root of the array in one step.

Consider the example on the next page. The program on top iterates 1024 times. Each iteration calculates a square root and throws the result away. (This program is for illustration purposes only, and does not do any useful work.) The program on the bottom creates an array of 1024 elements, calculates the square root of the array yielding an array of square roots, and throws the result away. Although they both yield the same results, the bottom program executes 52 times faster than the one on top.

You could increase your program performance by more than one order of magnitude just using this one technique. The basic principle behind this is simple. There is a fixed amount of overhead whenever an object executes, so you reduce the number of times an object executes by using arrays rather than scalar values.

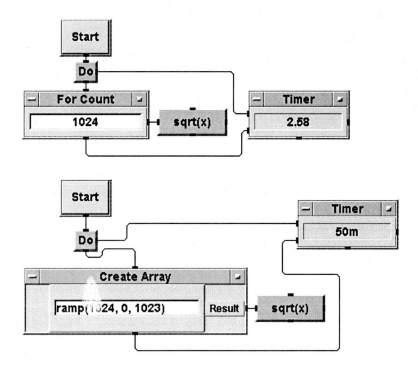

Fig. 11-1. Optimizing With Array Math

The object labeled Create Array is just a Formula object renamed. The ramp function generates an array with 1024 elements starting at 0 and ending at 1023.

Make Objects into Icons Whenever Possible

The more information HP VEE has to maintain on the screen the more time it will take your program to run. Using iconic views instead of open views will optimize your program several times. The example in the figure below operates 3.4 times faster using an iconic view for the For Count and Counter object.

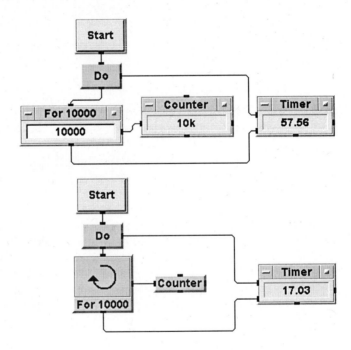

Fig. 11-2. Optimizing Your Programs Using Icons

Reduce the Number of Objects in Your Programs

As you become more experienced you will automatically use less objects, but there are two areas that lead to some additional optimization.

- First, try to use a single equation in a Formula object instead of using separate mathematical objects. For example, put the equation $((a + b) * c)/d$ into a Formula object instead of using separate objects for addition, multiplication, and division. Also, use constants in the formula instead of constant objects connected to inputs. (Set constants with Set Global.)

- Second, nest function calls within other function parameter lists. For instance, in the next two figures the function randomize uses the array generated by the function ramp. In the second program the function call to ramp is nested in the call to randomize resulting in faster program execution.

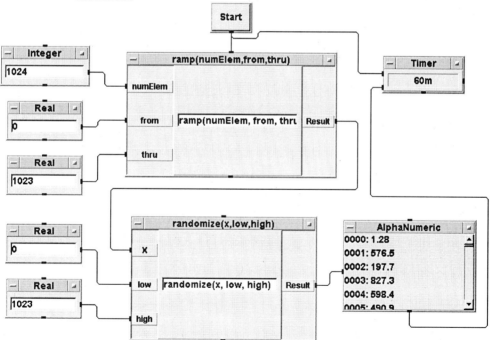

Fig. 11-3. Function Calls Without Optimization

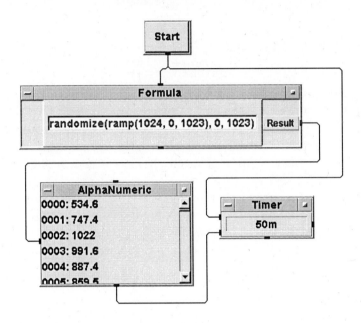

Fig. 11-4. Function Calls with Optimization

Other Ways to Optimize HP VEE Programs

Besides the three techniques mentioned already, the linking of compiled functions in other languages to your HP VEE programs affords the greatest execution speed gains. Compiled functions on UNIX platforms will be covered in the next section of this chapter. Compiled functions on PCs will be covered in chapter 12. Below we have listed a variety of other optimization techniques that you can use in your applications, when appropriate.

- Run your program from the panel view instead of the detailed view. HP VEE will have less objects to maintain on the screen.

- Use globals rather than pass values (especially large arrays or records) into and out of UserObjects and UserFunctions.

- Collect data for graphical displays and plot the entire array at once rather than plotting each individual scalar point. If the X values of a plot are regularly spaced, use an XY Trace display rather than an X vs. Y Plot.

- Use one If/Then/Else object with multiple conditions instead of multiple If/Then/Else objects.

- Set graphical displays to be as plain as possible. The settings that allow the fastest update times are Grid Type => None and Layout => Graph Only in the Edit Properties dialog box. Also, only use Autoscale control pins where necessary.

- When reading data from a file use the ARRAY 1D TO END: (*) transaction instead of performing READ transactions on one element at a time and using the EOF pin.

- Use the Sequencer to control the flow of execution of several User Functions instead of separate Call Function objects.

- When using the Sequencer, only enable logging for transactions where the Log record is required.

- On Strip Charts, set the Buffer Size in Edit Properties to the smallest number possible for your application.

- Use the triadic operator, *(condition ? expression1 : expression2)*, instead of the If/Then/Else object with Gates and a Junction. (See chapter 4.)

- When using bitmaps set to Actual or Centered rather than Scaled, since Scaled will take a few moments longer.

- On indicators such as the Fill Bar or Thermometer, turn off Show Digital Display.

- On Color Alarms, if you're switching between colors rapidly, turn off Show 3D Border.

Optimizing With Compiled Functions (HP-UX and Solaris)

The process of using compiled functions in other languages involves shared libraries on UNIX platforms and Dynamic Link Libraries (DLLs) on PC platforms. Shared libraries are discussed in this section; DLLs are covered in chapter 12.

You can dynamically link a program written in C, C++, Fortran, and Pascal with your HP VEE programs on HP-UX workstations. Although all the languages mentioned should work on Solaris, only C is supported there at this time. Note that Pascal compiled functions are only supported on the HP 9000, Series 700 workstations.

Benefits of Using Compiled Functions

- Faster execution speed

- Leveraging your current test programs in other languages

- Developing data filters in other languages and integrating them into your HP VEE programs

- Securing proprietary routines

For these benefits you will add complexity to your development process. Only use a compiled function when the capability or performance that you need is not available using an HP VEE User Function or an Execute Program escape to the operating system.

The Process of Integrating Compiled Functions (HP-UX and Solaris)

The following is an outline of the process.

Outside HP VEE:

1. Write functions in C, C++, Fortran, or Pascal and compile them (Only C is supported on Solaris currently).

2. Write a definition file for the functions.

3. Create a shared library containing the compiled functions.

Inside HP VEE:

1. Use an Import Library object to bind the shared library to your program at run time. Within this object you will specify that you're calling a library containing Compiled Functions, the file that contains the shared library, and the definition file.

2. Call any functions in the shared library as you would any internal HP VEE function using a Call Function object or a function call from an expression field within an object such as the Sequencer or the Formula object.

3. (optional) You may also delete the library to free up memory using a Delete Library object.

Design Considerations

- You can use any facilities available to the operating system including math routines, instrument I/O, and so forth. However, you cannot access any HP VEE internals from within the program to be linked.

- You need to provide error checking within your compiled function, since HP VEE cannot trap errors in an external routine.

- You must deallocate any memory you allocated in your external routine.

- When passing data to an external routine, make sure you configure your Call Function input terminals to the type and shape of data that your routine requires.

- System I/O resources may become locked, so your external routine should be able to handle this type of event.

- If your external routine accepts arrays, it must have a valid pointer for the type of data it will examine. Also, the routine must check the size of the array. If the routine changes the size, you need to pass the new size back to your HP VEE program.

- The compiled function must use the *return( )* statement as its last statement, not *exit( )*. If the compiled function exits, then so will HP VEE, since a compiled function is linked to HP VEE.

- If you overwrite the bounds of an array, the result depends on the language you're using. In Pascal, which performs bounds checking, a run-time error will result, stopping HP VEE. In languages like C, where there is no bounds checking, the result will be unpredictable, but intermittent data corruption is probable.

Importing and Calling a Compiled Function (HP-UX and Solaris)

Once you have created the shared library and definition file outside of HP VEE, you can integrate the library into your HP VEE program. The process is similar to importing and calling User Functions. First, you use an Import Library object found in the Device => Function menu. You can change the Library Type field to Compiled Function (the default is User Function). You will then see a fourth field added to indicate the definition file. See the figure on the next page.

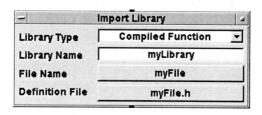

Fig. 11-5. Importing a Library of Compiled Functions

The Library Type can only be one of three choices: User Function, Compiled Function, or Remote Function. The Library Name field is simply the name HP VEE uses to identify your library, in case you would like to delete it later in the program. The File Name field will signify the file that holds the shared library.

Once you have imported the library with Import Library, you can call the Compiled Function by specifying the function name in the Call Function object. For example, the Call Function object below calls the Compiled Function named myFunction.

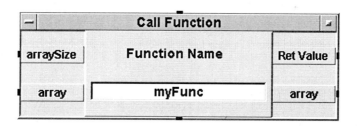

Fig. 11-6. Using Call Function for Compiled Functions

You can call a Compiled Function just as you would call a User Function. You can either select the desired function using Select Function from the Call Function object menu, or you can type in the name. In either case, provided HP VEE recognizes the function, the input and output terminals of the Call Function object will be configured automatically for the function. The necessary information is supplied by the definition file. (HP VEE will recognize it if its library has already been imported.) Or you can reconfigure the Call Function input and output terminals by selecting Configure pinout in the object menu. Whichever method you use, HP VEE will configure the Call Function object with the input terminals required by the function, and with a Ret Value output terminal for the return value of the function. In addition, there will be an output terminal corresponding to each input that is passed by reference.

You can also call the Compiled Function by name from an expression in a Formula object, or from other expressions evaluated at run time. For example, you could call a Compiled Function by including its name in an expression in a Sequencer transaction. Note, however, that only the Compiled Function's return value (Ret Value in the Call Function object) can be obtained from within an expression. If you want to obtain other parameters returned from the function, you will have to use the Call Function object.

You may also delete the library of Compiled Functions by using the Delete Library object in the Device => Function menu. Using the Import Library, Call Function, and Delete Library objects you can shorten your load time and conserve memory by importing and deleting them when the program has finished calling them.

Compiled Function Example Using C (HP-UX or Solaris)

In the following program, a library is imported and a C function is called. The C function accepts a real array and adds 1 to each element in the array. The modified array is returned to HP VEE on the Array terminal of the Call Function object, while the size of the array is returned on the Ret Value terminal. This example is located in:

<installation directory>/examples/manual/manual49.vee.

(A ".vee" extension indicates a program; a ".c" extension indicates a file containing C source code; a ".h" or ".def" extension signifies a definition file; and a ".sl" extension indicates a shared library file.)

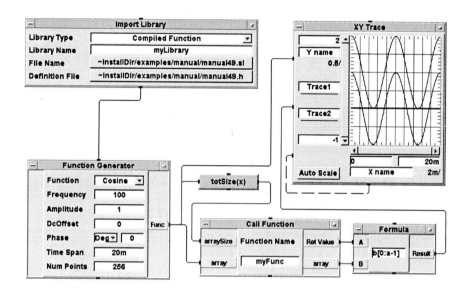

Fig. 11-7. Program Calling a Compiled Function

Note that one variable in the C function (and correspondingly, one data input terminal in the Call Function object) is used to indicate the size of the array. The arraySize variable is used to prevent data from being written beyond the end of the array.

Since *array* has been passed by reference, HP VEE automatically creates both an input and output pin on the Call Function object.

The arraySize variable has been passed by value, so HP VEE only creates an input terminal. However, here we've used the function's return value to return the size of the output array to HP VEE. This technique is useful when you need to return an array that has fewer elements than the input array.

Note that the C routine is a function, not a procedure. The Compiled Function requires a return value, so if you use a language that distinguishes between procedures and functions, make sure you write your routine as a function.

There are a few things to note about this program. First, the Import Library object executes before the Call Function object in the program. If you have any doubts about the order of execution regarding these two objects, use the sequence pins to assure the right order. Secondly, notice that the parameter variable *array* passed by reference to your function has both input and output terminals, but the variable *arraySize* passed by value has only an input terminal. Thirdly, the Formula object uses the size of the array in the Ret Value terminal to send the correct number of array elements to the display. Finally, the XY Trace uses a control pin to Auto Scale after it has received the two waveforms (note the dotted line from the sequence out pin to the control input pin).

Execute Program Object vs. Compiled Functions (HP-UX)

When you're deciding which method to use to integrate your compiled language programs with HP VEE, you should consider the following:

Execute Program Object

- Easier to use

- Longer start-up time

- Communication through pipes

- Protected address space

- Continuous execution

- Service of asynchronous events

- Safer (If your called program crashes, you simply get an error message.)

- Better for continuous data acquisition

**Compiled Functions Using the Import Library
and Call Function Objects**

- More complicated to use

- Short start-up time

- Communication by passing on the stack

- Memory space shared with HP VEE

- Synchronous execution

- Signals not blocked or caught

- Compiler required

- More risk in using (An array out-of-bounds error or overwriting memory will cause HP VEE to crash.)

Chapter 11 Checklist

You should now be able to perform the following tasks. Review topics, if necessary, before proceeding.

- Explain three basic techniques for optimizing HP VEE programs and give examples of each.

- Explain at least two more techniques in addition to the three above.

Unique Features on
PC and UNIX Platforms

Average Time To Complete: 2 hrs.

Overview

HP VEE programs port between the supported platforms, but there are some objects that are unique to particular operating systems. For example, when using compiled functions in textual languages on UNIX, HP VEE uses shared libraries; on a PC, Dynamic Link Libraries (DLLs). Named pipes on UNIX are equivalent to Dynamic Data Exchange (DDE) on a PC. In this chapter, we will describe the key differences between operating systems, and show you how HP has designed objects to handle them easily.

*In this chapter
you'll learn about:*

- The differences between the PC and UNIX platforms

- Using Dynamic Data Exchange (DDE) on a PC

- Using Dynamic Link Libraries (DLLs) on a PC

- Communicating with an HP BASIC/UX program

Differences Between the PC and UNIX Platforms

Programs

All features can be used to program on all platforms; however, if the object is dependent on the operating system, it will only accomplish its task on that operating system. You can allow for these differences when porting programs by using the Data => System Info objects: whichOS( ) or whichPlatform( ). They output the operating system (OS) or platform so that your program can detect whether to use an "OS-dependent" object. These objects will have "PC" or "UNIX" after the object name in the menu.

Named Pipes and Dynamic Data Exchange

The To/From Named Pipe (UNIX) object and the To/From DDE (PC) object accomplish the same task of communicating with another program or application on their respective operating systems.

HP BASIC/UX

The Initialize HP BASIC/UX (UNIX) and To/From HP BASIC/UX (UNIX) are only designed to work with HP BASIC/UX on HP-UX. HP BASIC for Windows works like any other textual language on a PC.

The Execute Program Objects

The Execute Program object has two versions: one for UNIX, one for the PC. Both are used for launching other programs or applications.

To/From Stdout, Stderr (UNIX)

Although these objects do work on a PC, they are implemented with files and are not recommended for general programming. You should only use them when porting an HP VEE program from a UNIX platform to the PC.

Fonts and Screen Resolutions

HP VEE on a PC chooses a font size that looks good with your screen resolution. The File => Edit Default Preferences... dialog box lets you easily alter the look and feel of your programs. Use the Edit Properties... selection in the object menus to customize individual objects. If necessary, HP VEE will translate the font saved in your program to one available on the destination machine. For best results, you may want to build your program on a computer with a screen resolution and font set similar to the destination machine. When porting programs, make sure the screen resolutions are similar to avoid problems.

Data Files

ASCII data files constructed with the **To File** object should be readable with the **From File** object on either the workstation or the PC platform. No binary files will work across platforms, since the byte ordering is reversed between workstations and PCs.

Using Dynamic Data Exchange (DDE)

DDE is a message-based protocol for exchanging information between Windows applications. A DDE conversation takes place between a DDE client and a DDE server. The DDE client is the program that makes the request for a connection in a conversational mode with a DDE server. Once this link is established, the client can then request data and services from the server application. A Windows 95 or Windows NT application supporting DDE may act as a client, a server, or both. HP VEE only supports DDE as a client application. You implement DDE with the To/From DDE (PC) object in the I/O menu. It offers similar functionality to the To/From Named Pipe (Unix) object on UNIX platforms. The DDE objects operate by sending transactions in much the same way a To/From File object works.

The most common terms associated with DDE are Application, Topic, and Item. When a client such as HP VEE wants to have a conversation with a DDE server, it must do so through an identification process using a server name, a topic name, and an item name. These three values get defined as strings in a DDE conversation.

The application name identifies a server in a DDE conversation. In most cases, the name of the application's .exe file is also the DDE server name. The topic name is a string that identifies a category of data. For example, if the server is a spreadsheet, a topic would be the name of a spreadsheet file. In general, most applications also support a topic by the name of "System". This topic is typically used to get more information on the application's available items. The item name usually refers to the data transmitted in the DDE conversation. (You can usually get more information on topics, items, and commands for particular applications by calling their online support.)

The client application starts a conversation by posting a message that includes the server's name (the application's name, such as a name of a spreadsheet program) and a name of a topic of its interest. If the server acknowledges this request positively, a link is established between the two. The client can then request data from the server. The server provides the data, if it has access to the data requested; otherwise, it replies negatively.

The client can also "poke" (write) data items to the server. The conversation stops when the client and the server send termination messages to each other.

The HP VEE DDE Object uses four types of transactions:

- **READ (REQUEST)** will read data from a DDE transfer.

- **WRITE (POKE)** will write data to a DDE transfer.

- **EXECUTE COMMAND: "[*<some command>]*"** sends the command to the DDE server and executes the command.

- **WAIT** waits for a specified amount of time.

> *Note: Experienced DDE users will notice the absence of DDEInitiate and DDETerminate commands in HP VEE for Windows implementation of the DDE object. You don't need to use them, because HP VEE automatically performs them for you.*

Lab 12 - 1: Building a Simple DDE Object

In the following exercise, you build a DDE object that communicates with the Windows Program Manager to create and delete a workgroup, workgroup item, and icon.

1. Select **I/O => To/From DDE (PC)** and place it in the left work area.

2. Change the **Application** input field to **progman**; change the **Topic** input field to **progman**.

   The application name progman identifies the Windows Program Manager application. Progman is the topic name too.

Now that you've identified the application and topic, you want to send a command to the Program Manager to create a Work Group.

3. Double-click the transaction bar to get the **I/O Transaction** dialog box. Click **READ (REQUEST)** to get the menu of DDE actions, highlight **EXECUTE**.

4. In the **I/O Transaction** dialog box, double-click the **COMMAND** input field to highlight the default quotation marks, type the command **"[CreateGroup(DDE Test)]"**, then click on **OK**. (You can also click in the COMMAND input field to get a cursor, then type between the quotation marks.)

   CreateGroup is the Program Manager command that creates a program group, and **DDE Test** is the title of that group.

   Your **To/From DDE** object should look like the figure below.

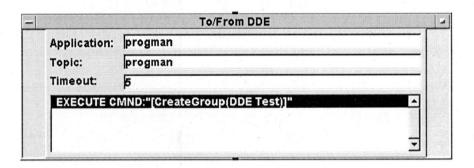

Fig. 12-1. The DDE Object With the First Transaction

Now that you've created a group with the Program Manager, let's add an item to that group.

5. Double-click just below the first transaction bar to get another I/O Transaction dialog box and configure it to execute the command:

   "[AddItem(C:\\WIN95\\NOTEPAD.EXE, Note Pad)]"

   (The double backslash is an escape character in HP VEE indicating a single backslash in the text. Replace WIN95 with the name of your operating system directory. I'm using WIN95, because that's the custom name I assigned to the Windows 95 directory.)

AddItem is the Program Manager command, and C:\\WIN95 \\NOTEPAD.EXE is the program that will be assigned to the new icon. Note Pad is the title that will appear under the icon. The icon bitmap is embedded in the NOTEPAD.EXE file.

The second transaction bar should now read:

EXECUTE CMND: "[AddItem(C:\\WIN95\\NOTEPAD.EXE, Note Pad)]"

6. Configure the next transaction bar to read:

WAIT INTERVAL: 5

7. Configure the fourth transaction to read:

EXECUTE CMND: "[DeleteGroup(DDE Test)]"

Your DDE object should now look like the figure below.

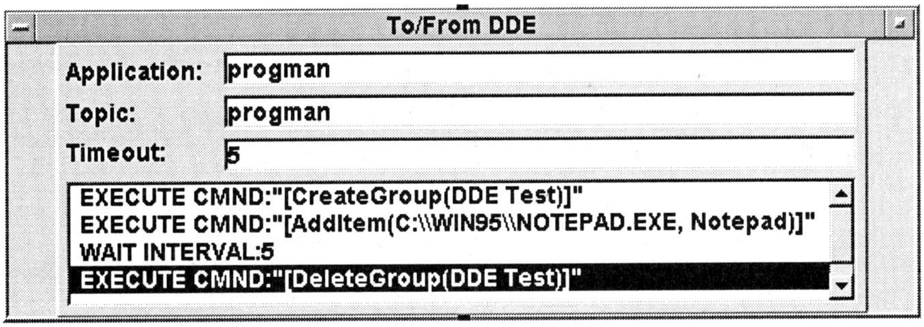

```
┌─┬──────────────────────── To/From DDE ───────────────────────┬─┐
│ │                                                             │ │
│  Application:  progman                                          │
│  Topic:        progman                                          │
│  Timeout:      5                                                │
│  ┌──────────────────────────────────────────────────────┬─┐   │
│  │ EXECUTE CMND:"[CreateGroup(DDE Test)]"               │▲│   │
│  │ EXECUTE CMND:"[AddItem(C:\\WIN95\\NOTEPAD.EXE, Notepad)]"│ │   │
│  │ WAIT INTERVAL:5                                      │ │   │
│  │ EXECUTE CMND:"[DeleteGroup(DDE Test)]"               │▼│   │
│  └──────────────────────────────────────────────────────┴─┘   │
└─────────────────────────────────────────────────────────────┘
```

Fig. 12-2. DDE Object With 4 Transactions Configured

Now you can test your DDE object.

8. Run your HP VEE program. Your DDE object should produce something similar to the figure below.

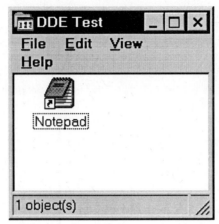

Fig. 12-3. Your DDE Object Creating a Workgroup

Now let's read data from the Program Manager.

9. Add another transaction to your **DDE** object. In the **I/O Transaction** dialog box, leave **READ (REQUEST)**. Change the **ITEM** input field to **"progman"**. Leave the **TEXT** input field at **X**. Leave **STRING FORMAT**. Change **SCALAR** to **ARRAY 1D**. Leave the default array size at **10**. Click **OK**.

X is the name of the data output pin, which will hold the contents of the data you read from the Program Manager. So you now have to add this pin to the DDE object.

10. Add a data output pin to the **DDE** object. The default will be labeled **X**.

11. Select a **Logging AlphaNumeric** display and connect it to the **To/From DDE** object output pin **X**.

12. Run your program. It should look similar to the one below.

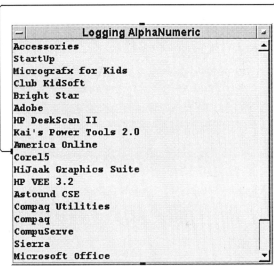

Fig. 12-4. The DDE Program

The workgroup named DDE Test with the Note Pad icon in Figure 12-3 has already been created and deleted in Figure 12-4 above. The text in the display will vary depending on the workgroups your Program Manager is displaying.

Note: *There is an excellent DDE program example in <installation directory>\EXAMPLES\ESCAPES\DDEPROGMN.VEE that demonstrates the use of the To/From DDE object to query the MS Windows Program Manager groups. If you study this example, it will increase your ability to utilize DDE.*

Using Dynamic Link Libraries

To write your own DLLs, contact Microsoft for documentation.

> *Note:* *HP VEE supports "_cdecl" and "_stdcall" calling conventions, which means that you could use most off-the-shelf DLLs as well as your own.*

Outside of HP VEE you create or obtain a DLL, then inside HP VEE:

1. Select **Device => Function => Import Library**.

   Change the **Library Type** input field to **Compiled Function**.

   The Import Library object automatically adds a fourth field for the Definition File.

   The **Library Name** field is arbitrary, since HP VEE uses it to keep track of this library in case you want to delete it later. You can use the default name, **myLibrary**, or type in a new name. Change the **File Name** input field to the name of the file that holds the DLL, and the **Definition File** input field to the appropriate definition file name (a *.h file, usually).

   You can load a library manually during your development phase by selecting **Load Lib** from the object menu.

2. Select **Device => Function => Call**.

   After you have loaded the DLL library by selecting **Load Lib** in the **Import Library** object menu, choose **Select Function** from the **Call Function** object menu, then choose the desired function from the list box presented.

   HP VEE automatically configures the Call Function object with the function name, and the proper number of input and output pins. Notice that the input pins have default names of A, B, C, ... that map to the first, second, third, ... parameters. The top output pin is the return value from the function. The second, third, ... output pins map to any parameters passed by reference to the function. If you've entered the function name, you can also configure the object by selecting Configure Pinout in the object menu.

Note: *You can also call a DLL function from an expression field provided the library has been loaded. When used in this way, you must enclose the parameters in parentheses after the function name, and the function only sends back its return value. Any parameters passed by reference can only be retrieved by using the Call Function object. For example, you might use the following expression in a Formula object:*

2 * yourFunc(a,b)

The a and the b would refer to two input pins on the Formula object, and the return value of yourFunc would be multiplied by 2 and placed on the output pin.

3. (Optional) Click **Device => Function => Delete Library**.

   While developing your program you can also select **Delete Lib** from the object menu. Deleting the library conserves memory.

An Example Using a DLL

In this exercise you will import a DLL and call a function from the DLL. You'll use a DLL that comes with HP VEE for Windows. This HP VEE program is located in:
<installation directory>\EXAMPLES\MANUAL\MANUAL49.
(The same program is designed to work on HP-UX, Solaris, MS Windows 3.x, Windows 95, or Windows NT.) Open this file in HP VEE.

Examine this example closely. It should look like Figure 12-5 on the next page.

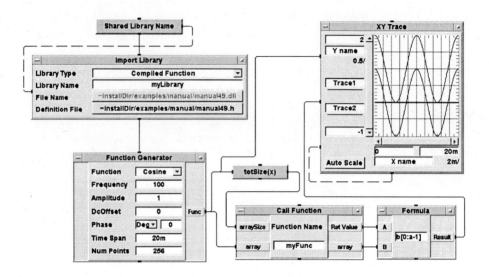

Fig. 12-5. A Program Using a DLL (MANUAL49)

Specifically, MANUAL49 calls a compiled function called myFunc.
MyFunc requires a C datatype called *long*, which is the same as an HP VEE
Int32. This number specifies the size of an array. The second input
parameter is a pointer to an array of reals. The definition file is located in
MANUAL49.H, and the source file for the C code is located in
MANUAL49.C. MyFunc adds 1 to every element of the array.

Before the first call to the compiled function, the DLL must be loaded using
the Import Library object (in the Device => Function submenu). The
Function Generator is used to create a waveform, which is output to the array
input pin on the Call Function object. The totSize object (in the AdvMath
=> Array submenu) is used to determine the size of the waveform, which is
output to the arraySize input pin on Call Function. The XY Trace object
displays both the original and the new waveforms.

Note: *The Call Function output pin labeled Ret Value holds the size of the returned array, so the expression B[0:A-1] in the Formula object will send the entire array to the display object.*

Run the program and notice that the second trace is one greater than the first trace at all points on the waveform.

Another key point to notice in the program is the method used for making it portable to all HP VEE platforms. The UNIX platforms use shared libraries compiled on either HP-UX or Solaris indicated by the filename extensions *.sl (on HP) or *.so (on Sun). The MS Windows DLL uses a Microsoft C 16-bit compiler; whereas, MS Windows NT and Windows 95 use a Microsoft C 32-bit compiler. These DLLs are both indicated using a *.dll extension.

The UserObject called Shared Library Name identifies which operating system you're using, then transmits the correct library name to the Import Library object, as shown below.

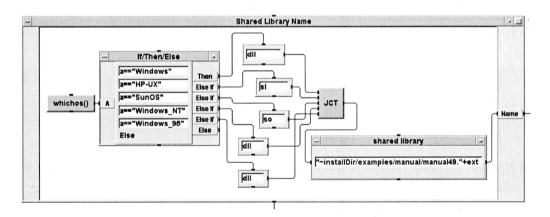

Fig. 12-6. The Shared Library Name UserObject

The whichos( ) function has been used in a renamed Formula object to identify the operating system. An expanded If/Then/Else object examines the output of the whichos( ) function, then triggers the appropriate text constant. This filename extension is then added to the MANUAL49 file using a renamed Formula object. (The input terminal on the Formula object labeled *shared library* has also been changed to *ext*.)

A control pin for a File Name has been added to the Import Library object; hence, you see a dotted line between the UserObject and the Import Library object.

> *Note: Investigate To/From Socket for sharing data in mixed environments - sending data to a database, for example.*

Communicating With HP BASIC/UX Programs

For HP BASIC on HP-UX, we provide a couple of additional objects to facilitate communication between the two languages. For Series 700 workstations (HP-UX 9.0 and 10.0) you can use HP VEE 3.2, the subject of this book. For Series 300 and 400 workstations (HP-UX 9.0), you need HP VEE 3.1. (HP BASIC for Windows can be used like any other textual language with HP VEE for all Windows operating systems.)

Using the Initialize HP BASIC/UX Object

The Init HP BASIC/UX object, as shown in the figure below, has a single field, in which you specify the HP BASIC program you'd like to run.

Fig. 12-7. The Init HP BASIC/UX Object

Enter the entire path and any options for the program. Here we've used ~installDir/examples/rmb/man34a.bas as an example. The program may have been stored or saved in HP BASIC. The object will spawn the HP BASIC/UX process and run the program. You can also use relative paths from the present working directory to specify the program, if you desire. This object doesn't provide any data path to or from HP BASIC/UX; use the To/From HP BASIC/UX object for that purpose. You can use more than one Init HP BASIC/UX object in an HP VEE program.

Note that there is no direct way to terminate an HP BASIC/UX process from an HP VEE program. Instead, you should use a QUIT statement in your HP BASIC program when it receives a certain data value from your HP VEE program. You could also use an Execute Program object to kill the HP BASIC process using a shell command, such as *rmbkill*. When you exit HP VEE, any HP BASIC/UX processes still attached are terminated automatically.

Using the To/From HP BASIC/UX Object

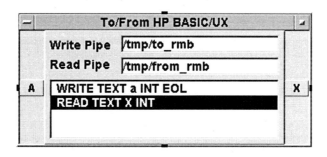

Fig. 12-8. The To/From HP BASIC/UX Object

The object above located in the I/O => HP BASIC/UX submenu facilitates data transfer to and from HP BASIC programs. This object creates and uses named pipes for interprocess communication. For simplicity HP VEE implements one pipe for READ transactions and another pipe for WRITE transactions. We have included two transactions writing and reading an integer as an example. You can use the default pipes or create your own by typing in new paths and filenames for Write Pipe and Read Pipe. Transactions are configured the same way as other transaction objects you've used in HP VEE. Note that the Write Pipe and Read Pipe fields can be added to the object as control pins.

All To/From HP BASIC/UX objects contain the same default names for read and write pipes. Therefore, be sure that you know which pipe you really want to read or write. Make sure that pipes to different programs have unique names. In your HP BASIC program check that you address OUTPUT and ENTER statements to the corect pipe.

If the pipes do not exist before To/From HP BASIC/UX operates, then they are created. However, there are some overhead costs; if the pipes exist beforehand, the program runs more quickly. These pipes are created for you automatically if they do not already exist:

/tmp/to_rmb
/tmp/from_rmb

To create additional pipes, use the operating system command *mknod*.

HP BASIC/UX pipes (which are simply named pipes) are opened when the first READ or WRITE transaction to that pipe operates after PreRun. All named pipes are closed at PostRun. (See HP VEE documentation for a detailed description of PreRun and PostRun.) The EXECUTE CLOSE READ PIPE and EXECUTE CLOSE WRITE PIPE transactions enable you to close pipes at any time.

Because of the behavior of named pipes, it is easiest to structure your transactions to transmit known or easily parsed data blocks. For example, if you are transmitting strings, determine the maximum length block you wish to transmit and pad shorter strings with blanks. This avoids the problems of trying to read more data from a pipe than is available and of leaving unwanted data in a pipe.

To help prevent a READ transaction from hanging until data is available, use a READ IOSTATUS DATA READY transaction in a separate To/From HP BASIC/UX object. The transaction returns a 1 if there is at least one byte to read, and a 0 if there are no bytes to read. To read all the data available on the read pipe, use a READ ... ARRAY 1D TO END:(*) transaction.

If you're running diskless, be certain you WRITE and READ to or from uniquely named pipes. Otherwise, several workstations on the same diskless cluster may attempt to access the same named pipe, which will cause contention problems.

Examine the following simple program to understand how to set up communication with an HP BASIC/UX program. It's located in *manual34.vee* in the *examples/rmb* subdirectory.

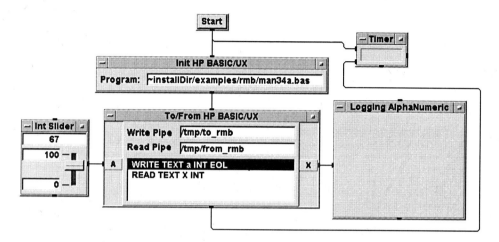

Fig. 12-9. Communicating With HP BASIC/UX

Chapter 12 Checklist

You should now be able to perform the following tasks:

- Explain the key differences between PC and UNIX platforms and what issues they raise in porting programs.

- Explain what DDE means and where you would use it.

- Explain the differences between a DDE client and DDE server using HP VEE as an example.

- Use the To/From DDE object to send commands to a DDE server application, wait for a specified interval, and read data from the server application.

- Explain the basic concept of a DLL.

- Import a DLL, call a function within it, then delete the DLL.

- Explain how to call and communicate with an HP BASIC/UX program.

Appendix A:
Ordering Information

HP VEE 3.2 for Windows 95 and Windows NT (E2120D)

- Options for unlimited run-time, graphics toolkit (PV-WAVE), localization, and upgrade.

HP VEE 3.2 for Series 700 / HP-UX 9.0 and 10.0 (E2111D)

- Options for unlimited run-time, graphics toolkit (PV-WAVE), localization, and upgrade.

HP VEE 3.2 for Solaris (E2112D)

- Options for unlimited run-time, graphics toolkit (PV-WAVE), localization, and upgrade.

HP VEE Site License for HP VEE 3.2 (E2117D)

- Low cost, covers all platforms in any mix.

- *Unlimited* run-time and lower cost upgrade available to owners of previous versions of HP VEE or any competitive graphical language.

For users of MS Windows 3.1 or Series 300/400 Workstations

HP VEE 3.1 for Windows 3.1 (E2120C)

Note: HP VEE 3.2 is not available for MS Windows 3.1.

- Options for unlimited run-time, localization, and upgrade.

Note: Free evaluation software for **HP VEE 3.1 for Windows 3.1** *is available currently under the name, "HP VEE for Windows Evaluation Kit." It should be used with an earlier version of this book,* **Graphical Programming: A Tutorial for HP VEE** *(Published by Prentice Hall PTR; ISBN: 0-13-362823-X). It can be obtained through HP Direct or HP sales offices listed at the end of this appendix. There is also a copy of this software on the evaluation CD that comes with this book.*

HP VEE 3.1 for Series 300 or 400 / HP-UX 9.0 (E2110C)

- Options for unlimited run-time, localization, and upgrade.

Note: HP VEE 3.2 is not available for Series 300/400 workstations.

Information for Referenced Products

PV-WAVE from Visual Numerics

- Available as Option VIS with HP VEE 3.2, PV-WAVE reads data from HP VEE's To File object and enhances HP VEE's rich data types by displaying 2D, 3D, and 4D tables, graphs, plots, surfaces, and projections for visual analysis and presentation.

Data Translation's Visual Programming Interface (VPI)

- Provides an additional HP VEE menu for controlling Data Translation's PC plug-in boards.

  Note: *VPI is not required to control the plug-in boards from other manufacturers. You can control those boards using DLLs that ship with the products.*

- To order VPI or obtain additional information, contact Data Translation directly at:

  U.S.: 800/525-8528
  International: 800/481-3700
  Fax: 508/481-8620
  100 Locke Dr.
  Marlboro, MA 01752-1192
  USA

How to Contact us in Colorado

To get current information on HP VEE and services such as an email forum, WWW information, or a monthly newsletter, please contact us in Colorado.

Voice: 970-679-3030
FAX: 970-679-5260
FaxBack: 970-679-3031
Email: pctm@lvld.hp.com

Where to Order HP VEE

HP DIRECT

The HP Direct organizations allow you to talk directly with HP without going through a sales representative locally. They can send you sales literature and take your product orders directly. They can send you the free HP VEE Evaluation Kit (for HP VEE 3.2 by Fall 95, or for HP VEE 3.1 now), which has software that can be used to learn the product with this book. Their country phone numbers are listed below:

U.S.A.

1-800-452-4484

Germany

(06172)16-1634

France

(1) 69-82-65-00

Italy

(02) 9212-2241

Netherlands

(020) 547-6669

Spain

900 123-123

Sweden

(08) 444-2000

Switzerland

(1) 735 7111

U.K.

01344-366666

HP SALES OFFICES

Call your local HP sales office listed in your telephone directory or an HP regional office listed below for the location of your nearest sales office.

United States of America:

Rockville, MD
(301) 670 4300

Rolling Meadow, IL
(708) 255 9800

Fullerton, CA
(714) 999 6700

Atlanta, GA
(404) 980 7351

Canada:
(416) 678 9430

Japan:
(8113) 3335 8192

Latin America:

Mexico
(525) 202 0155

Brazil
(11) 709 1444

Australia/New Zealand:
(03) 895 2895

Hong Kong:
(852) 848 7070

Korea:
(2) 769 0800

Taiwan:
(2) 717 9524

Singapore:
(65) 291 8554

India:
(11) 690 355

PRC:
(1) 505 3888

In Europe, Africa, and Middle East, please call your local HP sales office or representative:

Austria/South East Area:
(0222) 2500 0

Begium and Luxembourg:
(02) 761 31 11

Denmark:
45 99 10 00

Finland:
(90) 88 721

France:
(1) 69.82.65.00

Germany:
(06172) 16 0

Greece:
(01) 68 28 811

Ireland:
(01) 2844633

Israel:
(03) 5380 333

Italy:
(02) 95 300 930

Netherlands:
(020) 547 6669

Norway:
(02) 87 97 00

Portugal:
(11) 301 73 30

South Africa:
(011) 806 1000

Spain:
900 123 123

Sweden:
(08) 750 20 00

Switzerland:
(057) 31 21 11

Turkey:
(90 1) 4 125 83 13

United Kingdom:
(0344) 362 867

For countries not listed, contact Hewlett-Packard, International Sales Branch, Geneva, Switzerland.

Tel: +41-22-780-7111
Fax: +41-22-780-7535

Appendix B:
Additional Lab Exercises

The following exercises should be done to reinforce the HP VEE concepts you've learned in this book. Each programming problem will be classified under the main concept being stressed. You should develop a solution, then compare yours to the programs in this appendix. There are many ways to program any given task, so you have a valid solution if it meets the problem specifications. However, programs that execute more quickly and are easier to use should be considered better solutions. A short discussion of key points will follow each solution.

General Programming Techniques

Apple Bagger

You want to know how many apples it takes to fill a ten pound basket. Create an HP VEE program that counts how many apples it takes to fill the basket. Each apple weighs between 0 and 1 pound.

Suggestions:

This program can be created with 10 or fewer objects. Choose from the following:

> Start
> Until Break
> Random Number
> Accumulator

Break
Real
Conditional (A>=B)
Stop
Counter
If/Then/Else

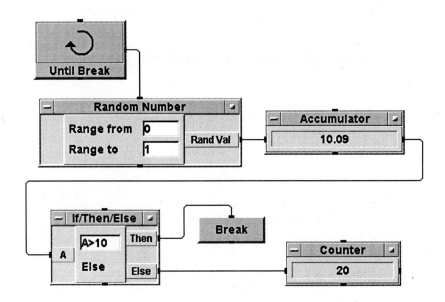

Fig. B-1. Apple Bagger, Solution 1

Key Points:

- **Optimal Solutions:** To optimize the performance of your programs, use fewer objects, if possible. Here we've used 6 objects; the program could also be implemented with 10 objects, as the next figure will show.

- **Until Break and Break Objects:** Use these objects for loops that require testing a condition. Here we want the loop to stop when the total weight of the apples is greater than 10 pounds.

- **Accumulator:** Use the Accumulator to keep a running total.

- **Counter:** Use the Counter to keep a running count. Here we use it to track the total number of apples in the basket. Note that when the total weight is over 10, only the Then pin fires on the If/Then/Else object giving us the correct answer in the Counter.

The following figure gives another solution using more objects:

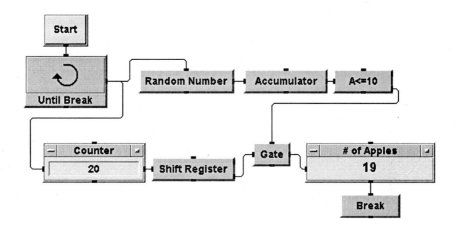

Fig. B-2. Apple Bagger, Solution 2

Key Points:

- **Start:** Using a Start object for this program is redundant, since you can use the Run button on the main menu bar. Start is best used when you have two programs on a screen, and you want to be able to run them independently. Or you have a program with a feedback loop, and you want to define where to initiate execution.

- **Shift Register:** You use a Shift Register to access the previous values of the output. In solution 2 the Counter is keeping a running count of every apple before it's weighed, so the count must be reduced by one when the total weight exceeds 10.

- **Gate:** The Gate is used to hold the output until another action occurs and activates its sequence pin. Here, when the condition A<=10 is no longer true the Else pin on the If/Then/Else object activates the gate.

Testing Numbers

Step 1

Create a program that allows a user to enter a number between 0 and 100. If the the number is greater than or equal to 50, display the number. If it is less than 50, display the message "Sorry."

Suggestions:

This program can be created with 7 or fewer objects. Choose from the following objects:

Start
Integer
Slider
Real
If/Then/Else
Formula
G ate
Text
Junction
AlphaNumeric

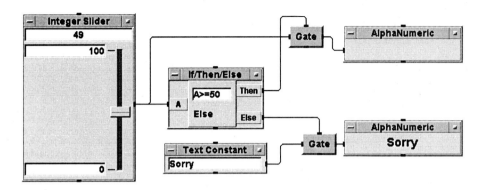

Fig. B-3. Testing Numbers, Step 1

Step 2

After the model is working with 7 objects, try programming it with 5 objects without using the Gate object.

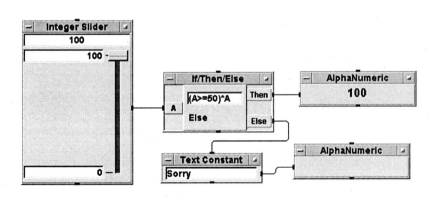

Fig. B-4. Testing Numbers, Step 2

Key Points

- **Auto Execute:** All input objects such as the Integer Slider have an Auto Execute selection in the object menu. If chosen, the object operates whenever its value is changed.

- **Eliminating Gates:** The expression (A>=50)*A in the If/Then/Else object evaluates to a 1*A, if A>=50 is true, or 0, if false. So A is put on the Then pin, if the expression is true, and a 0 is put on the Else pin, if the expression is false. (Any expression that evaluates to a non-zero is considered true, and the value is propagated on the Then pin.)

Step 3

Can you now program a solution using only 3 objects?

HINT: Try using a triadic expression in the Formula object. The format is: (<expression> ? <if TRUE,output value> : <if FALSE, output value>). For example, if A < 10 evaluates to TRUE, you want the value of A on the Result pin; otherwise, you want the string "FALSE" on the Result pin. You would use the following triadic expression: (A<10 ? A : "FALSE").

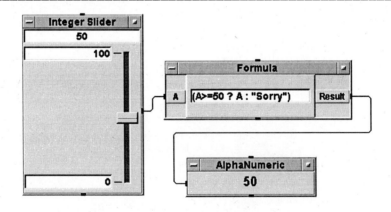

Fig. B-5. Testing Numbers, Step 3

Collecting Random Numbers

Create a program that generates 100 random numbers and displays them. Record the total time required to generate and display the values.

Suggestions:

This program can be created with 6 or fewer objects. Choose from the following:

> Start
> For Range
> Until Break
> Random Seed
> Random Number
> Collector
> Formula
> Set Values
> Allocate Array
> Logging AlphaNumeric
> Strip Chart
> VU Meter
> Date/Time
> Timer
> Now( )
> Break
> Do

HINT: To improve performance, send the data to the display only once by first collecting the data into an array using the Collector object. Note the performance differences.

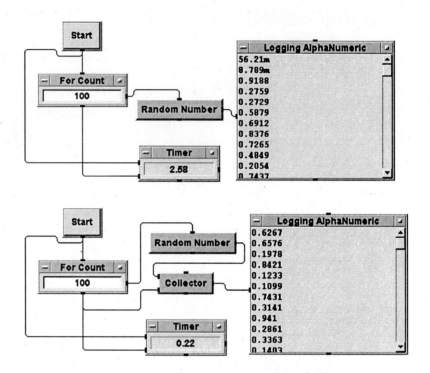

Fig. B-6. Collecting Random Numbers

Key Points

- **Logging AlphaNumeric vs. AlphaNumeric:** Use Logging AlphaNumeric to display consecutive input (either Scalar or Array 1D) as a history of previous values. Use AlphaNumeric to display data as a single value, an Array 1D, or an Array 2D. The Logging display gives you an array without index values; the AlphaNumeric display gives you the same array with index numbers and values.

- **Timing Pins:** Notice that we are timing from the execution of Start to the sequence output pin on For Count, because that pin fires after the thread has executed.

Random Number Generator

Step 1

Create a random number generator that requires external inputs. Display the numbers on a strip chart. Inputs should be allowed for:

Maximum random number
Minimum random number
Number of random numbers generated

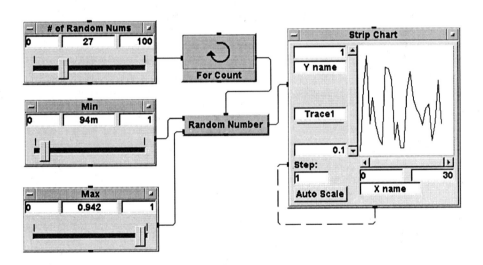

Fig. B-7. Random Number Generator, Step 1

Key Points:

- **Layout of Slider Objects:** You can select either a vertical or horizontal format for the screen image of the slider objects by clicking on Layout in the object menus.

- **Strip Chart:** Use a Strip Chart to display the recent history of data that is continuously generated.

- **The Auto Scale Control Pin:** By clicking on Terminals => Add Control Input... in a display's object menu, you can select Auto Scale as a control pin. By connecting it to the display's sequence output pin, HP VEE will automatically autoscale your graph after the data is displayed. Note the dotted line indicating the control pin connection.

Step 2

Collect the random numbers into an array. Find the moving average and display it with the numbers.

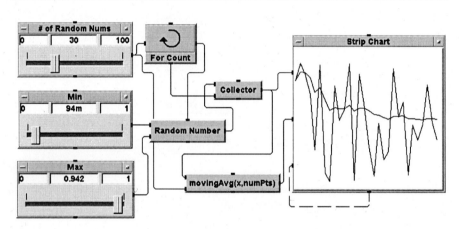

Fig. B-8. Random Number Generator, Step 2

- **MovingAvg(x, numPts):** Use this object located in the AdvMath => Data Filtering menu to smooth the input data using the average of a specified number of data points preceding the point of interest to calculate the smoothed data point.

Using Masks

Mask Test

Step 1

Create a 50 Hz sine wave with an adjustable amount of noise. Test the noisy sine wave to be certain that it stays below the following limits:

(0,0.5)
(2.2m, 1.2)
(7.2m, 1.2)
(10.2m, 0.5)
(20m, 0.5)

If the sine wave exceeds the limits, mark the failing points with a red diamond. HINTS: You can change the format of the displays from lines to dots to diamonds. Select Traces and Scales in Edit Properties... . Also, you may find the Comparator object helpful.

Step 2

Add to your program to calculate and display the percentage of failures.

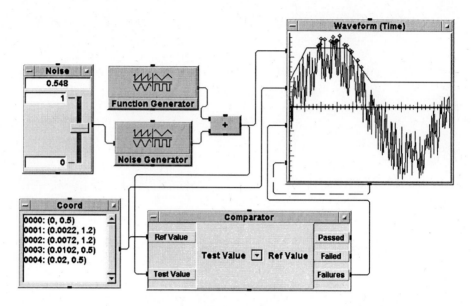

Fig. B-9. The Mask Test, Step 1

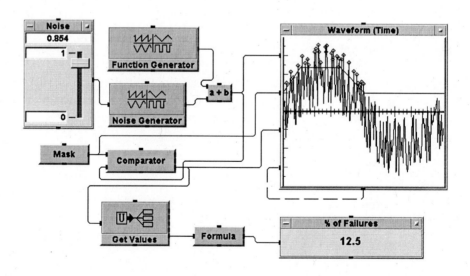

Fig. B-10. Mask Test, Step 2

Key Points:

- **Mask:** The mask is created using the Data => Constant => Coord object, then configuring it for 5 array elements. You simply input the coordinate pairs separated by commas and HP VEE will add the parentheses. The x values were chosen knowing that the time span of the waveform was 20 milliseconds. Also, note that the Waveform (Time) display will accept a Coord data type as an input. You could also have used a Data => Build Data => Arb Waveform object, which converts a Coord to a Waveform data type by specifying the number of points in the Waveform.

- **Comparator:** This object compares a test value against a reference value. Once again, you can compare a waveform to an array of coordinate pairs. The Failures pin gives you an array of the data points that failed, which you can send to the display and highlight with a different color or type of line.

- **Get Values:** This object is extremely useful for breaking down the information in an array. In this case, we've simply used the TotSize pin to get the number of failed data points for the percentage-of-failures calculation. (You could also use AdvMath => Array => totSize(x) to get the size of the array of Coord Failures from the Comparator.)

- **Formula:** *A/256*100* is the formula used to compute the percentage of failures, since the Function Generator and Noise Generator are set to put out 256 points.

Using Strings and Globals

Manipulating Strings and Globals

Using string objects or functions create a program that accepts a user's name in the following format: <space> <firstname> <space> <lastname>. After the user enters their name, have the program strip off the first name and only print the last name. Store the string into a global variable. Retrieve the string using the Formula object.

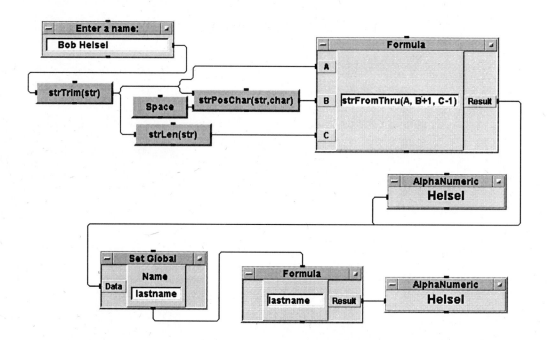

Fig. B-11. Manipulating Strings and Globals

Key Points

- **String Objects and Functions:** StrTrim(str) first strips off any spaces or tabs from the front and back of the name. StrPosChar(str,char) yields the index of the space character between the firstname and lastname. StrLen(str), of course, gives the length of the string. All of these were performed using the string objects, but they could also be done using string functions within a Formula object. StrFromThru(A,B+1,C-1) is used in the Formula object, and the function takes the string from input A, adds 1 to the index of the space from input B, and subtracts 1 from the string length at input C. (Recall that all indexing is zero-based.)

- **Set Global:** Notice how easily you can set a global variable called lastname, which can then be referenced in any expression field, such as the Formula object in this example.

- **Optimizing:** Three formulas and "space" constant on top could be combined into one formula. We would recommend leaving strTrim( ) on its own since its output is used multiple times, but the other three and the space could be combined into one to optimize speed. This could reduce readability, however.

Optimizing Techniques

Optimizing HP VEE Programs

Step 1

For this lab, you will build a simple HP VEE program two ways and note the difference in execution speed. Create a program that sends the range, 0 to 710 step 10, through both a sine function and cosine function. Put the results of the functions on an X vs Y display. Use the Timer object to clock how long the program takes. (Set your preferences for Trig Mode to Radians.)

Step 2

Clone all of the objects from the first program. Modify the new set to collect the range into an array. Now, the sine and cosine functions are run against an array of points, and only plotted one time. Note the time savings.

==

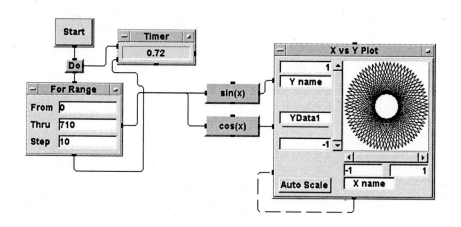

Fig. B-12. Optimizing HP VEE Programs, Step 1

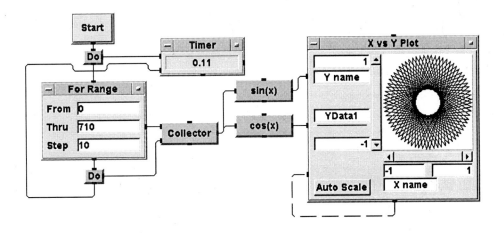

Fig. B-13. Optimizing HP VEE Programs, Step 2

Key Points

- **Optimizing with Arrays:** Note the increase in performance between step 1 and step 2 that comes from using arrays. Whenever possible, perform analysis or display results using arrays rather than scalar values.

- **X vs Y Display:** We used this display instead of the the Waveform or XY displays, because we had separate data for the X and Y data.

UserObjects

A Random Noise UserObject

Step 1

Create a UserObject that generates a random noise waveform. Display the noisy waveform and the noise spectrum outside the UserObject. Provide control outside the UserObject for the following: amplitude, number of points, interval (time span), DC offset.

> *Note:* *Do not use a virual source inside the UserObject. Use objects such as Build Waveform and Random Number to create your UserObject.*

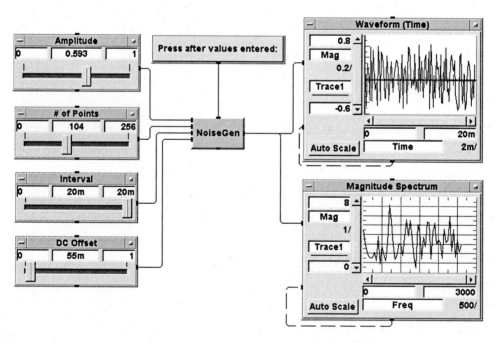

Fig. B-14. A Random Noise UserObject

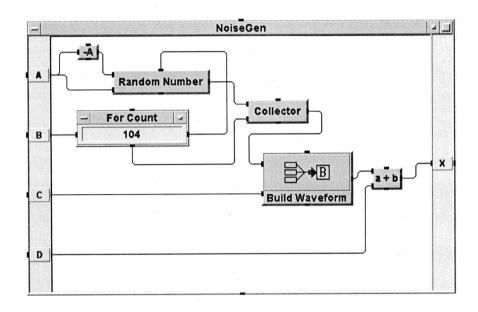

Fig. B-15. The NoiseGen UserObject

Key Points

- **UserObject:** Notice that the UserObjects you build are essentially customized objects that you've added to HP VEE.

- **Build Waveform:** This object creates a Waveform data type from a Real array of amplitude values and a time span (the length of time in seconds over which the y data was sampled).

HP VEE User Functions

Using User Functions

Step 1

Create a function called NoiseGen that accepts an amplitude value (0-1) from a slider and returns a noisy waveform.

Do not use: Virtual Source, For Count, For Range

Do use: Formula, Ramp(), Build Waveform

HINT: Use randomize(array, -a,a) where the array must be 256 points, and a is the amplitude.

Build a simple model to be certain this function works correctly.

==

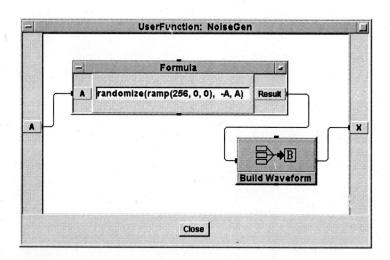

Fig. B-16. The NoiseGen User Function

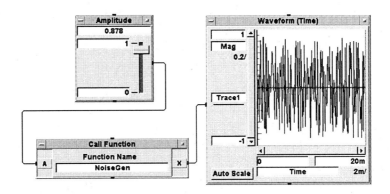

Fig. B-17. Using User Functions, Step 1

Key Points

- **Ramp():** Notice that the ramp( ) function is used to generate an array of 256 points within the parameter list for randomize( ).

- **Build Waveform:** Notice that the default time span here is 20 milliseconds, so that you only need to send an array to this object to build a waveform.

- **No Auto Scale on Display:** You don't need Auto Scale this time, because the amplitude will be no greater than 1, so the default scales are satisfactory.

Step 2

In the same program, create another function called AddNoise that calls the first function, NoiseGen. AddNoise should add the noisy waveform from your NoiseGen function to a sine wave. AddNoise should have two inputs, one for the NoiseGen amplitude and one for the sine wave; it should have one output for the result.

Build a simple model with a slider for the noise amplitude, and the Virtual Source => Function Generator (sine wave, Freq = 100 Hz) for the good waveform to add to the noise. Display the resultant waveform.

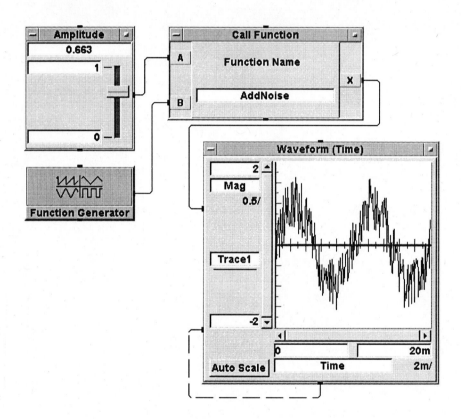

Fig. B-18. Using User Functions, Step 2

Step 3

In the same program, call the AddNoise function again, this time from a Formula object, taking the absolute value of the result. Display the absolute value waveform on the same display. Next prepare to edit the AddNoise function. Turn on Show Data Flow. Leave the edit window open and run the program. Notice how useful this capability would be for debugging purposes.

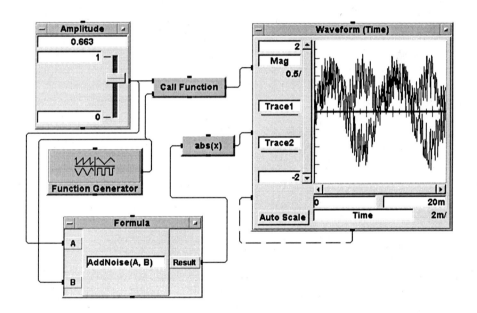

Fig. B-19. Using User Functions, Step 3

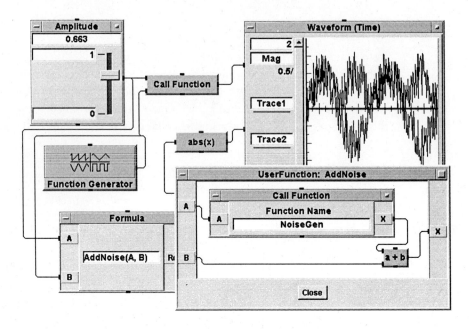

Fig. B-20. Edit Window Feature in Step 3

Step 4

Now change your program so that the slider sets a Global variable called Amplitude. Have the NoiseGen function use that Global (so NoiseGen will no longer require an input pin). Make the program run correctly. Save this file as uflab.vee.

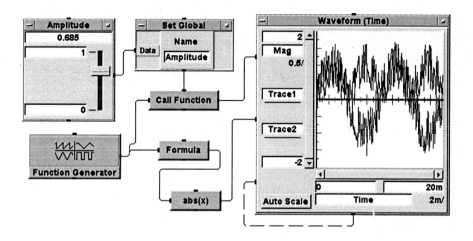

Fig. B-21. Using User Functions, Step 4

Importing and Deleting Libraries of User Functions

Build a simple program to import the uflab.vee (Using User Functions, Step 4 program name) functions, call the function that adds the noise, and then delete the functions programmatically. Use the Select Function choice in the object menu of the Call Function object.

===

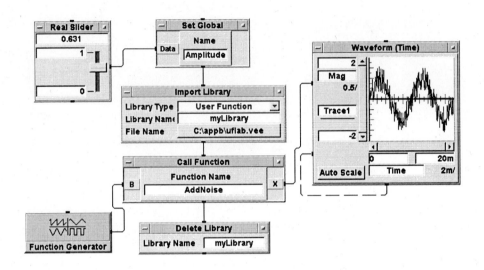

Fig. B-22. Importing and Deleting Libraries

Key Points

- **Load Lib:** You need to click on Load Lib in the Import Library object menu to manually load the library you specified, so that you can use the Select Function feature in Call Function.

- **Select Function:** Notice that this selection will configure the proper input and output pins for the function you select.

- **Editing User Functions:** If you import a library of User Functions programmatically, you will not be able to edit them. You can, however, view them for debugging purposes. If you want to edit the User Functions you import, use the Merge Library command instead.

- **Global Variable Caution:** Notice that when you use a global variable in a function, you have to remember to create that global when using that function in other programs. One of the advantages of explicitly creating inputs and outputs is that they are easier to track.

Operator Panels

Creating Operator Panels and Pop-ups

Step 1

Create a UserObject to interact with an operator. Use two inputs, A and B. If A and B are equal, send A to the output. If A and B are not equal, prompt the operator to select either A or B for the output, while the current value of each is displayed. If the operator does not respond in 10 seconds, generate an error message.

HINT: Each panel that pops up needs to be a separate UserObject. Also, remember to enable Show Panel on Execute when you want a panel to pop up.

===

Fig. B-23. Creating Operator Panels Program

Key Points

- **Iconized UserObject:** The entire program is in the iconized UserObject, AorB. When it executes, the appropriate pop-up panels will appear.

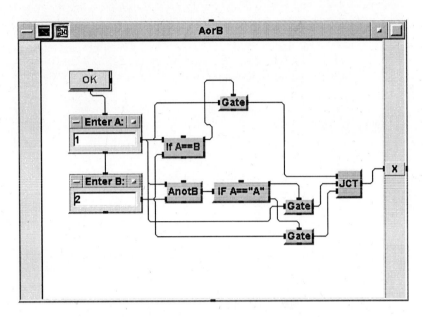

Fig. B-24. The AorB UserObject Detail View

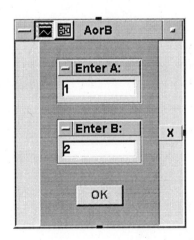

**Fig. B-25. The AorB Panel
View**

Key Points

- **Gating Selections:** In the AorB detail view, the If A==B simply gates A to the output, if A and B are equal. If not, then the UserObject AnotB is activated which will ask the user for her choice. The AnotB output is tested and the correct value is gated to the AorB output.

- **AorB Detail View:** The AorB pop-up panel gets the original two values from the user. Note the OK object is above the input boxes. Why? (You want the user to enter values before the input boxes execute.) If the two values are not equal, AnotB has its own pop-up panel for more user input.

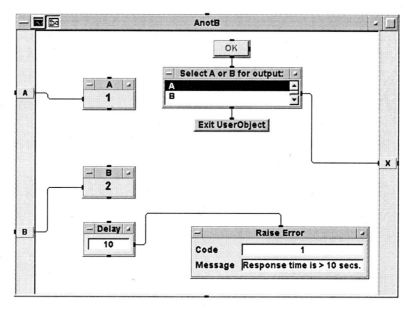

Fig. B-26. AnotB Detail View

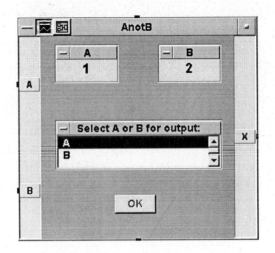

Fig. B-27. AnotB Panel View

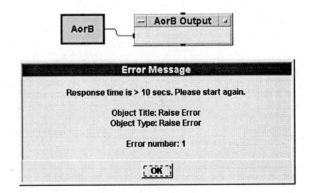

Fig. B-28. AnotB Error Message

Key Points

- **List Object as a Menu:** Note the use of the Data => Selection Controls => List object edited for two choices and formatted for a list. This configuration will output a text A or B. If you need the ordinal value (0 or 1), then put the output through the ordinal(x) function.

- **Exit UserObject:** If the user responds in under 10 seconds, this object will exit the UserObject, even though the Delay object may not have finished executing.

- **Delay and Raise Error:** After 10 seconds the Delay object pings the Raise Error object, which will pause execution of the program and display the Error Message you have typed in. A red outline will also appear around the object that caused the error, which goes away when you click on Stop or Run on the main menu bar.

Step 2

Change the UserObjects into UserFunctions.

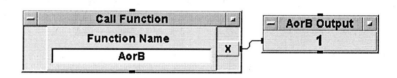

Fig. B-29. Creating Operator Panels Program, Step 2

Working with Files

Moving Data To and From Files

Step 1

Create an HP VEE program to write the time of day to a file. Generate 100 random points and write them to the file. Calculate the mean and standard deviation of the numbers and append them to the file in the following format:

    Mean: xxxxxx
    Std Dev: yyyyyy

Next, read only the mean and standard deviation from the file.

==

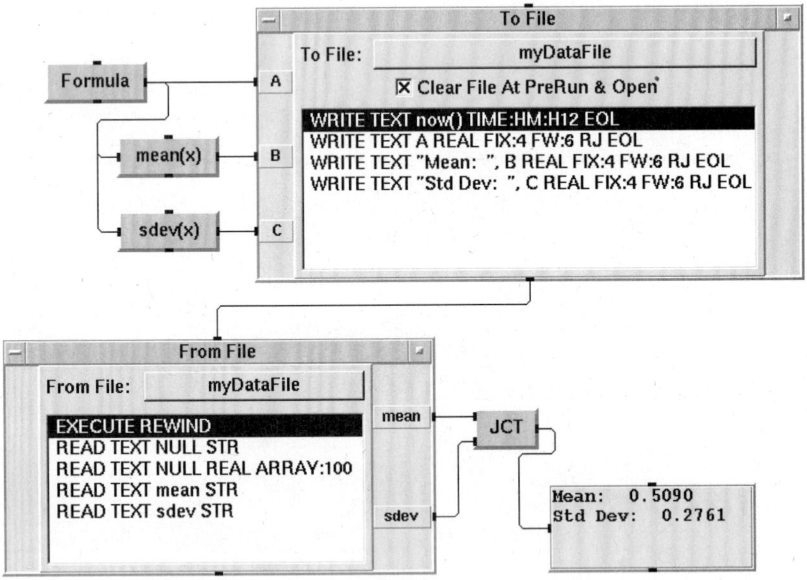

Fig. B-30. Moving Data To and From Files

Key Points

- **Generating an Array:** Use randomize(ramp(100,0,1), 0, 1) in the Formula object to create an array of 100 random numbers. The ramp( ) function generates an ordered array and delivers it to the randomize( ) function, which then generates random values between 0 and 1.

- **Time Stamp:** The now( ) function is used in the expression field of the I/O Transaction dialog box for transaction one in the To File object. When you change the format to TIME STAMP FORMAT, the dialog box gives you additional buttons to specify how the time will be stored.

- **Storing Two Values in a Line:** In both the third and fourth transactions in the To File object, we store a constant Text string, followed by a Real value. For example, in the third transaction you type **"Mean: ",B** in the expression field of the I/O Transaction box (assuming the mean value will be on the B input pin).

- **Extracting a Value From a File:** To get to the mean and standard deviation, you first have to send an EXECUTE REWIND to position the read pointer at the beginning. Then you use NULL with the proper format to READ past the time stamp and real array. Finally, you can read the last two lines in the file as strings.

- **Junction:** Use the Flow => Junction object when you want to connect more than one output to a single input - the mean and sdev outputs to the Logging AlphaNumeric display for example.

- **Deselecting Show Title:** Notice that we've deselected Show Title of the Logging AlphaNumeric display for a less cluttered appearance.

Records

Manipulating Records

Step 1

Build a record with three fields holding an integer, the time right now, and a four element array of reals. The fields should be named int, daytime, and rarry, respectively. Merge this record with another that holds a random number between 0 and 1, and a waveform. Name these fields rand and wave. The resultant record should have five fields.

===

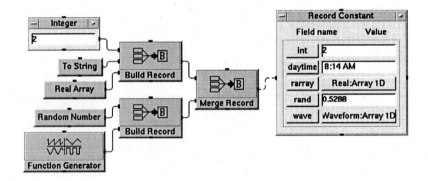

Fig. B-31. Manipulating Records, Step 1

Key Points

- **Time Stamp:** Use the now( ) function within the To String object to create your time stamp for this program.

- **Configuring a Data Constant as an Array:** Any data type in the Data => Constant menu can become an array by selecting Edit Properties => 1D array, then entering the size in its object menu, specifying the number of elements, and typing in the values.

- **Naming Fields:** By renaming the input terminals on the Build Record object, you can give your record specific field names such as int, rand, and wave.

- **The Default Value Control Input:** A Record Constant makes an excellent interactive display object by adding a Default Value Control pin. The Record Constant will automatically configure itself for the record it receives.

Step 2

Use a conditional expression in a Formula object to test the random value in the record, and display either the integer or a text string. If the value is less than 0.5, display the first field of the record; otherwise, output a text string "More than 0.5." Next, extract only the time and the waveform. (HINT: Do not use a Formula object.) Display this record with an AlphaNumeric object.

===

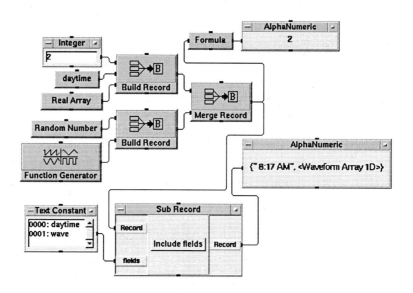

Fig. B-32. Manipulating Records, Step 2

Step 3

Replace the integer input for the first field with a For Count object and step through 10 iterations. Be certain to "ping" the random number generator and the time function on each iteration. Send the complete record into a To DataSet object. In a separate thread, retrieve all records from the dataset where the random value is greater than 0.5. Put the resultant records into a record constant.

HINT: You'll need a control pin for a Default Value on the Record Constant object.

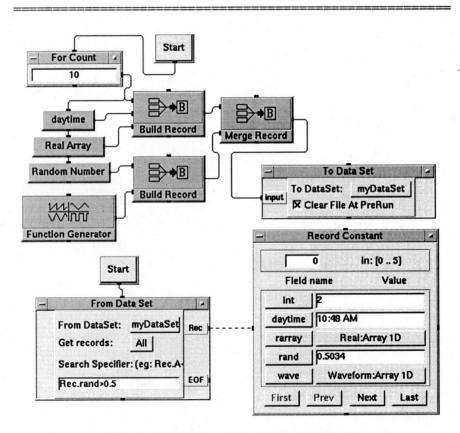

Fig. B-33. Manipulating Records, Step 3

Key Points

- **(Step 2) Using a Conditional Expression:** HP VEE supports a conditional expression, which provides an efficient way to implement an if-then-else action. For example, in this case we wrote the expression (A.rand < 0.5 ? A.int: "More than 0.5") in the Formula object. *If* A.rand is less than 0.5, *then* the condition is true and A.int becomes the result, *else* the string "More than 0.5" becomes the result.

- **(Step 2) The Sub Record Object:** Notice that we've put a Text array of the fields desired on the Sub Record input pin labeled *fields*. When you configure the Sub Record object to *include fields*, it will output a record that only contains the fields you have specified.

- **(Step 3) The To DataSet Object:** The *Clear File at PreRun* option only clears the file before data is sent the first time. Notice that the program sends 10 different records to the same file sequentially, and they are simply appended to the file.

- **(Step 3) The From DataSet Object:** Theis object is configured to retrieve all records where the *rand* field is greater than 0.5. In this case, six out of ten records meet that criterion.

Step 4

Create a panel display that allows you to edit the information from the dataset. Include a button that sends your changes back to the dataset. Run this program several times to see that your changes are being stored into the dataset.

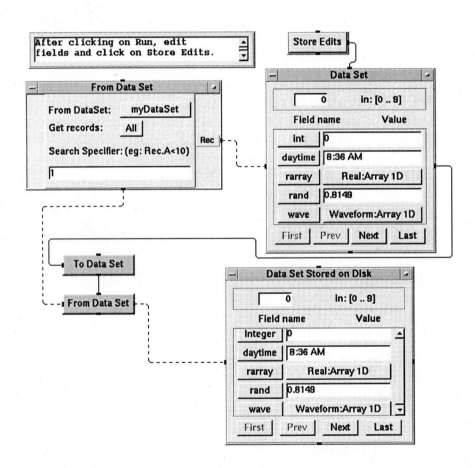

Fig. B-34. Manipulating Records, Step 4, Detail View

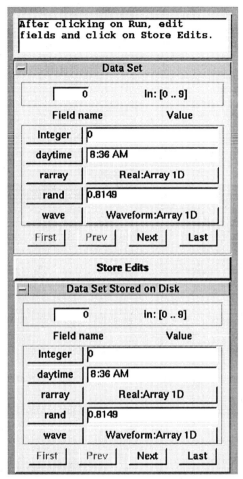

**Fig. B-35. Manipulating Records,
Step 4, Panel View**

Key Points

- **Renaming the OK Object:** Note that the OK object has been renamed *Store Edits.* This is a useful technique for making your program readable.

- **Rewind Control Pin:** Use it on From Data Set to reset the read pointer.

Test Sequencing

Using the Test Sequencer

Step 1

Create a simple user function called UpperLimit that is a pop-up panel with a Real Slider and a Confirm (OK) object. Send the output of the slider to a Global variable called UL and also to an output terminal.

Test1 in the sequencer should be an EXEC transaction that calls UpperLimit.

Create another function called AddRand that simulates the test you might actually call. This function should add an input value to a random value (0 to 1). Hence, one input pin and one output pin.

From the sequencer, make a tests2 call AddRand and send in a 0. Test the return value to do a limit comparison < the global UL value. If it passes, then return "PASS " +test2.result. If it fails, then return "FAILED " +test2.result.

Put an AlphaNumeric display on the Return pin of the Sequencer.

After the Sequencer object, ping a Get Global object (UL) and another AlphaNumeric display.

Run the program several times.

===

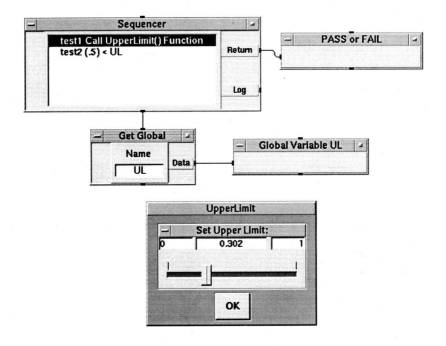

Fig. B-36. Using the Test Sequencer, Step 1

Key Points

- **Setting Global Variables with a User Function:** A typical use of the first Sequencer transaction is to call a User Function that sets Global Variables, as it does in this case. Then you can utilize these variables in any test that follows, as we have done here.

- **The Sequencer Return Pin:** We have used the Return pin in this example to deliver a pass or fail message plus the test value. You could use this pin to deliver any message or value from a particular test.

Step 2

Disable the first test step. Assuming you don't need the global anywhere else, you can call the UpperLimit function directly. Change test2 so that it compares the return value against the result of the UpperLimit function.

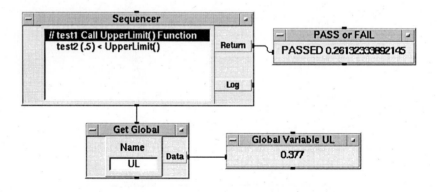

Fig. B-37. Using the Test Sequencer, Step 2

Key Points

- **The User Function in an Expression Field:** In this example, instead of comparing a test result to the UL variable, you can type the function name, UpperLimit(), in the expression field where the variable would go.

Logging Sequencer Data

Edit a test1 Sequencer transaction that simply calls the HP VEE function random( ). Compare the result against a limit < 0.5. Cut the test1 transaction and paste it back several times. You should have a total of 4 tests.

Build a program to run the sequencer five times with each Sequencer Log record going into an array and a dataset. Using the array, find the minimum, the maximum, the mean, and the standard deviation of the results of the second test.

HINT: Use a Formula object with a <record>.<record>.<field> in the expression field.

In a separate thread, get all of the records from the dataset where the first test passed or the second test failed. Print the timestamp field from the records on a Logging AlphaNumeric display.

HINT: You may need to access the Logging tab in the Edit Properties dialog box in the object menu of the Sequencer.

===

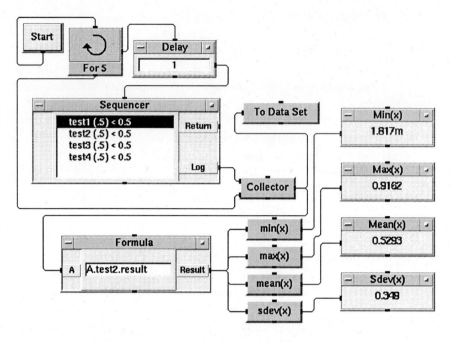

Fig. B-38. Logging Sequencer Data, First Thread

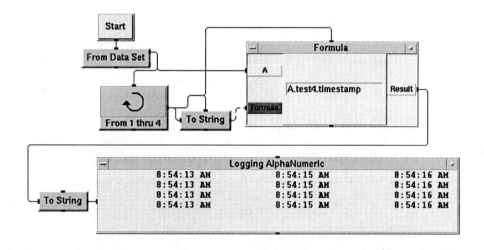

Fig. B-39. Logging Sequencer Data, Second Thread

Key Points

- **The Delay Object (First Thread):** This object simply holds execution flow for the specified number of seconds. Here we've used it to create time stamp values that varied between each run of the Sequencer.

- **The Data Format for Several Runs of the Sequencer (First Thread):** When the Sequencer executes once, it outputs a Record of Records — the first record has field names that match the test names, then each field holds a record containing the different pieces of data for that particular test. When the Sequencer runs several times, each Record of Records can be added to an array, which can then be investigated. If you use the <record>.<record>.<field> format in the Formula object, you will get an array of data - in this case, an array of real values giving the test results for five runs of test2. You then calculated the minimum, maximum, mean, and standard deviation from this array. You could have specified a single run of test2 by indicating a particular element in your array of records of records. For example, to get the first run result of test2 you would use the expression: *A[0].test2.result.* If you don't specify a particular element in an array, HP VEE assumes you mean the whole array.

- **The EOF Pin on the From Data Set Object (Second Thread):** We've added the EOF pin, in case there are no records that fit the criteria. If this happens then the EOF pin will fire, instead of HP VEE halting the program with an error message.

- **The Conditional Expression in the From Data Set Object (Second Thread):** We have used the expression *(Rec.test1.pass==1) OR (Rec.test2.pass==0)*. Again we've used the <record>.<record>.<field> format. We use Rec, since that is the name of the array of records being returned. Test1 and test2 specify which tests HP VEE should examine, and the field name *pass* is the default name for the pass-fail indicator (1 or 0) assigned by HP VEE. (You enable or disable different fields for all tests by selecting Logging tab in the Sequencer Edit Properties box.)

- **Formula Control Pin on the Formula Object (Second Thread):** Notice that you want to run the Formula object four times with a different formula each time accessing the runs of a particular test. The data output of the For Range object (labeled *From 1 thru 4*) is connected to the sequence input pins on the To String and Formula objects to make certain those objects execute after they have the new formula information. The For Range object will output the numbers 1 through 4 sequentially in this case. The general formula would look like this: *A.test<test number>.timestamp* (where *<test number>* is a number between 1 and 4). You can use the Formula control pin for this purpose. You use the To String and For Range objects to create the formula. The To String object holds the transaction *WRITE TEXT "A.test"+A+".timestamp"* (where A is the input terminal on To String that holds the test number from 1 to 4).

- **Converting Time Stamp Formats (Second Thread):** The To String object before Logging AlphaNumeric converts the time stamps from a Real format to a Time Stamp format for more clarity.

Extra Credit:

Load the example in the HP VEE subdirectory: **examples/mfgtest/mfgtest.ex**

Look at the two sequencer objects in this example. The first, Login Control, checks the user's name and password. The second sequencer uses the EXEC TRANS control pin and accepts an array of text strings to call specific tests.

Instrument Drivers

Using HP Instrument Drivers

Step 1

Using the HP driver for the HP3314A Function Generator, change the Frequency from 0 to 100 kHz with a step of 1 kHz, and clock the performance.

Step2

Repeat step 1 using a Component driver and characterize the performance differences.

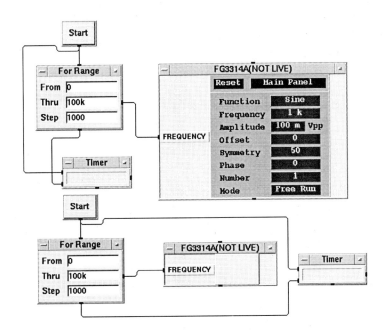

Fig. B-40. Using HP Instrument Drivers

Key Points

- **Component Drivers:** The component driver uses relevant parts of the instrument driver file and ignores the rest, so it will execute much faster than a complete instrument driver. In this case, it's about twice as fast. You could increase performance more by deselecting error checking when you're configuring either type of driver.

Compiled Functions (HP-UX)

This lab is to show you what is required from HP VEE to call C functions using the HP-UX platform. It does not address how to create the function in C or how to compile the function and build a shared library.

HP VEE includes an example C program designed to add the number 1 to a real array that is sent to the program. The C source code for the *myFunc* function is located in /usr/lib/veetest/examples/manual/manual49.c.

> *Note:* *The example program in manual49.vee in the same directory performs a similar task, but the program is written so that it will work on HP-UX, MS Windows, MS Windows NT, or SunOS.*

Step 1

Import and call the function from the following shared library: /usr/lib/veetest/examples/manual/manual49.sl.

The header file is stored in: /usr/lib/veetest/examples/manual/manual49.h

The function expects two input pins and one output pin plus the Ret Value pin.

Use a five element array to send to the array data input pin. Use the totSize object for the array size input pin. Display the results.

==

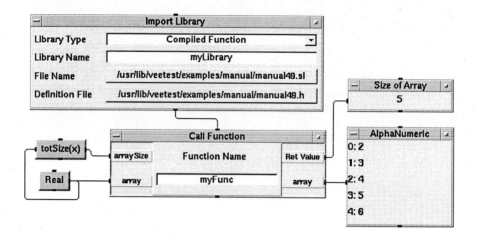

Fig. B-41. Using Compiled Functions, Step 1

Step2

Replace the totSize object with an integer value of 3. Subtract the array you sent to the Call Function object from the array you receive back from the function. Notice that this only adds 1 to the number of elements you specified.

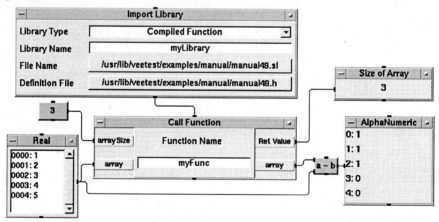

Fig. B-42. Using Compiled Functions, Step 2

Extra Credit:

WARNING...If you do this exercise, be prepared to kill your HP VEE process and re-start HP VEE. (See chapter 1.)

Change the integer value on arraysize to 50. Press Run.

This is telling the C program that although HP VEE is giving it a five element array, it is OK to use enough memory for 50 elements. This allows the C program to overwrite HP VEE memory. If this happens, you should always re-start your HP VEE process. This is why it's a good idea to use the totSize object.

Note: HP VEE may crash when you run this program!

Index

H

help
  instrument, 2-16
  on-line, 2-16
HP BASIC/UX, 12-14
HP VEE
  defined, 1-1
  exiting, 1-8
  objects, 1-11
  printing, 2-13
  programming with, 1-2
  quitting, 1-8
  saving programs, 1-8
  starting, 1-8
  work area, 1-4

I

icon, 1-13
instrument driver monitor, 3-30
instrument panel, 3-13
  configuring, 3-4
  programming, 3-13
  using, 3-13
instruments, 3-1
  help, 2-16

L

libraries
  creating and merging, 8-12
  importing and deleting, 8-16

M

masks, B-11
mathematically processing data, 4-11

menu, 1-5
  bar, 1-4
  object, 1-7
  pop-up, 1-7
  selecting, 1-5
  submenu, 1-5
merging, 8-2
modularity (UserObjects), 1-26
moving an object, 1-12
moving the work area, 1-16
MS Excel, 6-2
MS Word, 6-5

O

object menu, 1-7
  button, 1-7
  selecting, 1-7
objects, 1-11
  cloning, 1-12
  connecting, 1-20
  copying, 1-12
  deleting, 1-11
  dragging, 1-13
  moving, 1-12
  pasting, 1-12
  resizing, 1-14
  selecting, 1-14
  sizing, 1-14
online help, 1-11
opening a file, 1-10, 5-5
open view, 1-13
operator interface, 10-2
  creating, 10-15
  importing bitmaps, 10-23
  menus, 10-15
  status panel, 10-20

LICENSE AGREEMENT AND LIMITED WARRANTY

READ THE FOLLOWING TERMS AND CONDITIONS CAREFULLY BEFORE OPENING THIS CD-ROM PACKAGE. THIS LEGAL DOCUMENT IS AN AGREEMENT BE-TWEEN YOU AND PRENTICE-HALL, INC. (THE "COMPANY"). BY OPENING THIS SEALED CD-ROM PACKAGE, YOU ARE AGREEING TO BE BOUND BY THESE TERMS AND CONDITIONS. IF YOU DO NOT AGREE WITH THESE TERMS AND CONDITIONS, DO NOT OPEN THE CD-ROM PACKAGE. PROMPTLY RETURN THE UNOPENED CD-ROM PACKAGE AND ALL ACCOMPANYING ITEMS TO THE PLACE YOU OBTAINED THEM FOR A FULL REFUND OF ANY SUMS YOU HAVE PAID.

1.   **GRANT OF LICENSE:**   In consideration of your payment of the license fee, which is part of the price you paid for this product, and your agreement to abide by the terms and conditions of this Agreement, the Company grants to you a nonexclusive right to use and display the copy of the enclosed software program (hereinafter the "SOFTWARE") on a single computer (i.e., with a single CPU) at a single location so long as you comply with the terms of this Agreement. The Company reserves all rights not expressly granted to you under this Agreement.

2.   **OWNERSHIP OF SOFTWARE:** You own only the magnetic or physical media (the en-closed CD-ROM) on which the SOFTWARE is recorded or fixed, but the Company retains all the rights, title, and ownership to the SOFTWARE recorded on the original CD-ROM copy and all sub-sequent copies of the SOFTWARE, regardless of the form or media on which the original or other copies may exist. This license is not a sale of the original SOFTWARE or any copy to you.

3.   **COPY RESTRICTIONS:** This SOFTWARE and the accompanying printed materials and user manual (the "Documentation") are the subject of copyright. You may not copy the Docu-mentation or the SOFTWARE, except that you may make a single copy of the SOFTWARE for backup or archival purposes only. You may be held legally responsible for any copying or copyright infringement which is caused or encouraged by your failure to abide by the terms of this restriction.

4.   **USE RESTRICTIONS:** You may not network the SOFTWARE or otherwise use it on more than one computer or computer terminal at the same time. You may physically transfer the SOFTWARE from one computer to another provided that the SOFTWARE is used on only one com-puter at a time. You may not distribute copies of the SOFTWARE or Documentation to others. You may not reverse engineer, disassemble, decompile, modify, adapt, translate, or create derivative works based on the SOFTWARE or the Documentation without the prior written consent of the Company.

5.   **TRANSFER RESTRICTIONS:** The enclosed SOFTWARE is licensed only to you and may not be transferred to any one else without the prior written consent of the Company. Any unau-thorized transfer of the SOFTWARE shall result in the immediate termination of this Agreement.

6.   **TERMINATION:** This license is effective until terminated. This license will terminate automatically without notice from the Company and become null and void if you fail to comply with any provisions or limitations of this license. Upon termination, you shall destroy the Documentation and all copies of the SOFTWARE. All provisions of this Agreement as to warranties, limitation of liability, remedies or damages, and our ownership rights shall survive termination.

7.   **MISCELLANEOUS:** This Agreement shall be construed in accordance with the laws of the United States of America and the State of New York and shall benefit the Company, its affiliates, and assignees.

8.   **LIMITED WARRANTY AND DISCLAIMER OF WARRANTY:** The Company war-rants that the SOFTWARE, when properly used in accordance with the Documentation, will operate in substantial conformity with the description of the SOFTWARE set forth in the Documentation. The Company does not warrant that the SOFTWARE will meet your requirements or that the oper-ation of the SOFTWARE will be uninterrupted or error-free. The Company warrants that the media

on which the SOFTWARE is delivered shall be free from defects in materials and workmanship under normal use for a period of thirty (30) days from the date of your purchase. Your only remedy and the Company's only obligation under these limited warranties is, at the Company's option, return of the warranted item for a refund of any amounts paid by you or replacement of the item. Any replacement of SOFTWARE or media under the warranties shall not extend the original warranty period. The limited warranty set forth above shall not apply to any SOFTWARE which the Company determines in good faith has been subject to misuse, neglect, improper installation, repair, alteration, or damage by you. EXCEPT FOR THE EXPRESSED WARRANTIES SET FORTH ABOVE, THE COMPANY DISCLAIMS ALL WARRANTIES, EXPRESS OR IMPLIED, INCLUDING WITHOUT LIMITATION, THE IMPLIED WARRANTIES OF MERCHANTABILITY AND FITNESS FOR A PARTICULAR PURPOSE. EXCEPT FOR THE EXPRESS WARRANTY SET FORTH ABOVE, THE COMPANY DOES NOT WARRANT, GUARANTEE, OR MAKE ANY REPRESENTATION REGARDING THE USE OR THE RESULTS OF THE USE OF THE SOFTWARE IN TERMS OF ITS CORRECTNESS, ACCURACY, RELIABILITY, CURRENTNESS, OR OTHERWISE.

IN NO EVENT, SHALL THE COMPANY OR ITS EMPLOYEES, AGENTS, SUPPLIERS, OR CONTRACTORS BE LIABLE FOR ANY INCIDENTAL, INDIRECT, SPECIAL, OR CONSEQUENTIAL DAMAGES ARISING OUT OF OR IN CONNECTION WITH THE LICENSE GRANTED UNDER THIS AGREEMENT, OR FOR LOSS OF USE, LOSS OF DATA, LOSS OF INCOME OR PROFIT, OR OTHER LOSSES, SUSTAINED AS A RESULT OF INJURY TO ANY PERSON, OR LOSS OF OR DAMAGE TO PROPERTY, OR CLAIMS OF THIRD PARTIES, EVEN IF THE COMPANY OR AN AUTHORIZED REPRESENTATIVE OF THE COMPANY HAS BEEN ADVISED OF THE POSSIBILITY OF SUCH DAMAGES. IN NO EVENT SHALL LIABILITY OF THE COMPANY FOR DAMAGES WITH RESPECT TO THE SOFTWARE EXCEED THE AMOUNTS ACTUALLY PAID BY YOU, IF ANY, FOR THE SOFTWARE.

SOME JURISDICTIONS DO NOT ALLOW THE LIMITATION OF IMPLIED WARRANTIES OR LIABILITY FOR INCIDENTAL, INDIRECT, SPECIAL, OR CONSEQUENTIAL DAMAGES, SO THE ABOVE LIMITATIONS MAY NOT ALWAYS APPLY. THE WARRANTIES IN THIS AGREEMENT GIVE YOU SPECIFIC LEGAL RIGHTS AND YOU MAY ALSO HAVE OTHER RIGHTS WHICH VARY IN ACCORDANCE WITH LOCAL LAW.

ACKNOWLEDGMENT

YOU ACKNOWLEDGE THAT YOU HAVE READ THIS AGREEMENT, UNDERSTAND IT, AND AGREE TO BE BOUND BY ITS TERMS AND CONDITIONS. YOU ALSO AGREE THAT THIS AGREEMENT IS THE COMPLETE AND EXCLUSIVE STATEMENT OF THE AGREEMENT BETWEEN YOU AND THE COMPANY AND SUPERSEDES ALL PROPOSALS OR PRIOR AGREEMENTS, ORAL, OR WRITTEN, AND ANY OTHER COMMUNICATIONS BETWEEN YOU AND THE COMPANY OR ANY REPRESENTATIVE OF THE COMPANY RELATING TO THE SUBJECT MATTER OF THIS AGREEMENT.

Should you have any questions concerning this Agreement or if you wish to contact the Company for any reason, please contact in writing at the address below.

Robin Short
Prentice Hall PTR
One Lake Street
Upper Saddle River, New Jersey 07458

Installation Instructions for HP VEE Evaluation Software

You can use this software for up to 60 days to evaluate HP VEE with this book. The evaluation software has the same functionality as the full product. (See Appendix A for more information.)

To install on Windows 95:
1. Click Start, then select Run and enter: `D:` (or `E:)\VEE\SETUP.EXE` Then follow the instructions on the screen, until HP VEE is successfully installed.
2. Click Start, then select Run and enter: `D:` (or `E:)\HPIO\SETUP.EXE` Then follow the instructions on the screen, until the HP I/O software is installed.

To install on Windows NT:
3. Click File, then select Run and enter: `D:` (or `E:)\VEE\SETUP.EXE` Then follow the instructions on the screen, until HP VEE is successfully installed.
4. Click File, then select Run and enter: `D:` (or `E:)\HPIO\SETUP.EXE` Then follow the instructions on the screen, until the HP I/O software is installed.

NOTE: For HP VEE evaluation software for MS Windows 3.1, consult *Graphical Programming: A Tutorial for HP VEE* (Prentice Hall PTR, 1995, ISBN: 0-13-362823-X).